CONSTANT LEBASTARD

THE NORMANDY AMERICAN CEMETERY

An unforgettable testimony of the American sacrifice during the battle of Normandy

Translated from the French
by Anthony Lewis

OREP
EDITIONS

OREP
EDITIONS

Zone tertiaire de Nonant
14400 BAYEUX - France
Tél.: +33(0)2 31 51 81 31 - Fax: +33(0)2 31 51 81 32
E-mail: info@orepeditions.com
Website : www.orepeditions.com

Editor: Grégory PIQUE
Editorial coordination: Corine DESPREZ
Graphic design: OREP
Cartography: Jennifer LESAQUE

ISBN : 978-2-8151-0200-1
Copyright OREP 2014
Legal deposit: 2nd quarter 2014

"Visitor

Look how many of them they were

Look how young they were

They died for your freedom

Hold back your tears and be silent"

This quotation was previously visible in the vehicle park at the Normandy American Cemetery.

GENERAL INFORMATION

The cemetery is located 94 miles from Le Havre, 29 miles from Caen, 110 miles from Rouen and 50 miles from Cherbourg.

It can be reached easily by car via the main road N13, then by the secondary road D517 from Formigny to Saint-Laurent-sur-Mer, the secondary road D514 towards Colleville-sur-Mer and finally via its 875 yards approach road.

The cemetery and the Visitor Center are entirely free and the site is open all year round with the exception of 25th December and 1st January. Visitors may visit between 9 .00am and 5.00pm in winter and until 6.00pm from 15th April until 15th September.

The cemetery does not have any shops. Nothing is sold on the site and the American Battle Monuments Commission does not engage in any commerce.

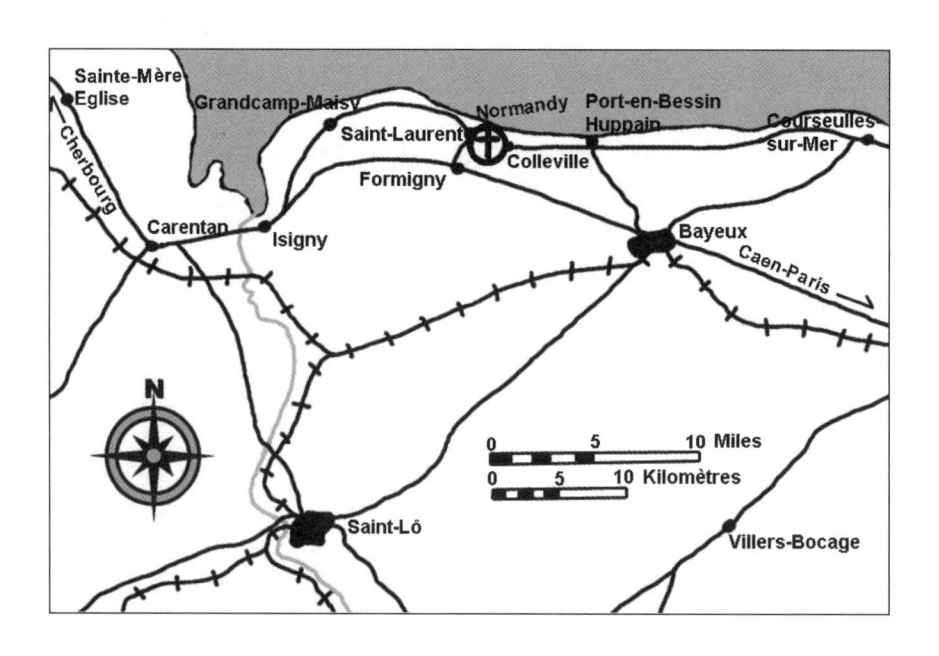

THE AMERICAN ORGANIZATIONS

ABMC: the American Battle Monuments Commission is a commission today in charge of the upkeep of American cemeteries outside of the United-States.

AGRC: the American Graves Registration Command was the organization responsible for the construction of the permanent American cemeteries of the Second World War.

AGRS: the American Graves Registration Service was the organization responsible for the collection, identification, burial of American soldiers and of the construction of temporary American cemeteries during the Second World War.

AMVETS: the American Veterans of World War II, Korea and Vietnam Wars is an association of veterans who commemorate the sacrifice of American soldiers, amongst other means, by the donation of a system of chimes one of which was given to the Normandy American cemetery.

AOMDA: the American Overseas Memorial Day Association is an association responsible for the organization of ceremonies on Memorial Day and who take part in the decoration of the graves and monuments of the American soldiers.

OQMG: the Office of the Quartermaster General was the Head of the Supply Corps of the American Forces responsible, amongst other things, for supervising all of the relevant operations relating to the cemeteries, prior to being given over to the ABMC.

PREFACE

More than 100 000 soldiers from all nationalities, victims of the confrontations of the summer of 1944, are resting today in Normandy soil. Whether civilian or military, all the cemeteries have a story, their story. We appreciate that Constant Lebastard is interested in that of the Normandy American Cemetery, more commonly known by the French as the American cemetery of Colleville, for it has become a mecca of memory, of recollection, but also of tourism. Each year, it is visited by hundreds of thousands of people. Who does not know of this vast green space of almost 172 acres where in an impressionable manner are aligned thousands of crosses in white marble, in impeccable rows, an army as such of the dead?

This publication is not just a simple tourist guide, as exist so many already. It is an innovative historical work, well written in the manner of research on the battle of Normandy managed by the University of Caen, looking more and more at changing its approaches, beyond that of the simple relationship with the fighting. Thus, Constant Lebastard first evokes the care of the dead by the Graves Registration Service, then the establishment of numerous provisional cemeteries, quoting many milestones at key stages of the battle. One of the most surprising cemeteries was certainly the one opened in haste at the top of the Vierville range, in the same bloody sand of Omaha, while the cannonade was still nearby. However, this situation could not continue forever, both for safety reasons and also to prevent the troops who continued to land from a totally demoralizing sight. The remains were exhumed and then in a few weeks carried not far close to the edge of the ridge in Le Ruquet, on the eastern part of the commune of Saint-Laurent-sur-Mer.

After the end of the war, the American Government decided to close the provisional cemeteries and to proceed with a regrouping into permanent cemeteries whose architectural creation and administration reverted to the American Battle Monuments Commission (ABMC). A singular fact – and we know little else – more than 15 000 bodies buried in Normandy (being more than half) were repatriated to the United-States at the request of the families. The others found themselves in one of only two places: the Brittany American Cemetery at Saint-James, in the south of the Manche department or the Normandy American Cemetery linked with Colleville-sur-Mer on land given to the United-States by France. Thousands of bodies were then transferred at first from Saint-Laurent, but also from Sainte-Mère-Église, Blosville, La Cambe, Saint-André-de-l'Eure… At the end of many years of work, its inauguration took place on 19th July, 1956. Constant Lebastard's book, fed by research into hitherto unexploited archives and often made available to him by the ABMC – at which point here it's convenient to thank them for their cooperation –is an enduring example of endeavor. One can only hope that he will open the way for other researchers in similar vein, for example on the British or German cemeteries, very different in their design and their appearance.

Jean QUELLIEN (PhD.)
Professor Emeritus
University of Caen, Lower Normandy

INTRODUCTION

Normandy was a key to the victory of the Allies against Nazi Germany following the Normandy landing of the 6th June 1944. The region has preserved numerous traces of the events that took place there. These are brought more alive today through the eye witness accounts of participants and local inhabitants. They are also visible, thanks to the remnants of fortifications, the many museums and the numerous battlefields, some of which have become heritage sites.

Today, in Colleville-sur-Mer, a village of only 170 inhabitants, the memory of the invasion and of the battle of Normandy remains alive. Thirty eight commemorative monuments are located in the three communes in the invasion sector of Omaha-Beach. Seventeen of them are to be found at Colleville-sur-Mer. Individuals can collect their thoughts in front of the monument to the 5th Engineer Special Brigade, the "wall of tanks", the column for the 60th anniversary or furthermore, the pebbled emblem of the First Infantry Division. However, it is at the American cemetery that the strongest links with the events of 6th June 1944 and the battle of Normandy remain.

This book has the object of discovering the cemetery of Colleville-sur-Mer, a place which has become one of the most well-known and visited memorial sites of the region. Its reputation is even international as is proved by the example of the interest of the composer Mark Camphouse who wrote his Prelude Symphony: "The cemetery at Colleville-sur-Mer" in homage to the men and women buried there. We find the cemetery in the film "The Omen" by Richard Donner (1976) and more recently in the film "Saving Private Ryan" by Steven Spielberg (1998). The site also has a location which adds to its reputation: situated on a bluff overlooking the Easy-Red sector on Omaha-Beach and the Channel Sea, it was established between the communities of Saint-Laurent-sur-Mer and Colleville-sur-Mer strengthening the relationship between the soldiers who are buried there and the feats that they achieved.

The Normandy American Cemetery remains one of the most well known and most visited military cemeteries in the area; however it is not unique. The necropolis of Colleville-sur-Mer is one of 27 military cemeteries situated in Normandy, ground which hosts the graves of over 100 000 soldiers of thirteen different nationalities. The region consists of sixteen British cemeteries, five German cemeteries, two Canadian cemeteries, two American cemeteries, one Polish cemetery and one French cemetery containing overall the bodies of 13 800 Americans, 17 000 British, 5 110 Canadians, 729 Polish, 246 French, 27 Australians, 19 New Zealanders, 7 South Africans, 7 Russians, 3 Czechs, 2 Italians, 1 Belgian and more than 70 000 Germans.

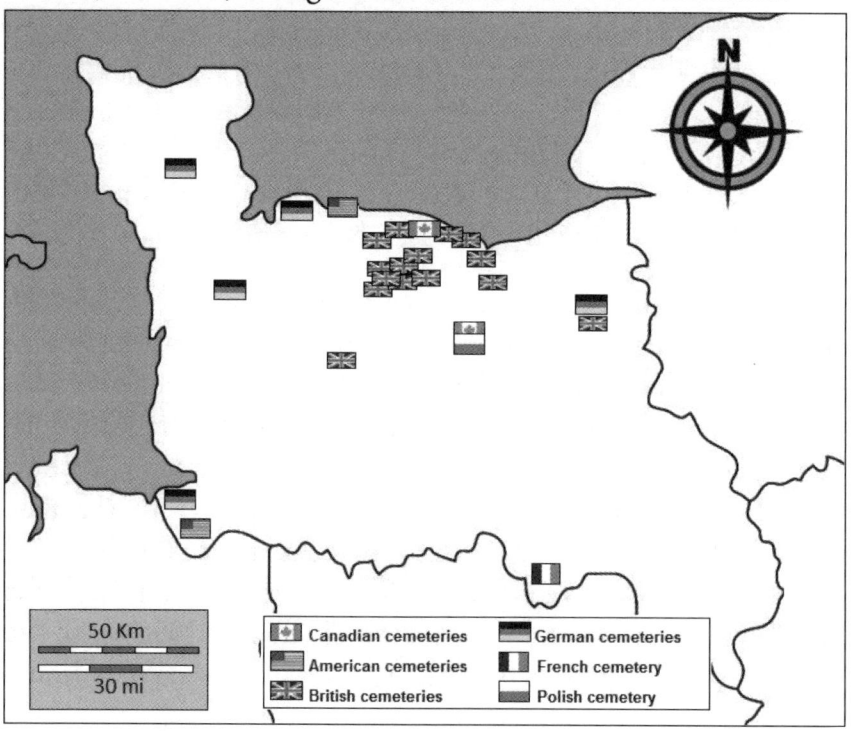

The Colleville-sur-Mer cemetery contains 9387 graves over an area of 170 acres, plus 1557 names of soldiers engraved on the Wall of the Missing whose bodies have never been found. It is not just a cemetery of the D-Day landing. It cares for equally a number of soldiers killed before, during and after the events of 6th June 1944. The cemetery of Colleville-sur-Mer is more commonly known under the name of the Normandy American Cemetery, especially by the Anglo-Saxons. The regional reference in its title is utilized to demonstrate its location and the fact that buried there are principally American soldiers killed in Upper and Lower-Normandy[1]. It also refers to events that occurred seventy years ago: the battle of Normandy.

***

On 7th December 1941, the United-States of America was attacked by surprise at Pearl Harbor by the Japanese which led to them actively entering into the Second World War against the Axis (Nazi Germany, the Japanese Empire and Fascist Italy). Very early on, the first invasion plans via the English Channel were envisaged. During the Trident conference in May 1943, the vast invasion project which the Americans had proposed in the spring of 1942 under the code name Round Up was taken from its boxes where the British had stored it. The Quadrant conference, held in Quebec in August 1943, decided in favor of the Bay of Seine coastline, in preference to that of the Pas-de-Calais, an objective judged to be too predictable for the Germans because of the short distance of the English coast. Initially, three invasion sectors were chosen: Omaha, Gold and Juno. But the British General Montgomery, Deputy to General Eisenhower, decided to extend the assault sector judged too narrow: by adding Utah

---

[1] However, there were some exceptions of soldiers killed in Brittany and in other regions and finally buried at Colleville-sur-Mer as we will re-call later.

to free Cherbourg more quickly and to allow the capture of a deep water port, and Sword, finally to reach Ouistreham. The first dates selected envisaged a landing in the early part of May 1944. But due to a lack of landing craft because of the increase in the number of landing beaches, D-Day was put back by one month. The Allies held onto the date of 5th June because of its favorable conditions: the assault had to take place at dawn, with a mid-rising tide to avoid the obstacles of the famous Atlantic Wall constructed under the orders of Hitler.

Because of bad weather, the invasion was finally effected on 6th June 1944. Except at Omaha-Beach, the Atlantic Wall did not hold and everywhere, the Allies made gains inland. The site of Omaha, situated between the communities of Vierville-sur-Mer, Saint-Laurent-sur-Mer and Colleville-sur-Mer, was because of its topography, easier to defend for the Germans. However, it was the only place which permitted a landing between the British sector of Gold and the American sector of Utah. The plateau where today is located the American cemetery of Colleville-sur-Mer was liberated by the American 1st Infantry Division several hours after the arrival of the first assault waves on the beach, which reflects the important difficulties encountered at Omaha-Beach. On the evening of D-Day, the bridgehead of Omaha did not exceed 1.2 miles in depth and the losses exceeded more than three thousand men (killed, injured and missing) being a third of the total losses of 6th June. Despite all, at midnight, 156 000 Allied soldiers of which 73 000 Americans had set foot on the Normandy coast.

The 29th Infantry Division landed between Vierville-sur-Mer and Saint-Laurent and was sent westwards to attempt to join up with the troops who landed at Utah, while that of the First Infantry Division landed between Saint-Laurent-sur-Mer and Colleville-sur-Mer and received the order to penetrate inland in the direction of Caumont-l'Éventé. On the 12th June, the 101st Airborne Division liberated Carentan, an important road junction enabling the connection of the Cotentin and the Calvados. In mid- June, the bridgeheads were considerably enlarged and joined up. The Americans who disembarked at Utah-Beach finally went towards Cherbourg which they liberated on 26th and 27th June, enabling them to have a deep water port indispensable for the re-supply of troops.

The difficulties encountered in Normandy can be explained by the painful battle of the hedgerows which followed afterwards: Saint-Lô was not liberated until the 18th July after violent fighting. After its liberation, the Americans, following an idea by General Bradley, put into place a major offensive starting on 25th July: Operation Cobra which resulted in the rapid liberation of Coutances on 28th July. This also permitted the troops of the 4th Armored Division to reach Avranches two days later. The advance was rapid and the Americans were in Brittany in the beginning of August. The Allies were then in a position to encircle the German troops. From 11th August, the Americans progressed in the direction of Argentan, then Falaise and on 20th August, the Germans were caught. Numerous German soldiers in spite of everything were able to cross the Seine and continued to slow down the American divisions in the Eure, more precisely in the Elbeuf region and Louviers. The 29th August is the date generally retained as being that of the end of the battle of Normandy: at this time, the Allied forces had progressed towards the north, the east and the south, in pursuit of the Germans who tried to re-organize. In total, there were sadly over 25 000 American casualties during this battle which lasted only two and a half months[2].

---

[2] For more information concerning the landing and the battle of Normandy see the books of Stephen AMBROSE, Joseph BALKOSKI or once more of Jean QUELLIEN.

Temporary military cemeteries were arranged to receive all these bodies then, the American Government undertook a program of repatriation, depending on the wishes of the families, together with the burial of the remaining bodies in two permanent American cemeteries situated in Normandy and constructed for this purpose. Thus, in addition to the cemetery of Colleville-sur-Mer, there exists another military American cemetery in the region: that of Saint-James (Manche Department) commonly called the Brittany American cemetery. This denomination was given to it above all to enable the worldwide visitors to distinguish between the two locations. This naming is equally justified by the place's location just some miles from the Brittany border; Saint-James marks the breakthrough of the German defenses which allowed the liberation of Brittany and the annihilation of German resistance in Normandy.

However, these two cemeteries would never have existed in the past because burials especially reserved for military soldiers are very recent creations. In fact, for a long time, heroes and military leaders were the only soldiers to be interred with dignity. This heritage old as time only changed from the 19th century, when Nations started to erect the first graves of simple soldiers fallen in battle. They were essentially ossuaries in which the dead were unknown: it was the case for the Mexican American war cemetery (1847 – 1850), for the French graves of the Crimean at Sevastopol (1856) or once more for the French and German graves of the war of 1870 – 1871. The first international agreements concerning the safeguarding of tombs, regardless of nationality, were signed in 1856, during the Treaty of Paris and in 1871, during the Treaty of Frankfurt. With the First World War, the belligerents equipped themselves with identification and burial services and, under pressure from the soldiers themselves, the individual grave became more common. Each nation created its own war graves organization: the Commonwealth War Graves

Commission for the British (1917), the *Commission nationale des sépultures militaires* for the French (1918), the *Volksbund Deutsche Kriegraberfursorge* for the Germans (1919) and the American Battle Monuments Commission (1923) for the Americans.

It is this latter institution which was entrusted with the upkeep of eight permanent American cemeteries from the First World War and fourteen permanent American cemeteries established after the Second World War including that of Colleville-sur-Mer. But outside of these twenty two cemeteries, the American Battle Monuments Commission, generally called the ABMC, is equally responsible for the maintenance of three other more unusual cemeteries: that of Mexico, Corozal and Clark cemetery. The National Cemetery of Mexico was established in 1851 to commemorate the sacrifice of soldiers killed during the fighting against Mexico. The responsibility for its maintenance was entrusted to the ABMC on 17th July 1947, by an executive order of President Truman. It consists of a cemetery where grouped together are 1 563 graves of soldiers killed during the Civil War, the Indian campaigns and of the Spanish American War. The administration of the Corozal (Panama) cemetery was assigned to the commission by an executive order dated October 1979 and signed by President Carter. This cemetery commemorates above all the sacrifice of all the men having worked on the Panama Canal operations and welcomes also, even today, any veteran wishing to be buried there. The Clark Veterans Cemetery is located in the Philippines and the ABMC assumed control of the site on 16th December 2013. It is the burial place for thousands of Veterans who died in conflicts other than the Second World War.

The commission maintains then actually a total of twenty five permanent cemeteries established outside of American soil of which eleven are located in France and a further twenty six monuments and memorials. The last ABMC monument was inaugurated on 28th July 2013 in the United Nations Cemetery in Busan, South Korea in remembrance of the American victims in the Korean War. The ABMC undertakes a considerable task in the maintenance of these monuments and of the graves of nearly 125 000 American soldiers of which 93 000 were killed during the Second World War.

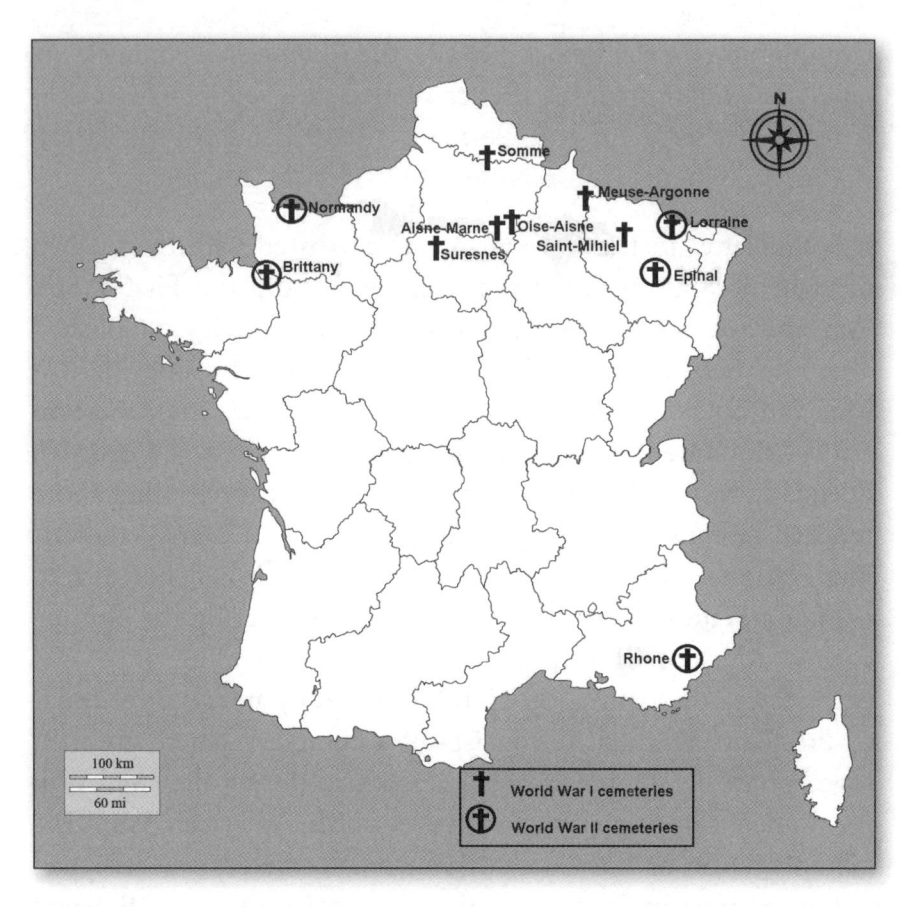

***

The Normandy landing and the Battle of Normandy have inspired numerous historians and authors whose works have multiplied over time. Over many years, historical research has concentrated on commemorative memorials, whether from the First or Second

World War, the municipalities keeping strong the memories of these events. One third of the municipalities of Calvados share a total of 370 monuments related to the Normandy landing. With such numbers it was evident that a study of the commemorations would become a field of research on its own. Much thought, including those of academics have flourished on the subject; a symposium was held in Caen in 1994 on the remembrance and the commemoration following the events of 1944. Similarly, many students have worked on the places of commemoration or the ceremonies. We can quote for example the study of Ahmed Elkhawaga on the memorable locations of the Normandy landing or the university thesis of Delphine Leneveu on the American commemorative monuments of the Normandy landing.

However, the history of the military cemeteries and the management of the dead were put to one side, even taking into account the few works on the subject and the trend which is likely to change soon[3]. The history of the Normandy American Cemetery has meanwhile never been written even though it is one of the most sacred sites of Normandy. No historian has ever really looked into this site, either by conviction that it was not essential for the understanding of the battle of Normandy and its consequences or, more likely, for lack of sources. The best study to this day of the cemeteries maintained by the ABMC is that of Ferdinand Dessente who portrays an interesting study of the American cemetery at Neuville-en-Condroz. It is true that certain works evoke Colleville-sur-Mer but they do so in a brief way. We can quote notably the very good guide of William Jordan called *"The Normandy American Cemetery"* or again that of Hugues Ozouf on the cemeteries of the Second World War in Lower Normandy. Thus, in spite of its reputation, the cemetery remains unknown: numerous errors or omissions can be

---

[3] Notably with the Doctorate thesis of Antonin DEHAYS at the University of Caen under the direction of Jean QUELLIEN.

recorded in the many articles or reporting realized by the media. In view of these errors and this lack of information we decided to undertake an in depth study of this location paramount to the remembrance of the D-Day landing and to Normandy tourism. A real symbol, the Normandy American Cemetery more than merits a book dedicated to its subject.

This study will therefore endeavor to look back on its history and especially its origins, to provide readers with a corrected vision of events that took place there and that is as close as possible to the historical truth. This study will not attempt to explain how death occurred during the Battle of Normandy on the American side, but it will try to answer the many questions about the history of the cemetery as well as work done by the Americans to honor their dead in Normandy. This book will look back over a long period of time and examine the ins and outs that made the cemetery a mecca of Normand tourism. In order to understand this site, it will be necessary to go back several decades before the events of 1944, keeping in mind that the history of the cemetery is still being written today.

The interest shown in this study by the ABMC and its help has enabled us to assemble documents not easily consultable in France including primary sources such as the manuscript left by General Thomas North (who led the commission during the construction of the cemeteries of the Second World War and whose information was of great help). Similarly, a lot of data has been received on the methods of burial or the services of American burials thanks to the works of Edward Steere and Thayer Boardman, *Final Disposition of World War II Dead 1945 – 1951*" or once more, "*Manuals of the American Armed Forces Graves Registration Services*". These documents were supplemented by the records of the Normandy American Cemetery accumulated since its creation but also by the French press which has published many articles and various private collections to which we had access.

These documentary sources allowed us to organize this book around several major themes. Thanks to them, we will understand how the United-States and its Armed Forces, then the ABMC have supported the American soldiers killed in Normandy following the Allied landing in 1944 and the methods utilized to pay tribute to them and to maintain their memory intact through the Normandy American Cemetery. Similarly, it will allow us to study the remarkable evolution which has occurred since its opening and the interest shown, up to today, in this site which has become, in addition to a must place of remembrance, one of the most visited sites of the battle of Normandy.

To do so, this book will consist of three parts. The first will look back on the first operations carried out upstream of the creation of permanent cemeteries and in particular the establishment of a burial service, the creation of a service to identify soldiers killed during the war, the implementation of temporary cemeteries and the difficulties in choosing permanent sites. The second part will focus on the creation and organization of the Normandy American Cemetery and in particular the final burial, the architecture and the soldiers buried there. The third and final section will attempt to highlight the cemetery's objectives and these are: the commemoration, the continuity of the soldiers' memory thanks to new projects and business developments as well as the work done to welcome families, veterans and visitors.

The American headquarters of the Graves Registration Service at Sainte-Mère-Église responsible for the organization and maintenance of nine provisional cemeteries established as fighting raged in Normandy. These nine cemeteries are: Sainte-Mère-Église No. 1 and 2, Blosville, La Cambe, Saint-Laurent-sur-Mer, Saint-Corneille, Gorron, Marigny and Le Chêne-Guérin.
National Archives USA.

FIRST PART

The origins of the Normandy American Cemetery

The creation of the Graves Registration Service and its first work

ORGANIZATION OF THE QUARTERMASTER GENERAL AND THE GRAVES REGISTRATION SERVICE

Necessary services

The American organization established during the Second World War to take charge of the bodies of the soldiers killed, emerged from a heritage of older practices established in the wake of various conflicts that crossed the country. During the Seminole Wars (between 1817 and 1858) and the Mexican-American War (1846 – 1848), the American soldiers were buried near the place where they died and very little effort was made to identify them. In 1861, with the outbreak of the Civil War, the War Department demanded a census and the identification of the soldiers killed. Thus in 1867, the U.S. Quartermaster Corps was for the first time responsible for the burial of the soldiers fallen in combat. The loss of human life and the trauma provoked by this war alone explained the measures taken in favor of the dead soldiers: nearly 620 000 men lost their lives between 1861 and 1865. In addition to the burial of the bodies of Unionists and Confederates soldiers, this new structure was also entrusted with the upkeep and maintenance of different national cemeteries. During the Mexican-American War, the United-States developed a new practice and began to repatriate the bodies of the soldiers killed to their families. It became the first nation in the world to practice the repatriation of soldiers killed abroad.

On 7th August 1917, at the request of General Pershing, a Graves Registration Service was created within the Quartermaster Corps to take over the dead of the First World War: the GRS

(Graves Registration Service). Major Charles C. Pierce, a chaplain in the army, was recalled to active duty to become the head of the organization in Europe. The operations were carried out in Belgium, Luxembourg, in Italy, in Russia and in Great-Britain, but the most important part of the work was carried out in France. At the peak of the activities in 1919, the Graves Registration Service had 350 officers and 18 000 employees.

After July 1919, the service continued its work under the direction of the American Expeditionary Forces. In November 1919, a complete reorganization of the work in Europe was instituted and the organization was henceforth known under the name of the "Graves Registration Service QMC" and placed under the leadership of Colonel Harry F. Rethers. The new service was responsible for exhumations and the preparation of the bodies for their return to the United-States or for their burial in a permanent cemetery abroad. At the end of 1919, there were 512 temporary American cemeteries in France, Belgium and Luxembourg to which must be added the soldiers buried in French and British military cemeteries, in communal cemeteries or isolated graves. Of nearly 80 000 dead Americans during the First World War, only 1 643 (or 2%) were not identified, thus demonstrating the important work that was undertaken by this organization. This success placed in evidence the necessity of a specialized service for the conflicts, accomplishing the tasks of recording burials, recovering the dead as soon as possible after the fighting and identifying them quickly and efficiently.

However, this service was dismantled between the two World Wars, explaining the difficulties of its reactivation at the start of the Second World War. Following the attack on Pearl Harbor, the United-States resumed a Graves Registration Service. The Technical Manual 10-630 had been redrafted some months before, in August 1941, to explain and detail the different techniques to recover dead soldiers. With the evolution of the conflict, all the theaters of military operation installed units of this new service for recording burials.

The restarting of the service suffered some difficulties which led to the Commanding Officer of the Army Service Forces developing a directive to instruct the Quartermaster General. This directive was titled *"To study and draw up a body of recommendations in reference to the problems of disposal of the war dead"*. The recommendations were orientated around three major aspects of the question: problems relating to graves abroad and the return of the dead to the United-States; then the necessity for a joint plan between the United-States and the foreign countries and lastly, the possibility to extend the national cemeteries in the United-States and the acquisition of sites for the construction of permanent cemeteries abroad.

With the increase in the number of troops (1.4 million soldiers in 1941 and 8 million in 1943) and by the same, with the increase in losses, it became evident that the office of the Quartermaster General was not sufficient to handle all cases. It was necessary to draw the attention of the highest authorities in the United-States to solve the burials problem. The establishment of a special service section dedicated to the recording of graves dominated the concept of the reorganization. Ensuring the management of the Memorial branch of the service installations division of the Quartermaster General, Colonel Harbold took personal responsibility in the preparation and study of these questions on 1st July 1943. On 14th August of the same year he submitted to the Quartermaster General Edward B. Gregory, a project named Policy Study No. 34 the second part of which was to reorganize the Graves Registration Service, renamed the American Graves Registration Service (AGRS)[4].

The AGRS had then to operate under the direction of the Quartermaster General, both in the United-States and anywhere else in the world. The program included a detailed presentation of the team and of the management structure.

The operation of the Graves Registration Service

The AGRS was subject to the direct authority of the office of the Quartermaster General of the U.S. Forces officially inscribed as head by a War Department circular No. 206 dated 11th September 1943. The service disposed of its own section in the United-States to serve as a clearinghouse to realize and record the reports of deaths and burials. The elements of the Graves Registration Service were divided into two principal sectors (Asian and European), then in twelve major command zones. In general, these zones embraced large regions corresponding to the progressive deployment of the American Army, being North America, the Hawaiian islands, Australia, the East Indies and Malaysia, the Philippines, India, China, the Middle East, Europe, Great-Britain and Ireland, Africa and to finish, the Caribbean. The headquarters of these areas were managed by a Colonel and consisted of 79 employees each.

The principal unit of the Graves Registration Service was a company – a company found itself generally attached to an Army Corps. The management of the company could be delegated by the Commanding Officer of the theater of operation to an officer of the Army Corps to which it was attached. In cases where no company was available, it was anticipated that each battalion, regiment, division, headquarters, hospital, etc. appointed a man to serve as officer of the Graves Registration Service.

---

[4] The name given during the Second World War is henceforth known as being the service of Mortuary Affairs.

The latter would be responsible for finding suitable personnel to undertake the tasks of the company. On the European front, all the companies were organized according to regulation 10-297. It provided that each company be composed of 6 officers and 119 men. The company included a company headquarters (two officers and nineteen men) and was subdivided into four platoons (one officer and twenty-two men each). Each platoon was itself divided into three sections of six men[5]. A platoon was empowered to serve one of the divisions of an Army Corps.

Organization of a Graves Registration company according to regulation 10-297

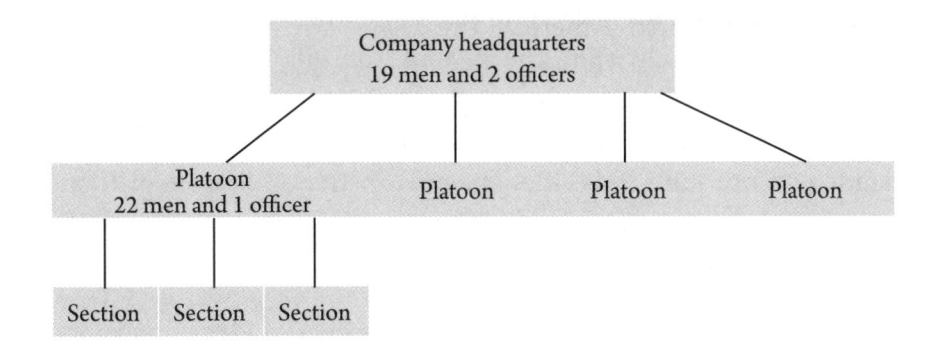

```
         A company of the Graves Registration Service
              119 men and 6 officers + 12 medics

                    Company headquarters
                     19 men and 2 officers
         ┌──────────────┬──────────────┬──────────────┐
      Platoon         Platoon       Platoon        Platoon
 22 men and 1 officer
   ┌────┬────┐
Section Section Section
```

---

[5] Graves Registration Services: the general board, *United-States Forces, European Theater*, [s.l.], 1945, 53p.

FIRST PART 27

Each company included a medical team of twelve people whose mission was not to treat the injured or sick but to help the service teams to identify the bodies and to find out the cause of their death. Amongst them, there were four qualified morgue employees on the basis of one man plus one medical technician by platoon. The company often included clerks and personnel for masses as well as four administrative assistants because of the amount of work administration (equally on the basis of one by platoon) and a fifth man for the company's headquarters administration. Finally, two men were specially trained to detect the trapped bodies. To these numbers were added thirteen trucks and ten trailers to enable the company to function. A medical team member was normally present during operations carried out by Graves Registration personnel.

In order to properly understand the organization of a company, let us take for example that of the 603rd Graves Registration Company, assigned to the VII American Army Corps in March 1944 in anticipation of the Normandy landing. The first platoon served the 4th Infantry Division, the second, the 9th Infantry Division, the third, the 90th Infantry Division and the fourth, the 82nd Airborne Division. In the V corps of the First Army which landed on 6th June 1944, the Graves Registration Service platoons were attached to each of the divisions in the Corps and also saw an additional platoon included.

For units smaller than divisions, the Quartermaster General planned smaller teams to carry out the work of burial and identification according to regulation 10-500. The Graves Registration Companies had staffing limitations and required a large workforce composed of civilians or of prisoners. In theory, they had to call upon them only when the front was more than 12 miles away. But this regulation was not often respected in Normandy as shown in the utilization of German prisoners with the provisional burials on Omaha-Beach.

"The doctors had to ensure that the individuals were dead. We were told that it was important to determine which type of weapon and weaponry was the most lethal in battle".
Source: http://in-honored-glory.info/.

African-American soldiers are collecting bodies with the aid of German prisoners on Omaha Beach.
National Archives USA.

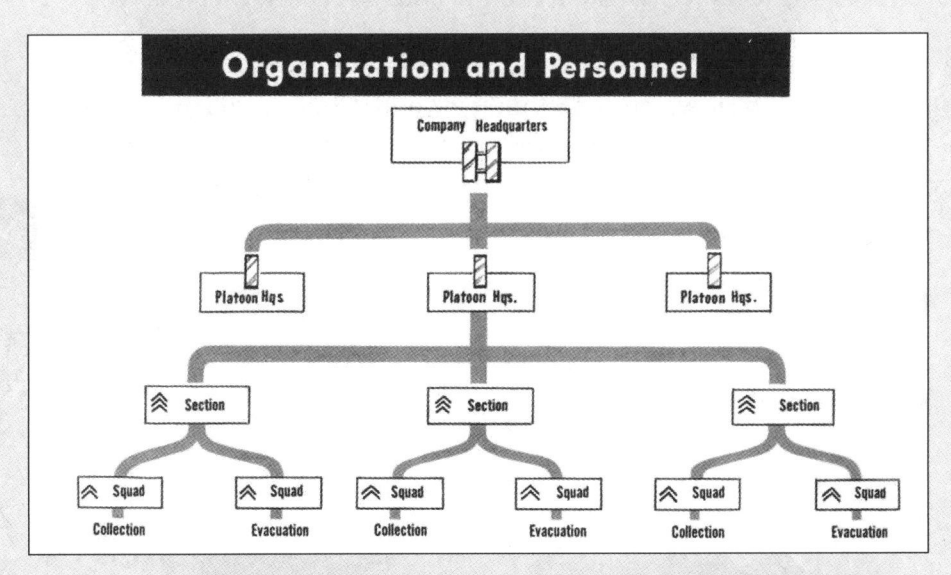

The chart describes the organization structure of a Graves Registration Company according to rule 10-298 of September 1944.
Source: http://in-honored-glory.info/.

The Graves Registration Service considered civilian help ineffective and difficult to control. This observation led to the realization of a second regulation in September 1944, a little after the battle of Normandy. Regulation No. 10-298 considerably increased the staffing of each company, going from 125 men (officers included) to 260. It was to create autonomous companies better able to manage the physical operations on the ground without a pressing need for civilian workers or of prisoners.

These well-structured companies knew nevertheless some weaknesses. In fact, information on their role was little circulated before the Normandy landing, which required the American military to each develop their work method for operations concerning the cemeteries. Communication was limited between the fighting troops and the Graves Registration Service. However, in the manuals, these companies had the task of maintaining operational links and of providing technical assistance to the units which they served.

At the end of the war the service's staffing was estimated at 22 792 men of which 3 189 military and 19 603 civilians. Among them were 2 442 administrative staff and 3 420 technicians. The logistics included, 5 895 motorized vehicles. The service employed more than thirty active companies before it was again dismantled after the war[6].

---

[6] Graves Registration Services: the general board, *op. cit.* and STEERE (Edward), BOARDMAN (Thayer M.), *Final disposition of World War II Dead 1945-51*, 1957.

THE PREPARATORY WORK OF THE GRAVES REGISTRATION SERVICE

To collect the bodies and personal effects

Firstly, it is important to indicate that the troops of the Graves Registration Service took care of the remains of all individuals serving under the American flag either in the Army, Air Force, Navy, Marines, Coastguards, American Red Cross, accredited correspondents, observers… as well as deceased deserters and prisoners. Similarly, they took care of bodies of Allied soldiers or Germans found by their teams even if, according to the Graves Registration Service manual, German bodies should not be buried in the same sections of cemeteries whether American or Allied. Under the principles of the Geneva Convention, the United-States assumed support for dead Germans; the information concerning them was then entrusted to the Information Office for Prisoners of War. The procedures required that the combat units evacuated themselves the bodies of the soldiers killed towards a collection point whose responsibility was assumed by the Graves Registration Service. Each army or division disposed of its own organization to manage the collections.

The best known example is that of Omaha-Beach. On 6th June 1944, the 18th Infantry Regiment, 1st Infantry Division organized its own unit to collect the bodies which was composed of eighteen men. The 6th Engineer Special Brigade which also landed on Omaha-Beach entrusted responsibility and the collection of bodies to an officer commanding one of the Beach Groups of the battalion. Each group was asked, thereafter, to appoint an officer of the battalion as Graves Registration Service officer. Things were done very much in the same way on Utah-Beach until the 603rd Graves Registration Company landed on 9th June to collect and bury the bodies of the VII Army Corps. However, some elements of the company had arrived on the 6th June, like Elbert E. Legg, sent by glider with the 82nd Airborne Division, who started to collect the bodies scattered along the pathways thanks to information brought by the soldiers.

The AGRS units also tried to deal with the evacuation of the bodies to the company control points in the combat zones: this explains the presence of the 607th Graves Registration Company at Utah and Omaha-Beach from the 6th June. This company was attached to the V Corps (two platoons for Omaha and two for Utah). Its 125 men had the task of collecting and burying the bodies as quickly as possible. At Omaha-Beach, they had the help of requisitioned German prisoners who carried the bodies from the beach and the surrounding hills towards the central collection point prior to transport to the then proposed cemetery. In the early hours of 7th June, it was asked to align the bodies in a unique zone out of sight. The report of the 6th Engineer Special Brigade informs us that two days later on 9th June, at the headquarters conference, officers insisted that the collection be systematic and that the dead had to be buried along road D, between Saint-Laurent-sur-Mer and Vierville-sur-Mer.

In each army, collection points were established to allow the assembly of the bodies before their transport to one of the provisional cemeteries where they would be buried. However, the bodies were most often evacuated directly to the provisional cemeteries when they were close enough. The following photographs show us how the Americans have had the bodies of the soldiers covered prior to being buried.

The companies of the Graves Registration Service aimed to collect the bodies and the personal effects of the dead soldiers. Initially, during the Normandy landing, the material taken off the dead soldiers (weapons, ammunition or rations) was made

Members of the 607th Graves Registration Company surrounded by the bodies of soldiers fallen at Omaha-Beach. *National Archives USA.*

Temporary collecting point at Saint-Laurent-sur-Mer, Omaha-Beach. *Conseil régional de Basse-Normandie/National Archives USA.*

available to the troops who continued to fight. But progressively as the beachheads were consolidated and as the troops were re-organized, personnel were assigned to secure the ammunition and to sort out the material. During the first days, the personal effects were placed in parachutes. The French, deprived for the most part after four years of occupation coveted the personal effects of the dead piling up. They hoped in particular to get the jump boots of the dead parachutists. From time to time they were allowed to recover the leather boots of the Germans whose bodies had been collected by the Graves Registration Service. The administration work of the Graves Registration Service companies was gradually organized and the personal effects were taken stock of to be sent later to depots after cleaning and disinfection.

There remains little evidence of these depots in Lower-Normandy. We only know, thanks to Colonel Ramsay of the Quartermaster Corps, that a detachment of thirty-nine men and four Quartermaster officers were sent to the continent twenty-eight days after D-Day and were organized in a cheese factory in Isigny-sur-Mer. The First Army had already accumulated more than 13 000 personal effects bags which had not yet been sorted, nor classified. In view of the scale of the task, this storage space quickly appeared insufficient and Cherbourg seemed to be the only town capable of storing all these effects. More than 35 000 personal effects bags were sent there and the factory at Isigny-sur-Mer was retained as a forward collecting point. At the end of the battle of Normandy, scarcely six weeks after the organization of the storage space at Cherbourg, it was necessary to move the unit nearer the fighting troops who had moved inland. Paris became the new and ideal place for storage thanks to its location and its important transport network[7].

---

[7] Testimony of Colonel A. C. Ramsey of the Quartermaster Corps, Extract from the Quartermaster Review of September-October 1945.

Collecting point at Saint-Laurent-sur-Mer temporary cemetery.
Conseil régional de Basse-Normandie/National Archives USA.

Collecting point at the temporary cemetery of La Cambe.
Conseil régional de Basse-Normandie/National Archives USA.

After the collection, the personal effects were sent to the office of personal effects in Kansas City, Missouri. This office was activated on 5th February 1942 and its principal aim was the careful storage and inventory of each personal effect. Each property was listed in an inventory printed in four examples. The original was placed in the personal effects bag, a copy was sent to the Adjutant-General in Washington, one other was left in the Quartermaster's depot in Kansas City and the last was stored in the Graves Registration Service archives. Once the inventory and classification work was completed, the widow or the legal representatives were able to recover the personal effects of the soldier[8].

Identification

Before the Normandy landing, the first identifications and burials of American soldiers in France was originated by the French civilians and the German authorities. It primarily concerned the teams of aircrew who took part in the operations above the French soil since 1942 (It explains why we find today a large number of soldiers killed before the 6th June in the Normandy American Cemetery). From the moment that the crash sites were recorded and the men identified, the International Red Cross was informed and transmitted the information to the American Government.

The AGRS was entrusted with the identification of the bodies of the American soldiers since its inception. The aim of the mission was considered to be priority and crucial. Following the excellent results obtained after the First World War and the impact it produced in the United-States, the Government consented

---

[8] Graves Registration, *War department Field Manual*, Washington, January 1945, 57p. and « Graves Registration search and recovery operations after World War II », *Quartermaster Review*, May/June 1946, Normandy American Cemetery.

Sorting and listing of the personal effects undertaken by an employee of the Quartermaster Corps. *National Archives USA.*

Collecting point at the temporary cemetery of Blosville.
Conseil régional de Basse-Normandie/National Archives USA.

to provide the necessary means to achieve this task under the best possible conditions. Each service company was perfectly prepared to undertake identifications and the different manuals developed described precisely the procedures to follow.

On D-Day, the first teams on the spot undertook the identification of the dead soldiers, whether American, Allies or enemies, in the same way and to the best extent possible. In fact, the identification "process" really started once the body was taken to the collection point. The team in charge of the site had to find the identity of the body before sending it to its burial location. The process was often helped by the famous identification plaques called dog tags. Each American soldier, whatever his unit, wore two permanently. They had their name, serial number, religion, blood group without indication of rhesus and from March 1944, a next-of-kin to contact in the event of death. Identification was rapidly established when at least a dog tag was found. In the case where the two tags were recovered, one was left on the soldier after a carbon copy had been taken and assigned finally to the Medical Officer in charge of drawing up the list of the losses; the other was placed with the personal effects until the arrival of the body in the temporary cemetery where the dog tag was hung on the grave marker[9].

However, the process was not always as simple because sometimes, the soldier killed was found without his plaques. In these cases, the work of the Graves Registration Service came into its own. The first thing to do was to go through the personal effects in search of clues; a wages slip, a vaccination card, an identity bracelet on the wrist of the dead, etc. These few elements were sufficient to assure the identification

---

[9] Graves Registration, *War department Field Manual, op. cit.* and "Testimony of a veteran of the 603rd Quartermaster Graves Registration Company, Colonel Legg", *Army Quartermaster bulletin*, 1994, Normandy American Cemetery.

even if taken in isolation. The soldiers received advice to write their whole name and their number under their helmet, on the reverse of their trouser belt, in their shoes or their leggings in case they might lose their identity plaque. Unfortunately, very few of them followed this advice.

In many cases, no document was discovered on the bodies which prevented identification. The Graves Registration units looked to see if the body did not come from a tank, an aircraft or other vehicle, including a list of team members allowing identification by elimination. If nothing was found, the Graves Registration Service attempted to collect testimonies from soldiers of the unit that could possibly identify the dead body. There had to be at least one or two members of the unit to be convinced with certainty of the identity of the body. As a last resort on the ground, the service was able to rely on the Battle Casualty Reports which were established and reported by each unit after combat.

On many occasions dog tags were found in the ground (as a result of bombing for example). The identification teams then performed research on the unknown soldiers lying close to the place where the plaques had been found.

If after all these searches an identity was finally obtained, the information was recorded and placed in a bottle (or a canteen if nothing else was available) to be buried with the body pending receipt of the subsequent exhumation directive issued by the office of the Quartermaster General. In the case where the body could not be identified, a copy of the burial report was slipped into a capsule and buried twelve inches into the ground near the body. These capsules were glass tubes around one inch diameter, some eight inches long and able to be easily recovered at any time to attempt a new identification of the body.

In spite of the existence of multiple elements enabling positive identification on the battlefield, frequently soldiers arrived as unknown in the research stations. In these cases the bodies were buried provisionally as unknown, during which time the combat receded or the war ended and further investigation could take place at a later date. Each Unknown Soldier was buried and designated under the name Unknown X-1, Unknown X-2 and so on, throughout the temporary cemetery. If several unknowns were found together but not identified – for example the crash of a bomber – each one was given a letter and a number to remember that these men died together. In the case where separation of the bodies was impossible, they were buried within the same grave.

The AGRS teams took care to first note for each unknown all the elements which could enable a future identification. They recorded each physical detail in a report called "Report of Interment" which detailed, for example, the physical anomalies or the particular characteristics such as birthmarks or tattoos.

The AGRS also photographed all personal objects: rings, private letters, etc. because identification sometimes hung by a thread. Here is one example: an American soldier killed during the Second World War remained an unknown despite extensive research. The only element that could allow his identification was a signet ring which he wore on a finger. The signet ring was engraved with the insignia of a military college in the United-States. Thanks to the system put in place by the Graves Registration Service and after months of enquiry, the research finally bore fruit. Thanks to identification efforts in collaboration with the school in question, the department was able to discover the identity of the soldier, allowing the family to be informed[10].

---

[10] Graves Registration, *Quartermaster Review*, May/June 1946.

American identification capsules buried with the bodies.
Source: http://med-dept.com/grs.php.

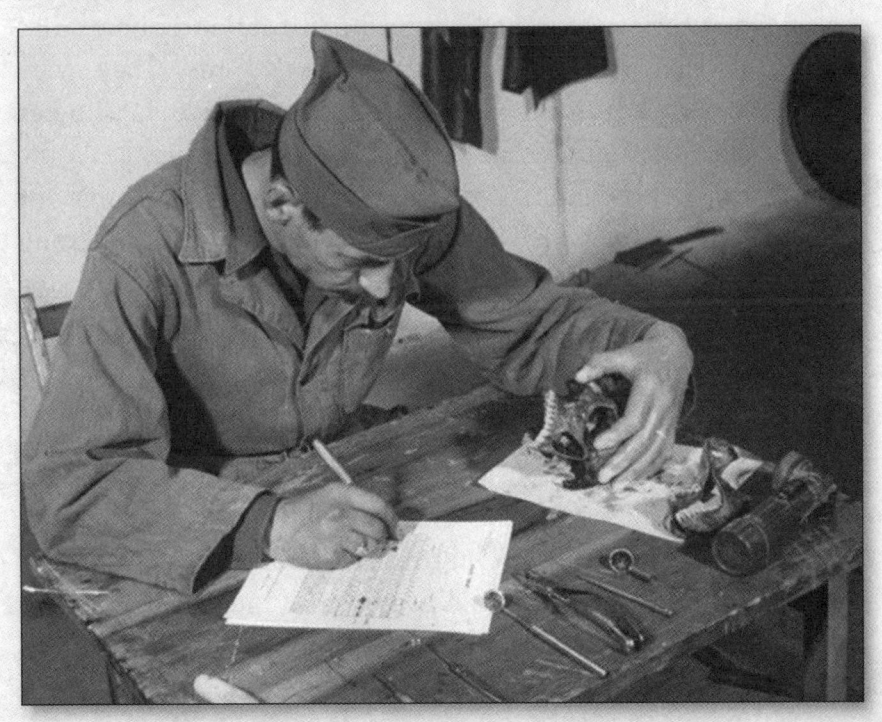

A soldier of the Graves Registration Service provides information for the Burial Report. *National Archives USA.*

If needed, the service could take the digital fingerprints for each unknown as well as an examination of the teeth that were recorded in black and white on the information sheet of the soldier. The set of all ten fingers was sent to the Adjutant General office in Washington and to the Federal Bureau of Investigation (FBI), who, thanks to a mathematical basis were able to search for the identity of the unknown. The report of the 6th Engineer Special Brigade informs us that just after the Normandy landing, digital fingerprints were taken from twenty bodies of soldiers on Omaha-Beach. This technique allowed the identification of seventeen bodies, the three other soldiers remained unidentifiable.

Once exhumed from the provisional cemeteries after the war, the bodies were sent to laboratories before being finally buried. These laboratories were the Central Identification Laboratories known also as the Central Identification Points. They were equipped with advanced material and responsible for bodies whose identification was uncertain or when differences were found during the exhumation. They were also responsible for the unidentified remains exhumed from individual or group burials. Each team was in general composed of four members: a supervisor and three assistants who examined the bodies to find potential clues.

Critics of the identification program insisted that the identification process considerably slowed the burial process, but in view of the results, it is clear that the work was a success. According to the Army Quartermaster Corps Foundation, American losses are estimated at 286 959 men of which 246 492 bodies had already been identified in 1946 being 86% of the losses. Among the 40 467 unidentified bodies, 54% had not yet been found (21 826 soldiers).

Units of the Graves Registration Service did not spare their efforts to establish the identity of the dead soldiers. Identifying a large number of soldiers as soon as they arrived at the collection points had as a result a sharp reduction in the number of unidentified bodies transferred in the temporary cemeteries. It also allowed the grouping of burials in a limited number of sites: after the First World War, several hundreds of cemeteries were disseminated for 79 000 soldiers "only" against 54 temporary American cemeteries in Europe, for 117 000 bodies at the end of hostilities in 1945. Finally, the unknowns represented no more than 3% of the 206 677 American soldiers killed in Europe following the final exhumations and the passage of the bodies via the identification laboratories.

The Establishment of Temporary Cemeteries in Normandy

THE CREATION OF THE CEMETERY AT OMAHA-BEACH

Rules to follow

The temporary cemeteries were located in the deadliest combat zones. The number of cemeteries was often determined according to the intensity of the fighting, the speed of the front's advance and the location of the combat hospitals. Division or Corps cemeteries were established solely during the first operational stages in Normandy. Later, each army set up one or several necropolis following its involvement in the conflict. The decision to create a temporary cemetery reverted to different people; it concerned in general the Commander of the Army Corps or of the Division but it happened that the decision was taken by an officer of the Graves Registration Service, as will be seen later on.

Whilst the Allies planned the landing, the AGRS also planned the implementation of temporary cemeteries in Normandy. It was necessary for future cemeteries not to be seen by hostile forces nor be within reach of the artillery. If the implementation of a temporary cemetery was judged impossible, the service recommended using local cemeteries. Furthermore, it was important to develop the cemeteries in the least fertile zones, in order not to deprive the local inhabitants of food which they could take from the soil. The officers of the Graves Registration Service, generally engineering surveyors qualified to take over the management of the sites, had an obligation to retain permanently with them a map locating the cemeteries a copy of which had to be sent to the Quartermaster General.

The choice of the cemetery location fell sometimes on members of the AGRS. However, the layout of the site and its boundaries were the responsibility of the Engineering Corps when these troops were available. The standard plans provided by the Quartermaster General had to be scrupulously followed especially concerning the organization of the plots and rows of the graves and in particular on the number of burials per cemetery.

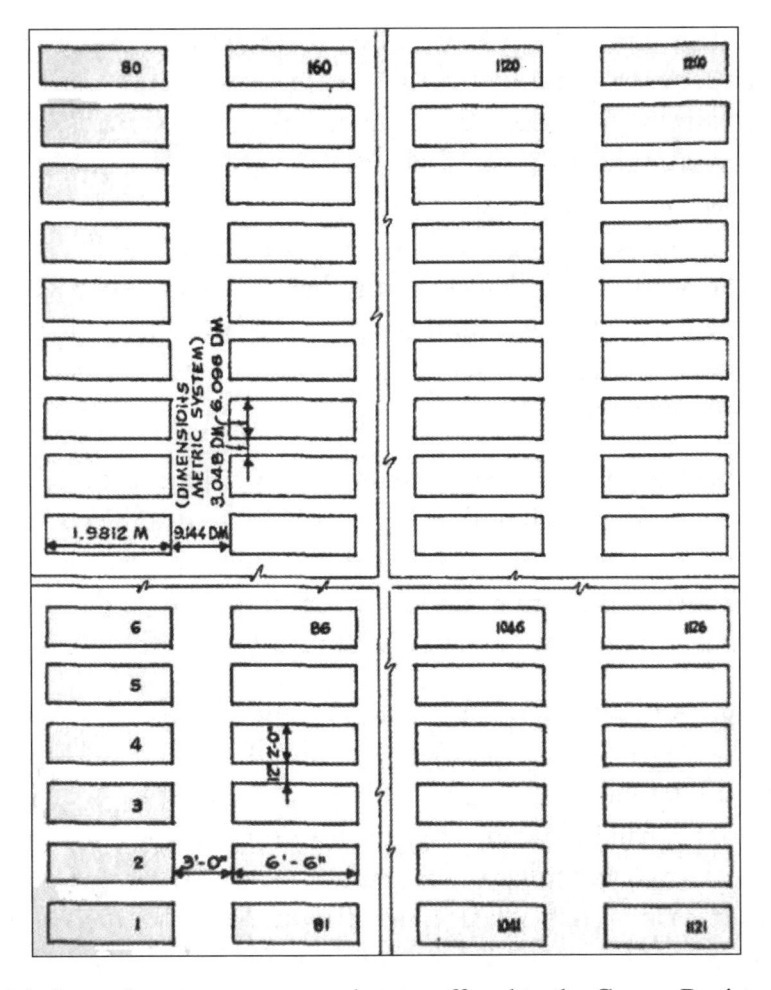

Model plans of temporary cemeteries are offered to the Graves Registration Service employees to help them in their task. *Photo ABMC.*

The installation of a first cemetery

The first burial plans provided for the Normandy landing envisaged the creation of two cemeteries in coordination with the V Corps close by Omaha-Beach: one to be situated south west of Sainte-Honorine-des-Pertes, in the zone of the 5th Engineers Special Brigade and the other, in the zone of the 6th Brigade, near Cricqueville-en-Bessin.

The 607th Graves Registration Company faced several problems which required them to change their plans when they landed on D-Day. In the first place, the dead on the beach and close inland were very numerous. Similarly, the troops did not advance in the way that was originally planned. It was imperative to secure the area before dealing with the dead. The men of the Engineers Brigade were again dealing with their primary task that was the opening of the exits and the clearance of supplies from the beachheads. Thus, they were not able to form the necessary work teams to bury the bodies.

The realization of a first cemetery on 6th June proved to be impossible. The two initial sites were still located at the end of the day under German control and many of the beach exits were still blocked. With the important loss it became vital to find a location to establish a first temporary cemetery.

Warrant Officer James W. Tucker landed on 6th June on Omaha-Beach, more precisely in the Easy-Red sector. His unit, 299th Combat Engineer Battalion, equipped with eight bulldozers, had for its objective to clean-up the beach exits. Once that job was accomplished, he had to undertake another equally delicate task: *"Part of our crew attempted to clear the beach of bodies but there was no place to put them. Orders came down to me to dig a temporary mass grave. I had one of my dozers do it. I had the driver go back and forth until he had a big enough trench dug.*

General view of the first temporary cemetery established on Omaha-Beach.
Conseil régional de Basse-Normandie/National Archives USA.

Ceremony at the provisional cemetery on the beach.
Conseil régional de Basse-Normandie/ National Archives USA.

FIRST PART   47

Then the Chaplain and I gathered men to collect the bodies. The job was not a pleasant one and they all eventually got sick, leaving only the Chaplain and I to finish the difficult job. The bodies were stacked in the trench like cordwood and covered over with sand. I understand it was the first American cemetery in Europe World War II" [11].

Thus, a mass grave was dug to counter the urgency. But finally on 7th June, the 3rd Platoon of the 607th Company attached to the 6th Engineer Special Brigade managed to establish a first cemetery directly on the beach, at the foot of the cliff between Vierville-sur-Mer and Saint-Laurent-sur-Mer in the Dog White sector of the Omaha-Beach landing. It became the first temporary American cemetery of the Second World War established by a company of the Graves Registration Service in France.

Subsequently, hundreds of prisoners of war were made available and African-American soldiers put them to work. George Ciampa, veteran of the 607th Graves Registration Company remembers that the graves were dug by German prisoners. The task was considerable in view of the number of bodies which were strewn on the beach. It was necessary to bury them quickly in order to avoid all risk of an epidemic and to prevent soldiers who continued to land seeing dead comrades. Many ceremonies took place in this first cemetery and many soldiers grouped together paying their respects to their brothers in arms fallen during the first days of the battle.

---

[11] http://www.6juin1944.com/veterans/tucker.php: testimony of James W. Tucker. From this, we learn that half of the men of the 299th Engineer Combat Battalion were killed or injured on Omaha-Beach. Those who survived could not advance inland until 9th June. In 1957, James returned to Omaha with his family and visited the Normandy American Cemetery. James died in 1983 and was buried at Arlington National Cemetery with full military honors.

The first soldiers buried were those killed on D-Day. In the book by
Raymond Daniel and Marie-France Benoist on Saint-Laurent-sur-Mer,
Edmond Scelles testified and remembered having seen dead Americans on
the beach. He recalled that African-Americans were responsible
for transporting them. After the ground mine clearance, a bulldozer was
used to dig the trenches.
Source: www.omahabeach.vierville.free.fr.

On June 10, 1944, at the time of its closure, this cemetery – later curiously named American cemetery No. 2 – contained the bodies of 457 American soldiers, some Germans, English sailors and RAF aircrew. According to the periodic report of the 6th Engineer Special Brigade on that same day at midnight, all the bodies around Omaha-Beach had been recovered.

The first site did not at all correspond to hygiene and morale standards. The smell and the flies made the atmosphere unbearable while at the same time, whole divisions of American soldiers continued to disembark to liberate Normandy. The first sight that the men had on arrival was that of the burials of their friends and the smell coming from the cemetery. For hygiene reasons and to maintain troop morale, the Graves Registration Service manual recognized that the graves had to be situated outside of advancing lines. It is why all the bodies were moved and buried in the new site delimited on the crest of a hill to the east of Exit E-1 at Saint-Laurent-sur-Mer.

Only one monument was erected to mark the memory of the first American temporary cemetery of the Second World War in France. Its location has been indicated for a long time by this commemorative plaque engraved with the following inscription: *"This marks the site of First American cemetary* [sic] *in France World War II since moved to American Cemetary* [sic] *No. 1"* This plaque has since been replaced by a small monument which can be seen in Vierville-sur-Mer.

The first memorial (below) situated at the location of the temporary
cemetery on Omaha-Beach and the memorial today (above).
Source: www.omahabeach.vierville.free.fr and C. Lebastard

FIRST PART

The second temporary cemetery at Omaha-Beach

Work on the new site started on 10th June with the progressive burial of 775 Allies (American and British) and of 200 Germans. During their transport, the bodies were covered so as not to affect the morale of the troops. In general, a priest from the confession of the deceased was responsible for performing the burial rites.

In less than ten days, all the bodies from the first cemetery were moved and reburied in cemetery No. 1. On 12th June officers from the Pentagon of which Eisenhower, Marshall, Arnold and Admiral King met at Omaha-Beach to see the situation and to assure themselves of the progress of the work in the cemeteries. The bodies continued to flow and the location was henceforth commonly called V Corps Cemetery because practically all the soldiers buried there came from this Army Corps. The 3rd platoon of the 607th Graves Registration Company received help from the 2nd platoon attached to the 5th Engineer Special Brigade. This 5th brigade was in charge of organizing the layout of the site. On 25th June, the 607th company was relieved and returned under the direct control of the First Army. This company established more than a dozen temporary cemeteries during the war.

By midnight on 26th June, a total of 1 510 Americans were buried at Saint-Laurent-sur-Mer with 48 Allies and 606 German soldiers making a total of 2 164 bodies. The work continued for more than three weeks post the Normandy landing. Finally there were 3 797 buried soldiers, to which must be adjusted the names of 1 185 American soldiers considered as missing in action. On 14th July 1944 (Bastille Day), a palm leaf was laid down during a ceremony at the cemetery in memory of the sacrifice of the American soldiers. Today, the permanent Normandy American Cemetery is in part constructed on the temporary cemetery whose traces could be seen for a long time after this cemetery had been demolished.

German soldiers digging graves at the temporary cemetery of Saint-Laurent-sur-Mer. *Photo ABMC.*

The temporary cemetery of Saint-Laurent-sur-Mer. We can distinguish in the background the plots which will be used to construct the permanent Normandy American Cemetery. *Photo ABMC.*

FIRST PART   53

Ceremony in the presence of General Eisenhower and his wife at the temporary cemetery of Saint-Laurent-sur-Mer. *Photo ABMC.*

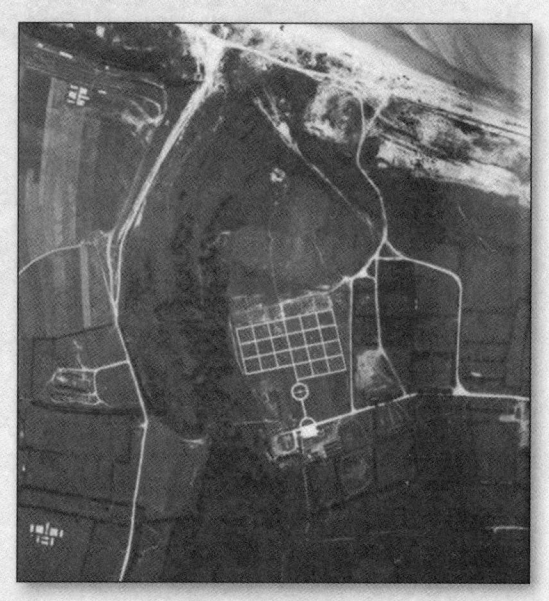

View on the temporary cemetery of Saint-Laurent-sur-Mer. *Collection Antonin Dehays.*

View outlining the permanent cemetery of Colleville-sur-Mer and the remnants of the temporary cemetery. This photograph was taken shortly after completion of the permanent burials. *Collection Geert Van den Bogaert.*

54

THE TEMPORARY CEMETERIES IN NORTH-WEST FRANCE

A gradual development

The two permanent American cemeteries located today in Normandy are those of Colleville-sur-Mer and Saint-James. They were constituted from twelve temporary cemeteries. Six of them were established in the Manche Department: Saint-Mère-Eglise (two cemeteries), Blosville, Marigny, Chêne-Guérin and Saint-James. Two other cemeteries were developed in the Calvados Department: Saint-Laurent-sur-Mer and La Cambe. Four others were dispersed across Normandy and in the bordering regions: Gorron (Mayenne), Saint-Corneille (Sarthe), Saint-André-de l'Eure (Eure), and Villeneuve-sur-Auvers (Essonne). All these sites were constructed in line with the American troop advancement in France.

The cemetery of Vierville-sur-Mer was the first to be laid out in Normandy. It was rapidly followed by another cemetery constituted on 8th June 1944 on Utah-Beach near the American campaign hospital *La Madeleine*. It was established by the 1st platoon of the 603rd Graves Registration Company in order to bury the dead of the 4th Infantry Division. This platoon disembarked with the troops of the 4th Infantry Division on 6th June and they were helped in their task by the 1st Engineer Special Brigade. Around 190 bodies were buried there before their rapid transfer to the larger temporary cemetery of Sainte-Mère-Église No. 1. Few documents were able to be collected on the Utah-Beach cemetery and even less concerning the temporary cemetery of Hiesville installed in *Château de la Colombière* which was removed shortly after.

On 9th June 1944, other platoons of the 603rd Graves Registration Company landed on the coast of Utah-Beach with the task of establishing the first temporary cemeteries in Europe.

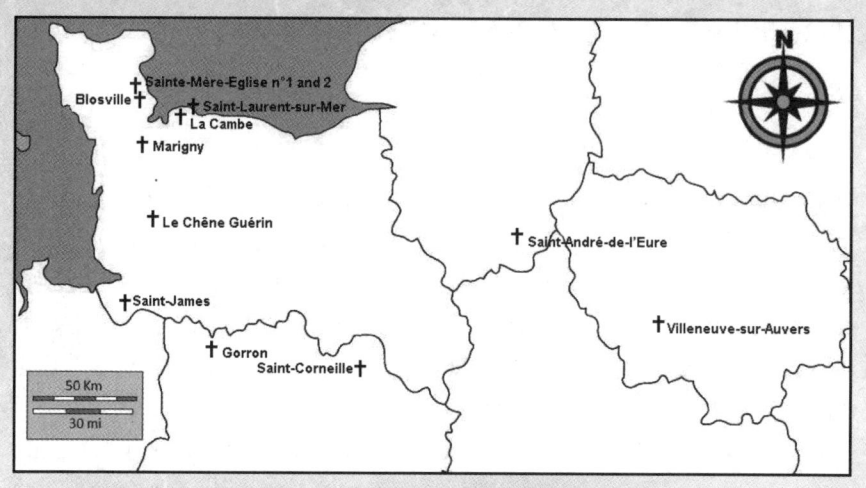

The temporary American cemeteries in North-West France.

The temporary cemetery of Hiesville.
Collection Antonin Dehays.

The temporary cemetery on Utah-Beach.
Utah-Beach Museum.

They put to work on the same day, the 3rd platoon constituting the first cemetery of Sainte-Mère-Église to bury the fallen soldiers of the 90th Infantry Division. However, on 12th June, in view of the number of losses in other units, the cemetery was transformed into the cemetery of the VII Army Corps. In fact, hundreds of bodies – a good number of whom were German soldiers - were waiting for identification and burial.

The Sainte-Mère-Église cemetery quickly became too small: 2 172 American soldiers and 13 Allies were buried there in a few weeks and the work still continued around the community. The huge losses of parachutists amongst others obliged the Graves Registration Company to undertake the construction of a second cemetery further south at Sainte-Mère-Église on the 25th June. The site became known under the name of Sainte-Mère-Église No. 2 and received the bodies of 4 812 American, Allied and German soldiers.

Thanks to the next photograph, we can see the proximity of the two Sainte-Mère-Église cemeteries. In the foreground of the first picture, we can see cemetery No. 2 – the most extended of the two – and in the background, cemetery No. 1. 6 997 soldiers in total were buried in these two sites. Today, at the location of Sainte-Mère-Église cemetery No. 1 is the municipal stadium, while at the location of cemetery No. 2, a monument recalls the cemetery location where since are shops.

On 11th June 1944, the troops disembarking at Omaha-Beach had finally succeeded in consolidating the beachhead and plunged into the heart of Normandy. During this offensive the American Army lost numerous troops and was forced to establish a new temporary military cemetery on high ground in the village of La Cambe. Six weeks later, whilst there were still bodies to be buried; the location was consecrated during a ceremony in the presence of General Gerhardt, Commander of the 29th Infantry Division.

Two photographs of the temporary cemeteries at Sainte-Mère-Église.
Photo ABMC.

A total of 4 534 U.S. First Army soldiers were buried there. The majority of them were from the 29th Infantry Division which explained why the cemetery took the name of this unit. After the exhumation of the American bodies in 1948, the area was transformed into a permanent German cemetery.

Around 20th June 1944, the 4th platoon of the 603rd Graves Registration Company was headed towards Orglandes to establish a new cemetery. As was originally planned for the American troops, it gathered up primarily the bodies of German troops: 6 074 of them were buried using the same procedures applied to the American soldiers. The temporary cemetery of Orglandes eventually became a permanent German cemetery where today are still buried 10 152 German soldiers.

In a little over a week, three new temporary American cemeteries were built in Normandy: Marigny on 31st July 1944 with 3 070 bodies, Saint-James on 5th August with 4 367 bodies and the Chêne-Guérin on 7th August containing the bodies of 1 202 soldiers. A second cemetery at Chêne-Guérin was established to bury 1 628 bodies of German soldiers.

The future permanent cemetery of Saint-James was established less than one week after the liberation of Avranches by the 610th Graves Registration Company. Subsequently, the cemetery was assigned to the 3042nd Graves Registration Company, attached to Patton's Third Army and supported by the 611th Company. Joseph J. Shomon, veteran of the latter, had quickly noticed the poor quality of the rocky ground where the Saint-James temporary cemetery was located. His company even said that the site's choice had been a serious error! That did not stop the burial of 4 367 American soldiers, 45 British, 38 French, 3 Canadians, 1 Australian and 1 New Zealander, who for the most part lost their lives during the liberation of Saint-Lo and the Cotentin and during the operations in Brittany to control the east bank of the Seine.

Sign established at the entrance of the temporary cemetery of La Cambe.
The insignia of the 29th Infantry Division was painted above the text.
Photo ABMC.

La Cambe temporary cemetery. *Photo ABMC.*

With the advance of military operations, the Americans continued progressively to establish new cemeteries: Gorron (15th August 1944), Saint-Corneille (16th August 1944), Saint-André-de-l'Eure (24th August 1944) and Villeneuve-sur-Auvers (25th August 1944).

Once the temporary cemeteries established, the 578th Quartermaster Battalion based at Carteret was assigned to the 3050th Graves Registration Company to deal with the cemeteries of the ten departments in the West. According to data from the American Graves Registration Command, the cemeteries of the North-West of France (not including the cemeteries of Utah-Beach and Hiesville) contained in total 24 698 bodies of American soldiers. It is necessary to add to these figures the exact number of American soldiers buried in Saint-Laurent-sur-Mer and in Sainte-Mère-Église No. 2 cemeteries which unfortunately remain unknown as we only have numbers for all nationalities in these two cemeteries.

Table of temporary American cemeteries in the North-West of France

Cemeteries	Date of Opening	Number of American soldiers buried
Blosville	7th June 1944	5 701
Sainte-Mère-Église No. 1	9th June 1944	2 172
La Cambe	10th June 1944	4 534
Saint-Laurent-sur-Mer	10th June 1944	3 797 (and other nationalities)
Sainte-Mère-Église No. 2	25th June 1944	4 812 (and other nationalities)
Marigny	31st July 1944	3 070
Saint-James	5th August 1944	4 367
Le-Chêne-Guérin	7th August 1944	1 202
Gorron	15th August 1944	752
Saint-Corneille	16th August 1944	521
Saint-André-de-l'Eure	24th August 1944	2 066
Villeneuve-sur-Auvers	25th August 1944	303

American soldiers are paying their respects at the grave of a comrade in arms killed during the liberation of Normandy. *National Archives USA.*

Saint-James temporary cemetery. *Photo ABMC.*

Some figures give us an idea of the scale of the work undertaken: in April 1945, 73 360 American soldiers were buried in twenty four temporary American cemeteries on French soil including the cemeteries in Normandy. In total, 190 985 soldiers were buried in the temporary American cemeteries in Europe (117 322 Americans, 1 733 Allies and 71 890 Enemies). 12 441 soldiers of the Axis powers were buried by the Americans in fifteen cemeteries which had been entirely reserved for them. On the 6th April 1946, the office of the Quartermaster General compiled a register of 359 temporary American cemeteries in the world containing the remains of 241 500 soldiers.

The first burials: the example of Blosville cemetery

The cemetery of Blosville was constituted from 7th June 1944 by Elbert E. Legg, then sergeant in the 603rd Graves Registration Company. This unit was made up of novices who had never been in contact with bodies, except for two of them who worked before in civil burial services. Legg was sent to Normandy on the 6th June 1944 with the task of marking out on his own the first temporary cemetery of the 82nd Airborne Division. The remainder of his unit joined him several days later, after the landing on Utah-Beach. From his testimony we have learned how the men of the Graves Registration Service organized the temporary cemeteries.

When he arrived in Normandy with the 82nd Airborne Division, his first task consisted of choosing a site in order to outline and lay out a first cemetery. He chose a field near the cross roads of Les Forges and started to collect the bodies. The manual advised the choice, as far as possible, of open fields with easy soil to dig and located near a service road. Legg received help from some men and notably from that of Lieutenant James M. Fraim who himself proposed to recruit civilians in order to lend him a helping hand. Lieutenant Fraim had at his disposal a pool of French francs, reserved from the start to pay for French workers. He decided to look for French civilians who would agree to bury soldiers. Legg did not have all the necessary material available to give the cemetery a proper appearance but decided meanwhile to arrange the grave stones in rows of twenty. When Lieutenant Fraim returned and informed Legg that he had found 35 Frenchmen ready to help, fifty bodies had already been collected.

These soldiers were buried in the cemetery the next day, on 7th June, after having secured their personal effects but without having taken an inventory. One of the two Dog Tags they each wore was left on the remains and the second was placed on the grave marker. The combat troops brought in information on the location of bodies whose whereabouts were pinpointed on a map. Fraim attempted to obtain German prisoners to help him retrieve the bodies as quickly as possible. On the 9th June, the bodies amassed at the cemetery were counted in their hundreds: nearly half of the bodies were of German soldiers. Around 70 French came as reinforcements to dig the graves. Some German prisoners were also routed to the cemetery but due to a lack of tools, they were evacuated to the beach to be conducted to prison camps.

Finally, on 10th June 1944, a first platoon of the 603rd Graves Registration Company arrived with materials and tools as well as 150 German prisoners. A second plot of two hundred graves was drawn to help the work of the teams responsible for digging the ditches. It was not until 13th June that the 4th platoon of the 603rd Graves Registration Company (Legg's platoon) arrived in the cemetery. 35 Americans and 100 Germans had already been buried. Among the collected remains, there were less than one hundred American soldiers to bury while there were hundreds of German bodies waiting.

From then on, combat units of the 82nd Airborne Division directly evacuated the bodies to the cemetery. New plots were established of two hundred graves and a start was made on an inventory of personal effects. The burial procedures described in the technical manuals could at last be followed. These manuals advised for example to use mattress covers to realize the first burials. Legg did not have any and so first used the parachutes utilized the day before. It was only with the arrival of reinforcements that the covers were finally available. On 20th June, his platoon headed towards Orglandes but the work continued however on the site. Today, a small monument at Les Forges shows the location of the temporary cemetery of Blosville where more than 5 700 soldiers' bodies were buried[12].

Yves de la Rue is another witness to the construction of Blosville cemetery. He was employed by the Americans to bury the bodies of the soldiers stored in the cemetery, just opposite his farm. Two days after the landing, he remembers that an officer came to find labor: *"Trucks passed in the countryside to collect the bodies and brought them to us. I was responsible for taking the personal effects, and putting them into a small bag closed by a parachute cord. We also took weapons, cigarettes and at the end of the day, we distributed packets between those who had dug the ditches. In the beginning, we buried them in parachutes then in special bags. After, coffins arrived. So we had to unearth those that had been put in parachutes and bags to put them into coffins. I did that for two weeks. It was very hard on my morale.*

---

[12] "Testimony of a veteran of the 603rd Quartermaster Graves Registration Company, Colonel Legg" *op. cit.* After having completed the cemetery at Blosville, Legg asked to be transferred with the 82nd Airborne Division and was assigned to the 407th Graves Registration Company. In September, he took part in the Market-Garden operation in the Netherlands and started a new cemetery five miles from Nijmegen. He served in three other wars: in Korea, in the Dominican Republic and in Vietnam before retiring with the rank of Colonel in 1970.

The first days hurt me to see them. I found two soldiers who had arrived on 6th June in front of the farm and to whom I had poured some cider. They were both burnt, it was horrible, monstrous. After, I got "used" to fiddling with all these dead."

THE GRADUAL ORGANIZATION OF TEMPORARY CEMETERIES

The installation of grave markers

The marking of each grave was necessary for many reasons. Everyone agreed on the fact that the graves dug during the conflict were just temporary graves and that it would require a further exhumation. It was indispensable to mark the precise spot of each body by means of a symbol and to be able to immediately differentiate the grave of an American soldier with that of a soldier from the other side. The marker and the Dog Tag secured thereto had to enable positive identification of the buried body. We understand therefore the importance emphasized in the Graves Registration manuals to the marker.

During the initial interments, the burials were carried out with urgency and the War Department advised the use of materials directly available on the ground: a large stone, a stake, a bayonet on which was hung a helmet… …

These funerals were often performed without any record being made. It was necessary that the marker used to identify the resting place allowed the Graves Registration Service to be able to find it again so as to achieve the future burial correctly. The War Department recommended to the men of the Graves Registration Service to produce markers in wood in the form of a triangle 36 inches in height by 6 inches wide at the top when it was possible. These stakes were commonly called Name Pegs. If the installation of a Name Peg was impossible it

Two examples of grave markers used during the first
burials by the fighting troops.
Conseil régional de Basse-Normandie/National Archives USA et ABMC.

Civilians are unloading bodies in the temporary cemetery of Blosville. Yves de La Rue can be seen in the photo.
National Archives USA.

was recommended to put in place traditional stakes to enable the fixing of the Dog Tag. These stakes could be found in many of the temporary cemeteries, notably in the first cemetery at Omaha-Beach or once more at La Cambe.

With the positive development of the front for the Allies, the Americans henceforth were capable of installing more informative markers and of a better quality: the famous white wooden cross already used in the First World War and Stars of David for the soldiers of the Jewish faith, also in wood and colored white. The German soldiers, buried by the Americans, received for their part crosses in black wood[13] and were often buried in plots of specific graves.

On the front face of the cross, was painted in black stencil the full name of the soldier (Christian name, initial of the second Christian name as well as the surname) and just below, his Dog Tag number as we can see in the stencil utilized to mark the grave location of Allen J. Roscoe, a soldier in the 29th Infantry Division killed on 1st August 1944. He is today buried in the Normandy American Cemetery.

The maintenance of cemeteries

All the Commanding Officers paid frequent visits to the soldiers killed and buried in the temporary cemeteries. General Collins, Commanding Officer of VII Army Corps, for example, even

---

[13] Graves Registration, War department Field Manual, *op. cit.* It seems that legend attributes to the Treaty of Versailles the obligation for the vanquished to use black crosses to mark the graves of their soldiers and to the victors to mark their graves by crosses in whitewood. However, no document referring to such a decision has been found in the archives (for now?). One article in the Treaty of Versailles exists on graves but makes no reference to the different colors. Black crosses seem to have been imposed by the victors because black is not a color found in German mortuary tradition.

Ceremony in the presence of civilians at the temporary cemetery of La Cambe.
Conseil régional de Basse-Normandie/National Archives USA.

7th July 1944: an American Army carpenter prepares wooden crosses which will be used to mark the graves of soldiers fallen in Normandy.
Archives départementales de la Manche.

Stencil used for Private Allen J. Roscoe of the 29th Infantry Division.
Collection Alain Dupain.

The progressive installation of wooden markers in the temporary cemetery of Saint-Laurent-sur-Mer.
Conseil régional de Basse-Normandie/National Archives USA.

tried to ensure that each American body be buried on the day of its arrival in a temporary cemetery. This interest shown by the generals in the bodies of their soldiers is important because it explains why all the efforts were made to improve the overall appearance of the sites. Progressively, the different temporary cemeteries were closed to new burials and final inspections were conducted by officers of the Graves Registration Service. It was intended to leave sufficient space in each cemetery in the eventuality that bodies would be found in fields close by.

On 1st July 1945, the American Graves Registration Service AGRS was replaced by the American Graves Registration Command AGRC entirely autonomous. The AGRC took over all the responsibilities undertaken hitherto by the AGRS. The war was over and this new service could now deal in more detail with each cemetery. AGRC realized quickly that the cemeteries would remain active for several years with the regular visits paid by families to the grave of their loved one(s). It is why, from 1945, the service decided to improve the appearance of each temporary cemetery and notably that of Saint-Laurent-sur-Mer. The Quartermaster General then authorized numerous work projects in the temporary cemeteries of both a minor and major nature in order to make them more attractive. Gradually, numerous installations were put into place: signage erection; bush, hedge and shrub planting; fence building; curb installation around the grave plots; establishment of gravel driveways...

In November 1945, the AGRC appealed to British landscape contractors to refine the design of certain temporary cemeteries that could eventually be retained as permanent cemeteries. During the spring of 1946, the service supervised renovation operations at the Saint-Laurent-sur-Mer cemetery: the painting of the grave markers, their re-alignment, the planting of bushes and flowers and undertook the construction of structures considered to be indispensable: a small chapel and a reception building.

All these projects enriched the landscape of the different cemeteries that became much more welcoming. However, contractors had to keep in mind that lands used had to be returned to their owners when the permanent cemeteries would be built. The contracts signed between the American nation and the owners stipulated that the original appearance of the land had not to be significantly altered under penalty of having to pay compensation. These sites had been acquired with a careful eye to economy and in order to avoid having to pay too high a sum. Every effort was made to retain the land's original appearance.

The searches after the War and the results obtained

Once the work of collecting the bodies in the battlefields was completed by the campaign units of the Graves Registration Service, the AGRC focused on the search for and the recovery of bodies. This work had already started just after the end of the military operations in Normandy. It consisted of finding the listed or unlisted mortal remains resting in isolated graves often dug by civilians. The AGRC considered as isolated graves, all graves made outside of the temporary American cemeteries as well as those groups of graves of less than twenty-five American soldiers. The units of the AGRC also looked for bodies which had not been buried. These were subsequently recovered, identified whenever possible and buried.

Efforts intensified in a significant way at the end of 1945 when the AGRC had the responsibility to conduct the plan clarifying the status of the victims. The aim of this work was primarily to confirm or modify the status of military losses: "presumed dead", "missing in action", "prisoner of war" or again "captured"; such status having been provisionally allocated during the hostilities.

Chapel erected in the temporary cemetery of Saint-Laurent-sur-Mer.
Photo ABMC.

One other example of the development of infrastructures: the temporary cemetery of Marigny. *Photo ABMC.*

From 1st January 1946, three types of teams of the AGRC were sent to find the bodies of the American soldiers. Firstly, the so called "advertising" teams who requested relevant information from civilians; then the "research and field investigation" teams who located the isolated graves. Lastly, the "recovery teams" or "exhumation teams" who recovered, exhumed and undertook the identifications if possible.

This research was made possible thanks to many American, German and French documents. The AGRC used initially the reports established by each combat unit following the daily actions: the After Action Reports. Missing Air Crew Reports were used for aircrew which indicated aviation bases' losses. German "green cards" established in German hospitals for prisoners of war were also taken into account together with the "beige cards" which recorded the burials of 14 000 American airmen who fell behind the front lines during air raids. Records from the French Military Graves Service represented sixty per cent of the information gathered by the Graves Registration Service. For others, they were gathered thanks to field research work (30%) and to various documents (10%) including those written by the Germans.

A few figures can give us an idea of the work accomplished: on 31st March 1946, of the 40 467 American soldiers initially unidentified 18 641 of them were located by units of the Graves Registration Service. Of those 18 641 soldiers, 10 986 were resting in military cemeteries and 7 655 were buried in isolated graves.

Towards the Establishment of Permanent Cemeteries

THE CHOICES GIVEN TO FAMILIES

The first projects

The first plans concerning the soldiers' graves and of war memorials were envisaged whilst the battles were still raging. This issue was not brought about by the end of the Second World War in Europe. The first proposals concerning the bodies of the soldiers were planned with the directive Policy Study No. 34 undertaken by Colonel Harbold and submitted on 14th August 1943.

The first part of this Policy Study No. 34 recommended the repatriation of all the dead buried temporarily overseas if seventy per cent or more of the families concerned so requested. The bodies would be taken in charge of by the War Department. In the absence of individuals' requests, the remains would be transported by ship to the United-States and consequentially under the control of the Quartermaster General[14]. However, the report specified that if the soldier had expressed to his family or to his friends the wish to be buried overseas, his choice should be respected. A rule was established concerning the return of the bodies to the United-States or for burial in foreign lands:

---

[14] The National cemeteries were created by an act of 17th July 1862. The American President proposed land to be used as National cemeteries so that those who had lost their life for their country could rest in peace. It is with an act of 15th April 1920, that, henceforth, all veterans from all wars could be buried there. At the end of the First World War, the practice of burying the wife alongside the soldier became widespread. In 1929, there were 84 National cemeteries dispersed in the country. See: STEERE, BOARDMAN, *op. cit.*

the return or the burial overseas would be made in any event according to the wishes of the closest member of the immediate family.

Even if burials overseas were not excluded, the report observed in its third part that it was still too early to establish permanent cemeteries. Policy Study No. 34 advocated that the choice of the location of sites for new cemeteries had to be undertaken quietly once peace would return to the United-States. It would also allow easier routing of construction materials.

It was necessary to consider the construction or expansion of National cemeteries in the United-States. However, during the First World War, 85% of soldiers killed and repatriated to the United-States were buried in private cemeteries and only 5 300 in National cemeteries. There was then no reason to change that policy after the Second World War. The project of Policy Study No. 34 was a first step but it was still insufficient to resolve the problem of repatriation and of burial of the bodies. Thus, nine more months elapsed before another plan was considered.

In June 1944, Colonel Harbold Director of the Memorial Division proposed that the overall responsibility for repatriation of the American bodies be entrusted to the Quartermaster General. According to him, concentrated action would thus achieve better coordination. The greatest difficulty was to know the number of staff required for the repatriation of the soldiers killed. On 25th August 1944, a meeting was organized at the Headquarters of the Office of the Quartermaster General (OQMG) bringing together Agencies and Government Departments interested by the repatriation program. The concept of repatriating all the soldiers if seventy per cent of the family at least so wishes was abandoned. In July 1945, General Eisenhower questioned the War Department on its intentions but it had not yet decided anything. Finally, the Quartermaster General worked on a new plan for the soldiers' repatriation or burial in the new cemeteries overseas according to the family wishes. The War Department on 8th September 1945 developed a plan in the same vein in favor of a repatriation of the dead of the Second World War called: *"Plan for repatriation of the dead of World War II and establishment of permanent United-States military cemeteries at home and abroad".*

"Tell me about my boy"

The United-States finally decided to put in place a similar program to that achieved during the First World War and to thus leave the choice to the families of the fate of their loved one(s) killed in combat. This program was in line with the information policy of the U.S. Government established with families since the beginning of the conflict.

In fact, when a soldier was killed, the family was informed of the death of his or their loved ones on average one month later by telegram. Its content was relatively brief: *"The Secretary of War desires me to express his deep sympathy that your husband / son... was killed in action on (date) in France. Letter follows".*

"Tell me about my boy": this request was frequently made to the Quartermaster General by families who wanted more information on the progress of the War Department's program. These requests were most often written to obtain information on the return of the body and on the final burials of the soldiers killed overseas. In 1946, a document entitled *"Tell me about my boy"* was realized by the Quartermaster Corps for the families. Its objective was to answer numerous questions. The Quartermaster's office started to send the documents to the families at the start of 1947. During this period, the operations to search for bodies in the battlefields continued.

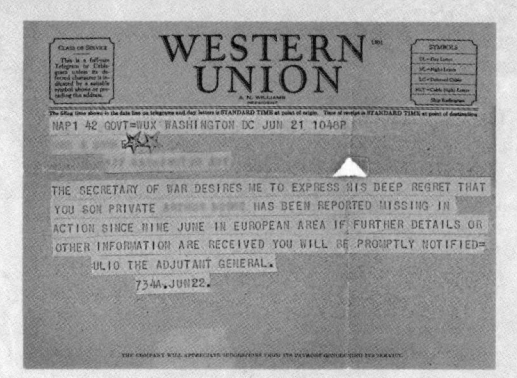

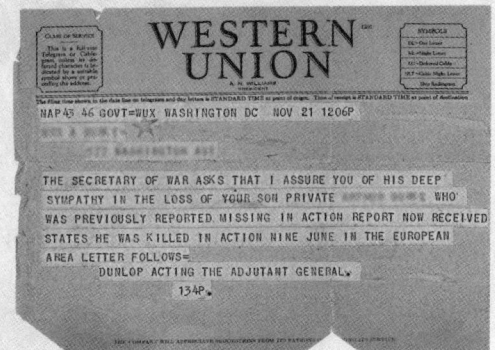

Two telegrams of the Western-Union received by the family of an American soldier. He was reported missing on 9th June 1944. The first message informs the family of his missing in action and the second changes the status of "missing" to "killed-in-action". *Source: Bellevillesons.com.*

The chaplain Francis L. Sampson of the 101st Airborne Division is blessing the bodies of American soldiers who fell during the battle of Normandy. In the background can be seen German soldiers guarded by American soldiers together with another priest blessing graves freshly dug.
Source: Flickr.com.

The Government succeeded in agreeing on a common project and suggested that the burials remain subject to the choice of the next of kin. It undertook to respect their wishes without regard to ethnicity, rank or religion of the deceased. As a first step, it was necessary to remind those concerned who had the right to a burial in an eventual permanent cemetery or repatriation: members of the American Armed Forces dead in service and U.S. citizens who served in the Armed Forces of any country at war against Germany, Italy and Japan and dead in service. American citizens whose death was a direct result of the war or because of their involvement in activities related to the prosecution of the war were also eligible. On the advice of the Secretary of the Army a motion was added concerning all U.S. citizens whose repatriation was in the public interest. However, their death had to have accrued in the period between 3rd September 1939 and 30th June 1946 included.

It was decided that the final burial would be subject in the first place to the choice of the wife, except that in the case of remarriage or if the two parties had divorced or were separated. In this case, the decision revoked to a son if 21 or older and in the order of birth. In the case of absence of or of minority children, the choice was up to the closest relative in the following order: the father of the deceased, his mother, the brothers if 21 years or more and in order of birth, then the sisters of majority age and in birth order. A relative could refuse to make the decision which then reverted to the next relative.

The Quartermaster gave to families four burial options: the repatriation of the deceased to the United-States (or a U.S. territory) for burial in a private cemetery or secondly in a National cemetery. Families also had the opportunity to obtain the return of the relative to a foreign country in which they had been installed for burial in a private cemetery. The last option was burial in an American cemetery abroad.

The War Department officially had no preference for one or other of the four burial options. It was planned that all the burial charges, from the preparation of the body to the putting into the ground would be borne by the Government. The United-States undertook to provide for deceased military personnel a flag to cover the coffin during the funeral service and to give it to the family after the ceremony. In the case of repatriation for burial in a private cemetery, the religious service was met by the family, even if the grave stone had been purchased by the Government. If the family wished, an honor guard could be present.

The Government engaged to pay all the expenses for a burial in a permanent military cemetery abroad and to ensure the presence of a priest of the deceased's religion as had already been respected as far as possible in temporary cemeteries. The Government wished as well to reassure the families that the bodies – from their exhumation until their return – would always be under military guard.

Finally the arrangements made for the remains of the soldiers were confirmed by law 368 of the 80th American Congress (meeting between 3rd January 1947 and 3rd January 1949) as had been the arrangements made after the First World War by law 389 of the 66th Congress. The law was called: *"For the next of kin to select permanent interment of a family member's remains on foreign soil in an American military cemetery designed, constructed and maintained specifically to honor in perpetuity the dead of those wars, or to repatriate the remains to the United-States for interment in a national or private cemetery"*.

THE AMERICAN BATTLE MONUMENTS COMMISSION

Origin of the Commission

Following the establishment of the temporary cemeteries and the sending of requests to the families, the American Battle Monuments Commission (ABMC) was assigned a key role in the future of thousands of deceased soldiers waiting repatriation and final burial. The Commission was originally created just after the end of the First World War not to take charge of the permanent cemeteries but as a symbol of U.S. involvement in the First World War by means of erecting monuments. It is in March 1919 some months after the end of the conflict, that General Pershing requested the completion of a preliminary study to mark the American battlefields of the first World conflict. He had noticed that troops were already in the process of erecting monuments with inscriptions sometimes inaccurate or not politically correct. Furthermore, some brave units were not represented on the monuments. The General concluded that someone had to take responsibility for telling and explaining through the monuments, the history of the American Expeditionary Forces. The War Department appointed a War Monuments board chaired by General John Mc Auley Palmer on 11th June 1921. The Board realized very quickly that its objectives went well beyond the jurisdiction of the War Department.

This is public law 534 of the 67th Congress in 1923 which created the American Battle Monuments Commission. Made up of seven volunteer members and an officer of the regular Army serving as secretary, they were all nominated by the President of the United-States. General Pershing himself was elected as the first president of the ABMC. Other personalities were also nominated: Senator David A. Reed of Pennsylvania, Senator

Thos. W. Miler of Delaware and Robert G. Woodside, veteran of the 3rd Infantry Division who had twice been Director of the Association for Veterans of Foreign Wars.

During the decade of 1920, the ABMC project took shape: the main duties would be to build multi-confessional chapels in the eight permanent cemeteries outside of the United-States constructed by the Graves Registration Service after the First World War as well as a series of monuments which would mark the participation of the United-States in the war. Each chapel had to have on its walls the names of the soldiers missing in action, totaling 4 452 names. Following the creation of the ABMC, a memorial could no longer receive assistance from an Agency of the American Government without the project having received the prior approval of the Fine Arts Commission.

At the end of 1923, the commission began writing a program. In order to do this, it visited the battlefields of Europe. After this first visit it judged it necessary to establish an office in Europe under the leadership of Thomas North. This man had joined the commission at the end of 1923 as its agent in Paris. The office of the commission in Paris was first located in a suite at the U.S. embassy in *rue Chaillot*. Then on 1st June 1924, the commission's first real office opened its doors at 18 *rue de Tilsitt* (around from *Place de l'Etoile*). On 1st July, the seat moved again to 20 *rue Molitor* into a small villa already occupied by the Graves Registration Service with whom the ABMC collaborated.

The War Department had not yet written the official history of the First World War. General Pershing requested that a group of historians work on the subject. In June 1925, Doctor Cret and Major Price visited Europe to formulate a concrete program for the commission: the exact location of the future chapels as well as their architecture.

Finally, the ABMC decided to erect monuments in areas of major American operations: Aisne-Marne, Chateau-Thierry, Saint-Mihiel, Montsec, Meuse-Argonne and Montfaucon. Smaller monuments were envisaged. Some were constructed between Kemmel and Ypres, at Bellicourt, Cantigny, near Montdidier, Sommepy, Audenarde, Tours, Brest and Gibraltar. Other projects for monuments were abandoned due to lack of finance: it was 1929 and the time of the Great Depression.

The eight permanent American cemeteries of the First World War

Location	Graves of identified soldiers	Graves of the Unknowns	Number of Missing in Action	Total
Belleau, Aisne, France	2 038	251	1 060	3 349
Bony, Aisne, France	1 706	138	333	2 177
Brookwood, Great-Britain	427	41	563	1 031
Fère-en-Tardenois, Aisne, France	5 415	597	241	6 253
Romagne-sous-Montfaucon, Meuse, France	13 760	486	954	15 200
Suresnes, Hauts-de-Seine, France	1 535	6	974	2 515
Thiaucourt, Meurthe-et-Moselle, France	4 036	117	284	4 437
Waregem, Flanders, Belgium	347	21	43	411
Total	29 264	1 657	4 452	35 373

In September 1933, the commission's Paris office was moved into the new buildings of the U.S. Embassy, 2 *Avenue Gabriel* in Paris. Under the executive order no. 6614 of President Franklin D. Roosevelt and at the suggestion of General Pershing, the responsibility for the maintenance of the cemeteries overseas and for the maintenance of the war monuments was transferred from the War Department to that of the ABMC on 21st May 1934.

General Pershing nicknamed "Black Jack" was born in 1860 and died on 15th July 1948. He commanded the American Expeditionary Forces during the First World War. He was regarded as a mentor by generations of American Generals and notably by Marshall, Eisenhower, Bradley and Patton. In 1919, Congress authorized the President to promote Pershing General of the Armies in recognition of his services.
Library of Congress USA.

Stamp of the American Battle Monuments Commission. *Photo ABMC.*

The monument at Bellicourt a few miles from Saint-Quentin in the Aisne department commemorates the American offensive in September 1918 and the sacrifice of 90 000 American soldiers who lost their lives during the conflict.
Photo ABMC.

With the expansion of its duties, the ABMC needed more personnel and when the neighboring office of the Graves Registration Service in Paris was closed many of its employees joined the ranks of the commission.

The commission during the Second World War and its reorganization

Until 1939, routine maintenance of the monuments and of the cemeteries held the attention of the commission. A revised edition of the Battlefield sites guide was published the previous year under the title *"American Armies and Battlefields in Europe"*. Following international tensions, Major Holle in charge of the Paris office of the ABMC moved the headquarters to Dreux on 9th October 1939. A second move was necessary to Gujan-Mestras between Bordeaux and the Bay of Biscay on 9th June 1940 because of the advance of the German Army. The French capitulation allowed all the personnel to return to the Paris embassy 10 days later. The commission learned that the chapel at Belleau had suffered machine gun and shell damage. Difficulties imposed by the Germans considerably slowed down the maintenance at the sites. The situation worsened and General Pershing decided on 13th May 1941 to repatriate to Washington the twenty two American civilians working for the ABMC in Belgium and France. In July 1941, the Paris office was moved to the Superintendent quarters of the Suresnes cemetery until April 1944. Then, from May until August 1944, they were accommodated in a building on the *Avenue Hoche*. In September 1944, the ABMC office returned to the U.S. embassy after the complete liberation of Paris and the vicinity.

It should be noted that the German troops during the occupation treated the cemeteries with respect, apart from a few Jewish graves destroyed in the cemetery of Thiaucourt or the destruction of the monument of Brest which gave way for an observation post part of the Atlantic Wall. The cemeteries did not fall into disuse during the war. Vichy sent funds at first then the Swiss Government ascribed funds to the French Minister of Finance.

After the end of the war and because of numerous American losses, a letter from President Truman dated 30th September 1945 and signed by Secretaries Stimson and Forrestal, recommended that the President wrote an executive order to increase the functions of the ABMC to include the cemeteries of the Second World War. Similarly it recommended that the commission should determine the rules for the construction of private monuments. The President gave his approval and the executive order was signed on 4th March 1946.

A new law (law 456 of the 79th Congress) was passed to provide the necessary means for the scope of the functions of the commission: the members went from seven to eleven. The President nominated the new members of the ABMC: General George C. Marshall, General Alexander A. Vandegrift, the Senator of South-Carolina Burnet R. Maybank and Joseph C. Baldwin a former Congressman. The law also increased the mission of the commission on the international scene including authority over the construction of private monuments.

In early 1946, Vice-President Robert G. Woodside asked General Eisenhower to recommend Thomas North as Secretary of the ABMC. The President approved this request on 18th April 1946. In the same year, nearly all the superintendents reverted to their posts in the First World War cemeteries and Lieutenant-Colonel Krueger Jr. assumed the position of Director, Paris office. The ABMC gradually reorganized itself in preparation for its new role: the selection and the maintenance of the Second World War cemeteries[15].

---

[15] NORTH (General Thomas), Manuscript, American Battle Monuments Commission,[s.l], [No date], [n.p.].

THE SELECTION OF THE PERMANENT CEMETERIES

The different projects

Long negotiations were necessary to obtain a final list of the permanent cemeteries. In the plans submitted to the General commanding the Service of the Armed Forces, the Quartermaster Corps recommended that the War Department select the sites for permanent cemeteries of the Second World War. Furthermore it negotiated the acquisition of necessary land in collaboration with the ABMC. The commission would be responsible for the general management of land, buildings and monuments of the cemeteries while the War Department would take care of re-burial in accordance with the architectural development of the sites. It was agreed that the ABMC would take charge of the cemeteries' administration and their maintenance once the entire procedures were completed.

The War Department listed a proposal for cemeteries overseas including nine sites in Europe in its plan for the repatriation and the establishment of permanent cemeteries of 8th September 1945. Five sites were located in France: Saint-Laurent-sur-Mer, Saint-James, Épinal, Limey and Solers. Major-General Robert M. Littlejohn discussed the selection of all these sites but confirmed the first proposition for a permanent cemetery at Saint-Laurent-sur-Mer. This site was for him a concrete example and an historic war location which had all the essential technical prerequisites. He also suggested the construction of a permanent cemetery at Saint-Mère-Église No. 2 with its emotional impact and historical importance.

This request was in line with the wishes of the local mayor of Sainte-Mère-Église at the time Alexandre Renaud who tried to conserve the temporary cemeteries and transform them into permanent cemeteries. He even requested the help of

Mrs. Roosevelt (whose husband was buried in Sainte-Mère-Église cemetery No. 2) who supported him. Facing successive American administration refusals, the mayor attempted to obtain the right to retain only a few burials, which he was also refused[16].

In spring and in the early summer of 1946, the interested parties in the program put forward new proposals for the permanent sites. An attaché from Bern suggested the use of a small military cemetery at Munsingen as a tribute to airmen killed on Swiss territory. His suggestion was not retained because it was necessary that the number of permanent cemeteries be as low as possible, at the time for material and financial reasons.

At the same time, the AGRC authorized a detailed study of the cemeteries proposed by Stevenson, Alexander and Jennings, landscape consultants, who travelled to Europe. Different teams were effectively sent to carry out reconnaissance and topographic surveys of various sites. During their studies, the officials recognized that the sites ought to have above all a sense of history, an intelligent geographic location, expansion possibilities and a relationship with military organizations which fought in the zone. The Saint-Laurent-sur-Mer site offered all these advantages: moreover, it was the first temporary military American cemetery in France[17].

Finally, the consultant architects and the representatives of the ABMC decided to submit the names of ten localities to the office of the Quartermaster General in March 1946.

---

[16] Testimony of Henri-Jean RENAUD received on 20th April 2010 at the Normandy American Cemetery.

[17] We can question this assertion because the cemetery of Saint-Laurent-sur-Mer was constituted after the cemeteries of Blosville, Sainte-Mère-Église No. 1 and La Cambe. However, the Americans do not necessarily make any distinction between the first cemetery on Omaha-Beach and that of Saint-Laurent-sur-Mer.

The first six cemeteries listed were retained in priority and the last four came in second place. Here is the list of the cemeteries with in brackets, their maximum supposed grave capacity: Saint-Laurent-sur-Mer (12 000), Cambridge (5 000), Hamm (7 500), Margraten (12 000), Épinal (6 500) and Henri-Chapelle (12 000) to which was added Sainte-Mère-Église No. 2 (5 500), Limey (8 000) and finally Neuville-en-Condroz or Saint-Avold[18] (8 000) giving a potential total of 84 500 graves. The Quartermaster General Horkan approved this list but estimated that the first six sites should be sufficient.

General North accompanied by Leslie Biffle, also a member of the ABMC, undertook inspections of potential sites in North-Africa during the summer of 1946. They clarified the essential characteristics required for the formation of the permanent cemeteries. It was paramount that the sites reflect the advances of the military operations and have an easy access. Each cemetery and its surroundings would be required to have a certain natural beauty, present a calm context and their environmental planning and maintenance costs should be reasonable. None of them had to be situated in enemy territory apart from Italy which joined the Allies at the end of the war. The last criterion was essential: no cemetery had to contain more than 10 000 graves[19].

---

[18] At this time they hesitated between Neuville-en-Condroz and Saint-Avold; ultimately, they will choose both sites.

[19] The inherent problems in the construction of the permanent cemeteries in the continent of Asia were revealed during this inspection. In fact, the "low" death rate in this area as well as the politics made their establishment unthinkable. The attitude of the Russian authorities discouraged the establishment of military cemeteries on their territory. The choice of Florence, Carthage and Manila visited much later was easier and natural. The selection of entirely new sites was necessary for numerous reasons: accessibility, impossibility of construction on the planned places because of archeological discoveries... NORTH, op. cit.

A meeting was held in Washington in July 1946 to consider the different proposed plans whose evaluation was entrusted to the ABMC. Harbeson proposed a list of sites divided into three groups. The first is interesting to list since the sites of Cambridge, Margraten, Henri-Chapelle, Hamm, Saint-Avold, Épinal and Saint-Laurent-sur-Mer are the same locations proposed in March of that year and approved by the Quartermaster General. Even if the cemetery of Saint-James had been emphasized in the 8th September 1945 plan, the officials did not mention it until September 1946.

The final decision was that of the War Department who requested that the final report of the ABMC be submitted before 15th February 1947. It had to be accompanied by a general plan of the site grave plots for the 1st July. The Government was harried by the families who wished that the burials and the repatriation procedures were able to start. The time limits were respected and on 15th April, a new meeting was organized in Washington in the presence of the OQMG, the AGRC and the ABMC. An agreement was reached for the site of Saint-Laurent-sur-Mer fully allowing the burial planning. The agreement also provided for operations to be realized in four other envisaged permanent cemeteries: Saint-Avold, Draguignan, Saint-James and… Blosville; one of the Normandy temporary cemeteries.

In the meantime, responses from the families tended to indicate that around twenty-two per cent of the soldiers would be buried in the permanent cemeteries, being a reduction in the estimations which provided for approximately fifty per cent. This new trend caused the ABMC to reconsider the number of overseas cemeteries in favor of projects taken up by the War Department and a majority of Graves Registration Service officials. The choice of ten permanent cemeteries presented a compromise between the two points of view. The office of the Quartermaster General was favorable to the use of Saint-James and Draguignan and preliminary plans were established.

On 1st May 1947, the AGRC studied different methods to be applied for the realization of new cemeteries. It proposed that the sites be constructed by local contractors who had to provide all of the machinery, staff and spare parts. Other solutions were proposed: the use of the American Army providing the necessary equipment and the spare parts or contracts with American companies. Finally, the good reputation of the fully equipped businesses of France, Belgium and the Netherlands weighed the balance in favor of the first choice.

The final choices

Before proceeding to the final choice of the permanent sites, views were sought from the Generals commanding the operational theaters like Eisenhower or MacArthur, amongst others. These choices were progressive: on 15th April 1947, the Saint-Laurent-sur-Mer cemetery was confirmed as a future permanent cemetery at the same time as the cemetery of Neuville-en-Condroz which will later become known as the Ardennes cemetery. On 22nd April, the Secretary of War officially endorsed these choices. The selection of the Saint-Laurent-sur-Mer was relatively easy. It must nevertheless be noted that the site entrance was constructed in Colleville-sur-Mer and not in Saint-Laurent-sur-Mer, which explains why today the cemetery is known by its name of the American cemetery of Colleville-sur-Mer especially by the French, a misnomer that lingered on many years after its creation. The last element which motivated the Government in its choice was the advantageous location of the Colleville-sur-Mer site: the installation of the cemetery was planned five miles from the national road and near the towns of Caen, Bayeux and Carentan giving assurance to the visitors of the necessary commodities once the war damage would be repaired.

During the summer of 1947, the representatives of the different organizations met once again and decided to plan the burials on the basis of forty per cent overseas and sixty per cent in the United-States. On 20th October 1947, a new meeting was held in Washington: the officials decided on the final creation of two cemeteries only in Normandy: Colleville-sur-Mer and Saint-James. They insisted also that the cemetery at Colleville-sur-Mer should not contain more than 13 000 graves. The AGRC headquarters granted that the Saint-James cemetery should not exceed 5 200 graves.

The organizations concerned in the creation of permanent cemeteries thought it more interesting to have smaller cemeteries instead of large ones. This is why Saint-James was added to the list. It was decided to place the bodies of the temporary cemeteries of Saint-Corneille, Villeneuve-sur-Auvers, Gorron, Le Chêne-Guérin and Marigny at Saint-James and those of Blosville, Sainte-Mère-Église No. 1 and 2, La Cambe and Saint-André-de-l'Eure at Colleville-sur-Mer cemetery, as well as the bodies contained in the temporary cemetery of Saint-Laurent-sur-Mer. This last temporary cemetery would then be removed to allow the construction of the large permanent Normandy American Cemetery.

Finally, the Secretary of the Army and the ABMC selected a total of fourteen new locations as permanent cemeteries in 1947: Saint-Avold, Saint-James, Épinal, Colleville-sur-Mer, Draguignan for France; Neuville-en-Condroz and Henri-Chapelle in Belgium; Florence and Nettuno in Italy; Margraten in the Netherlands; Cambridge in England; Luxembourg; Carthage in Tunisia and Manila in the Philippines. It seemed unreasonable to the American authorities to construct a second cemetery near Paris while there already existed the permanent American cemetery of Suresnes with 1 541 American soldiers of the First World War buried. In March 1949, they chose to symbolize in this place the fighting around Paris by burying twenty-four unknowns of the Second World War in a vacant zone of the cemetery. The ABMC also decided to enlarge the chapel to commemorate henceforth the memory of the dead of the two world wars in adding two loggias to the building.

It was planned that the temporary cemeteries constituted during the Second World War would return to the host country ownership after their dismantling. Following the selection of the permanent sites, it just remained to acquire them.

Are these cemeteries American territories?

Once the grounds were chosen, it was essential to deal with the host nations to acquire the necessary lands and to establish a viable jurisdiction. The territorial principle often forwarded by the media demonstrates ignorance of the regulations governing these cemeteries[20]. After the First World War, the necessary land for the construction of the permanent cemeteries had been purchased from France, on most occasions, for a symbolic one franc with the guarantee of a concession in perpetuity, without rent, tax or taxation. The Montfaucon site was an exception because it was conceded by France. The treaty had been signed with France on 29th August 1929 and on the 4th October 1929 with Belgium. The concessions were sometimes sensitive: on the Chateau-Thierry site for example, the twenty-seven acres necessary corresponded to 575 different parcels!

As far as the Montfaucon cemetery, concessions in perpetuity were made by the host countries for the new permanent

---

[20] See: "Un nouveau memorial à Omaha" (A new memorial at Omaha-Beach) in the French Newspaper *Ouest-France* on 3rd June 2007. The journalist interviewing Daniel L. Neese, Superintendent of Normandy American Cemetery, seems obliged to pose the eternal question: "Who owns the land?"

American cemeteries after the Second World War. In October 1947, once the fourteen sites were chosen, France and the United-States signed a first agreement concerning the conception of five new permanent cemeteries on French soil. Then, on 19th March 1956, a second agreement was concluded between Christian Pineau, Minister of French Foreign Affairs and Clarence D. Dillon, United-States Ambassador in Paris, representing the American Government. On many occasions, French, Belgium, Holland or Luxembourg Government officials had demonstrated goodwill to expropriate any land required for the construction of a permanent cemetery – the British for their part made no statement. They asked only in exchange that the land was limited to the necessary essential.

We have chosen to evoke the legislation of the American cemeteries of the Second World War in France through the 1956 agreement since it replaced the agreement signed on 1st October 1947.

The first article of this treaty guarantees the American Government the free disposal, without any limit in time, of necessary land for the constitution of cemeteries namely: for Draguignan, 11 acres; for Épinal, 47 acres; for Saint-Avold, 113 acres; Saint-James, 28 acres and for Colleville-sur-Mer, 170 acres. It was stipulated that these grounds had to be used solely for the burial of members of the American Armed Forces, the bodies of American citizens who died contributing *"to the pursuit of world war II"* or for the construction of buildings and annexes necessary in maintaining the cemeteries.

It was expected, according to the third article, that the lands be exempted of all taxes present or future. At the same time the ABMC was offered the possibility of expanding the surface areas of the cemeteries at any time, in agreement with the French Ministry of Veterans or its successor. The fourth article is without doubt the most interesting: *"It is understood that the Government of the United-States will submit and conform to the French laws and regulations on the policing of burial grounds and that the provisions of the decree of March 7, 1808 relative to the protective zone which must surround cemeteries located outside the perimeter of populated parts of communes will be applicable to the cemeteries which are subject of the present agreement".* This article breaks the legend that the American cemeteries are American territories since here, it is clearly indicated that the cemeteries must conform to French law. Nevertheless, the Americans took advantage of the many benefits they had and still have to execute all necessary facilities and beautification of the cemeteries while taking advantage of a tax exemption.

In article 7, it was detailed that if the American Government decided one day to remove one or several cemeteries, it would revert in the loss of rights over the land in question. Thereby, if it was decided one day that Colleville-sur-Mer should disappear; all the plots would revert to France.

This treaty shows us that the American cemeteries of the Second World War in France are concessions in perpetuity, exempt of all charges or taxes but which remain nevertheless under French legislation and which are not American territories! The ABMC and the American Government would not draw real benefits if their cemeteries became American enclaves because, as noted by General North, this arrangement was and remains more advantageous: in the case, for example, where it would be necessary to intervene with security forces, it is much easier and quicker that the French Police intervene rather than the American Police stationed outside French territory. In the same way, if the cemeteries were American territories, the Gendarmerie would be obliged to ask for special authority in order to intervene. Moreover, it could be embarrassing for the United-States if a fugitive took refuge in one of its cemeteries[21]!

---

[21] NORTH, *op. cit.*

However, one can ask if it is also the case for the other cemeteries of the commission situated outside French borders? According to Ferdinand Dessente in his book on the Neuville-en-Condroz cemetery, the agreement signed in Brussels on 27th November 1959 between the American Government and the Belgium Government specifies though that it is a right to use the land, not a gift of the land. It is exactly the case for all the other cemeteries of the commission, whether of the First World War (like that of Brookwood in England) or of the Second World War. The only exception is the case of the Manila cemetery: according to the agreement of 14th March 1947, the site was conceded to the United-States not in perpetuity but for a lease of ninety-nine years. Furthermore in the Philippines, the burials were limited by agreement with the host country, however allowing scouts and Philippine soldiers who fought on the American side to be buried there.

For the cemeteries of other nations installed in France, each country realized its own agreement. They were nevertheless practically similar to those signed with the United-States: the Commonwealth War Graves Commission and the French Government, for example, signed an agreement for the concession of the cemeteries to be maintained in perpetuity by the British. France passed an agreement with the Federal Republic of Germany which stipulated the free use of the lands on which cemeteries were constructed, freely and without a time limitation but which remained properties of the French Republic. In conclusion, the Americans have not enjoyed legislatively more benefits than other nations who fought and lost men on French territory.

"Agreement concluded between the Government of the United States of America and the Government of the French Republic relative to the grant of plots of land located in France for the creation of permanent military cemeteries or the construction of war memorials.

Signed at Paris March 19, 1956.

The Government of the United States of America, on the one part, and the Government of the French Republic, on the other, desirous to implement and complete the agreement dated October 1st 1947, as regards the creation in France of permanent cemeteries in calm and dignified sites, destined to receive the bodies of American nationals victims of the 1939-1945 war, and the erection of memorials to commemorate their sacrifice, have agreed to the following provisions:

Article 1: The Government of the French Republic grants to the Government of the United States of America, with a view to the creation of permanent American military cemeteries of World War II or the construction of War memorials, the free disposal without limitation of duration of the plots of land enumerated in the attached documents with maps annexed thereto.

Article 2: The plots of land thus placed at the disposal of the Government of the United States of America shall be exclusively utilized as provided in Article 1, either to bury therein the remains of members of the American Armed Forces or of American citizens who died while contributing to the pursuit of World War II, to build war memorials thereon, or for buildings and utilities needed to maintain these cemeteries.

Article 3: *The plots of land placed at the disposal of the Government of the United States of America by virtue of the provisions of the present agreement are and shall remain exonerated from all present and future taxes. They are handed over free from all charges and easements incompatible with the use to which they are destined.*

All questions concerning the extension or modification of boundaries of the said plots – as shown in the documents attached to the present agreement – which later on might be deemed necessary, will be settled by direct agreement between the "Ministère des Anciens Combattants et Victimes de Guerre" or its successors and the American Battle Monuments Commission or its successors.

Likewise, the placing at the disposal of the American Government of additional land located outside the cemeteries but whose attribution might be deemed necessary in the future to their maintenance will be the subject of a direct agreement between the said Ministry and Commission.

Article 4: *It is understood that the Government of the United States will submit and conform to the French laws and regulations on the policing of burial grounds and that the provisions of the decree of March 7, 1808 relative to the protective zone which must surround cemeteries located outside the perimeter of populated parts of communes will be applicable to the cemeteries which are the subject of the present agreement.*

Article 5: *The Government of the United States of America will be able to execute directly all installations or embellishment works in these cemeteries.*

Article 6: *The provisions of the present agreement will come into force on the day of its signature. They will be applied, of a common accord, to the measures which may have been previously taken with a view to insuring the planning and installing of cemeteries already existing on the plots of land referred to in Article 1.*

Article 7: *The suppression, by decision of the Government of the United States of America, of one or several of military cemeteries listed in the attached documents will result ipso facto for the latter in the loss of the right to use the plots of land where such cemetery or cemeteries are installed, the plots in question being affected to another use.*

Article 8: *The present agreement is drawn up in two originals one in French and the other in English, both texts being authentic.*

Done at Paris on 19th March 1956".

Signed by C. Pineau for the Government of the French Republic.

Signed by C.D. Dillon for the Government of the United States of America.

We are in 1954, the Normandy American Cemetery is nearly completed and the families are able finally to pay their respects in front of the final graves of their loved ones killed during the Second World War. *Photo ABMC.*

SECOND PART

The creation and organization of the Normandy American Cemetery

The Last Operations

EXHUMATIONS AND REPATRIATIONS

The preparations for repatriation

The United-States developed the idea of a mass repatriation while establishing the first burial projects during the Second World War. But the plans for repatriation of bodies were suspended during the course of the war. The success of repatriation during the Great War had confirmed to the Americans the idea of using the same plan after the end of the Second World War. However, this American practice differed from that of other European countries including Germany, Great-Britain or France. These countries chose to bury the bodies near where they were killed without considering repatriation.

It was difficult for the Americans to get the Europeans to understand this policy of repatriation which they were not familiar with even if this statement can be qualified. In 1948 for example, the French Minister of Veteran Affairs managed a similar operation to repatriate the French soldiers' bodies fallen in the Italian Peninsula during the fighting of 1943-1944. 1 800 soldiers were exhumed and their bodies were sent to Marseille before being directed to dispersal centers and directed to families.

Nevertheless, this type of choice was difficult to understand for European society. The British author Stephen Graham had already written in 1921 that the American repatriations of the First World War had made the American sacrifice less visible and less powerful. Others felt that the cost of repatriation was an excessive expense. However, the American Government had observed that the cost of repatriation was not superior to that of burial in a permanent cemetery abroad. It was estimated that around

700 dollars would be required for the repatriation operations of a body back to his family (the same operation during the First World War had cost 400 dollars). If the United-States had to bring back all the 300 000 bodies to their families this operation would have cost 210 million dollars. In the case of a final burial worldwide, 200 dollars were necessary to transfer each body into a permanent cemetery abroad in addition to 200 dollars for the burial and 300 dollars for the maintenance of the grave for fifty years (six dollars per annum) thus a total of 700 dollars. This sum was identical to that necessary to affect repatriation.

This American practice of repatriation explains why the American Government recommended to the Graves Registration Service to build temporary cemeteries near ports or train networks during the Second World War. This would facilitate the transport of bodies and their eventual return to the United-States and as a consequence would reduce the costs, the number of temporary cemeteries and their dispersal.

A first repatriation project was formulated early on during the war and envisaged the division of the cemeteries into six sectors. It was planned to begin the repatriations with the European sectors in the following order: Belgium, Netherlands and Luxembourg first (sector No. 2) then the British Isles, Norway, Sweden and Denmark (sector No. 1), the West of France (No. 5), the South of France and Switzerland (No. 4), the East of France (No. 3) and to finish, Central France (No. 6). Sectors No. 5 and 6 had to be evacuated via Cherbourg, sector No. 1 via Southampton, sector No. 3 via Marseille and the last two sectors (No. 2 and No. 4) via Anvers. However, this plan was very optimistic and premature. It necessitated that the boxes and regulatory burial coffins would arrive in the temporary cemeteries by July 1946, that the exhumations would start in August and that the first ships would leave on the following month. The task was so considerable that nothing was ready for the dates provided.

They considered not only merchant ships as possible means of transport but also planes which they finally rejected. They insisted on one thing: that the sanitary conditions of the means of transport should be satisfactory.

The Quartermaster General, responsible for the program, was the only one able to give written instructions for the final disposition of American remains. In mid May 1946, the OQMG realized that the production of coffin boxes required a delay to the year end, forcing a planning revision. In the same way, it was necessary to think about exhuming hundreds of bodies scattered around the world in temporary cemeteries before undertaking the construction of future permanent cemeteries. The AGRC got down to the task.

During 1947, a large part of the family responses finally reached the American authorities: the repatriation program in Europe would eventually start from July 1947 and would be of some two years duration. The first exhumations started at the temporary cemetery of Henri-Chapelle which was closed to the public after a very moving ceremony. While the first operations were undertaken in Belgium, similar activities started in France. The preparations and the last audit started in mid-August 1947 in the temporary cemetery of Saint-Laurent-sur-Mer.

In September 1947, the AGRC headquarters announced that the repatriation program in the Saint-Laurent-sur-Mer temporary cemetery would officially start with a blessing on Sunday 14th September. This cemetery became the second cemetery closed in Europe because of exhumation operations. In spite of bad weather, several thousands of French and Americans participated in the funeral rites, in the presence of officials and of American Armed Forces representatives. The dignitaries made their speeches and laid wreaths during the ceremony.

The exhumations really started on 16th September and were performed by three sections of the AGRC. The bodies to be repatriated were stored in Cherbourg whilst those for final planned burial in Colleville-sur-Mer cemetery remained at Saint-Laurent. The same operations were progressively carried out in the different temporary cemeteries: on 22nd October at Lisnabreeny, on 27th at La Cambe, 2nd November at Épinal, 23rd at Blosville, in December at Varois and Saint-Juan, in spring 1948 at Sainte-Mère-Église No. 2, at Saint-James, Hamm, Saint-Avold, Limey…

The temporary cemetery of La Cambe was an exception. This location was destined to become a permanent cemetery for German soldiers. It closed from 19th October 1947 in order to allow the Graves Registration Service teams to perform the exhumation work, after a last blessing made in the presence of the Sub-Prefect of Bayeux, the American Vice-Consul of Cherbourg and of Colonel Lewry. In November 1947, the location was ready to become the permanent German cemetery which can still be visited today. The bodies of the American soldiers killed during the war had been exhumed from their provisional burial to allow repatriation and final burial. The American government had specially designed a standard coffin accompanied by its shipping case studied to resist potential impacts on transfer to the United-States. The coffins weighed 200 lbs. less than those provided during the First World War, but were still a weight of 400 lbs. with the remains inside. The shipping case was in wood containing the coffin which was of anodized cast aluminum and of bronze exterior. This coffin was bolted to the bottom of the shipping case to avoid any movement.

Delivery of the coffins in Europe was made thanks to the ports of Anvers, Cardiff and Cherbourg chosen only a few weeks before the start of the repatriations. While the first bodies were exhumed, operations were performed in the storage areas. On 20th August 1947, a first loading of nearly 2 800 coffins and shipping cases and of twenty-eight tons of equipment from New-York were discharged in Cherbourg. The cases were then sent immediately to Saint-Laurent-sur-Mer cemetery and to the Cherbourg storage area.

The progress of the exhumations

The construction of all the permanent cemeteries of the Second World War was scheduled partially or totally on the sites of the temporary cemeteries with the exception of the permanent cemetery of Saint-Avold. It was probably thought that the choice of these locations would reduce the body transport operations, but it had not been the case since all the bodies in the temporary cemeteries had to be exhumed to allow the preparation of the sites for final burials.

The Quartermaster General accorded a delay of three months to the families to give their decision on the fate of their loved one(s) and before returning the available form on the mortal remains. When the time came to an end, the Quartermaster General gave to the officials of the AGRC the authorization to proceed with the exhumations. The remains exhumed and positively identified were moved to areas corresponding to the family choice; when the AGRC did not know the family wishes, the bodies remained in the pre-fabricated morgues.

Each team was composed of an embalmer and of two assistants who only worked on one exhumation at a time. Each exhumed body had to be prepared and placed in his final coffin before the end of the day. Ferdinand Dessente in his book detailed the procedures followed during exhumations: the bodies deposited in the final coffins were removed from the cemetery if possible on the same day. Otherwise, they were placed overnight under

Photograph of a standard coffin with its shipping case. This type of coffin was used to bury the soldiers in all the Second World War permanent cemeteries abroad. *Edward Steere, Thayer Boardman.*

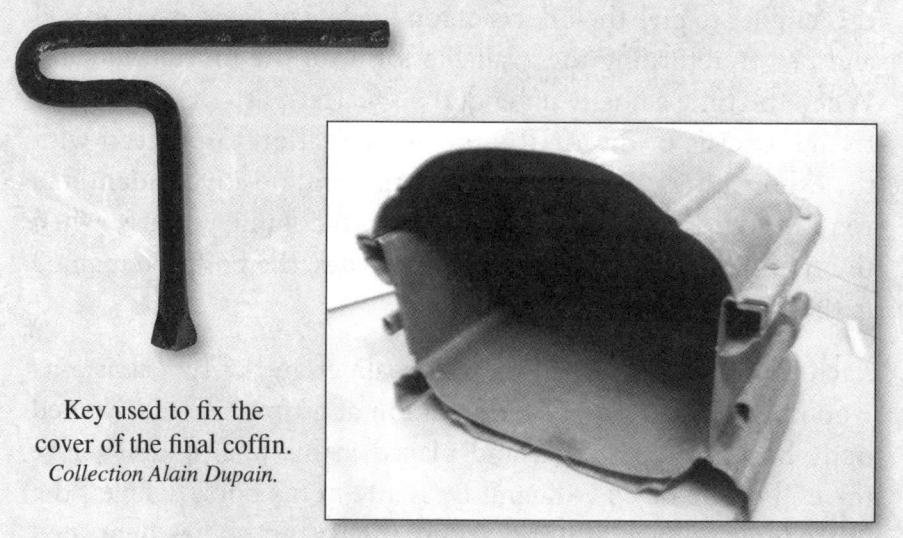

Key used to fix the cover of the final coffin. *Collection Alain Dupain.*

Side view of a coffin similar to those used to bury American soldiers killed during the Second World War. *Photo C. Lebastard.*

a tarpaulin or in a morgue under guard. The future Normandy cemetery disposed effectively of such a morgue. The burial directive was completed by an auditor indicating the nature of the temporary grave and the manner in which the body had first been buried (in a mattress cover, a parachute, a temporary coffin…). This auditor also indicated the state of the mortal remains: general condition and integrity of the body. The remains were generally buried at a depth of five foot in the temporary cemeteries but there were many exceptions. This explains why the Graves Registration Service teams regularly used the method of trenching: they exhumed the bodies by row starting with digging a shallow trench, leaving about 20 inches above the presumed position of the body. Each body was then treated individually: the AGRC teams proceeded to extract the provisional coffin. They descended into the pit to collect the remains on a stretcher if the coffin was too damaged. A check was made that no personal effect remained in the pit or the coffin. During the extraction operations of the bodies, the local employees did not have the authorization to handle the remains. The AGRC employees were the only employees allowed to take care of the remains. All the provisional coffins were systematically burnt after the exhumation. Once exhumed, the body of the soldier was prepared: a coating of liquid deodorant DDT based, formaldehyde, a curing compound and liquid intended for cavities was applied. The body was wrapped on a second work table in a blanket and a new bed sheet. Following the number of dog tags found on the body, one, two or three new identification tags were produced. Whenever possible, an original tag was pinned on the blanket at chest height.

If no problems were noted during the preceding operations, the body was placed in the final coffin. The last dog tag was fixed to the coffin handle at the head side held by a metal wire itself sealed with a seal by a clamp stamped with the initials "US". The body was then wedged with "padded socks" which arrived with the coffin to prevent it moving in transit. The funeral "installation" was held by several straps fixed to the interior of the coffin.

Once the operations on the body completed, the inspecting officer personally undertook the final check. He examined the identification record, the dog tags, the cleanliness of the coffin, the strength of the attachments and ensured that there was no strange smell outside that of the chemicals. The coffin was then sealed thanks to a key in the form of a T which locked 24 points closing the lid of the coffin. Once locked, the coffin was fixed to the shipping case. This case was marked by Stencil on the basis of the information contained in the burial directive. This marking included the name of the deceased, his rank, the section of the Armed Forces in which he served, as well as the region of the AGRC. For the unknowns, the first two lines indicated "Unknown" or "Group Burial" followed by the letter X, a dash and an order number. Finally, the name of the temporary cemetery where the remains were previously interred followed by the name and address of the consignee or of the cemetery of destination was indicated. On the left hand handle of the shipping case at head level were nailed the regulatory health certificate and the last dog tag of the deceased. The shipping case was then ready to be transferred to the designated permanent cemetery or to one of the three ports for repatriation (Cherbourg for Saint-Laurent-sur-Mer). Once all the bodies in the temporary cemetery were exhumed, the workers filled in the holes and spread quicklime to disinfect the soil, under order of the officer in charge.

The AGRS also buried military or civilian allies or enemies in the temporary cemeteries and made the remains available to the authorities in the country of origin.

The return to the country

Before repatriating the coffins to the United-States, it became necessary to group the fallen soldiers in the ports provided for this purpose. The coffins were carefully protected in their individual shipping cases and each covered by an American flag. The bodies exhumed from the cemeteries in North-West France ready to be repatriated, were all sent to Cherbourg which was named as port of shipment for the return to their families.

Lengthy preparatory work was necessary to make possible an operation of this magnitude: the distribution centers and the American ports were informed in advance of the next shipment of coffins to best co-ordinate the flow of supplies abroad. On 30th October 1947, all of the bodies at Saint-Laurent had been exhumed and ready to be moved. Similar operations had started at La Cambe whose team was scheduled to finish at the end of November. Thus, the first stage was about to be completed which marked the beginning of the repatriation. The first repatriations were carried out in Belgium: 7 060 bodies in the Henri-Chappelle cemetery had been exhumed and sent to Anvers of which 5 060 were boarded on the *USAT Connolly* on 30th September 1947.

The American people awaited the return of their heroes with impatience more than two years after the end of the war. An immense crowd gathered to pay a last tribute to the bodies of the first soldiers repatriated to the United-States on 26th October 1947 on the occasion of a large ceremony at Central Park (New-York). A few days later, on 4th November the *Robert F. Burns* left Cherbourg with a loading of 1 052 coffins originating from temporary cemeteries in North-West France and notably that of Saint-Laurent-sur-Mer. The ship then headed for Anvers where it loaded more than 3 150 remains. The ship left the port heading for New-York on 9th November with a total of 4 200 American coffins.

Loading of a flagged coffin intended for repatriation.
Photo ABMC.

A truck loaded with coffins containing the bodies of soldiers exhumed from the temporary cemeteries.
Photo ABMC.

The American Government finally decided that the repatriations will be made aboard the famous Liberty ships. The soldiers killed in Europe had to arrive in New-York (those of the Pacific in San Francisco) and were then routed by rail to the fifteen distribution centers spread across the United-States to serve each of the forty-eight American States at the time. These centers were situated in New-York (2 centers), Philadelphia, Charlotte, Atlanta, Memphis, Columbus, Chicago, San-Antonio, Fort-Worth, Kansas-City, Ogden, Seattle, San-Francisco and Mira-Loma.

Once docked at the military base of Brooklyn (New-York), the coffins were unloaded, sent to the distribution centers and routed by train to the family households. These trains conveyed fifteen railcars on average each with sixty-six coffins. Each stop was punctuated by ceremonies and the Government had asked that each body be accompanied by military escort and that the coffin remained covered by the American flag until rendered to the family.

These repatriation operations were globally conducted without problem. However, an incident occurred in January 1948 which could have had dramatic consequences. The ship *Joseph V. Connolly* left New-York on 8th January with forty-three crew members onboard and sank in the middle of the Atlantic. The engine room caught on fire while on board were thousands of empty coffins destined for soldiers killed in Europe. The captain appealed for help and the crew had to take to the lifeboats. The ship was transformed into a torch in the Atlantic: the fire was fed by the thousands of coffins on board. The shipwrecked sailors were helped by the *General Callan* and the *Union Victory*. Fortunately, there was no human loss to be deplored but the affair might have had far more serious consequences: during her previous voyage, the *USAT Connolly* was carrying more than 4 000 bodies to the United-States and the loss of so many

A consignment of coffins ready for repatriation.
Photo ABMC.

An impressive crowd gathered for a ceremony in New-York City on the occasion of the repatriation of the first soldiers killed in Europe.
Edward Steere, Thayer Boardman.

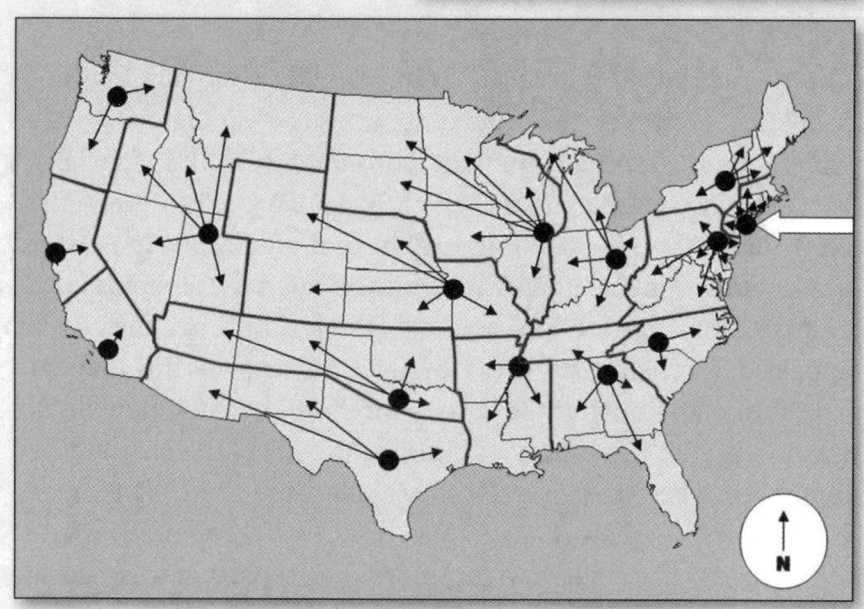

The different distribution centers spread across the United-States and their operational zones.

114

bodies would have had a significant negative influence for the American Government vis-à-vis public opinion.

In early 1948, all the bodies at Saint-Laurent-sur-Mer were accounted for, a total of 3 808 soldiers[22]. 1 909 of them had been repatriated, 1 786 still awaited a final burial in a permanent cemetery and 113 awaited a response by the families. The situation at La Cambe progressed more slowly even if nearly all the bodies had already been exhumed: 2 814 bodies were ready for final burial in the permanent cemetery of Colleville-sur-Mer and only 896 soldiers had been repatriated. The other remains awaited a reply by families (2 205 bodies) or awaited repatriation (578). During the same period, the operations were just starting in the temporary cemetery at Blosville: 621 bodies had been exhumed of which 99 awaited final burial at Colleville-sur-Mer, 169 bodies pending repatriation and the AGRC still awaited replies from 353 families, meaning more than half of the bodies exhumed. The advance taken in the operations at the temporary cemetery at Saint-Laurent can be explained by its location. The bodies had to be taken care of as a priority in order to make room for construction operations at the permanent Normandy American Cemetery. The location of the temporary Saint-Laurent-sur-Mer cemetery encroached on the site of the permanent cemetery and therefore had to be evacuated and dismantled quickly. At the beginning of 1948, 11 565 soldiers had been sent to the United-States, 8 982 still awaited final burial and 2 670 repatriation. 7 403 families still had to respond. On 9th July 1948, the AGRC reported that it had repatriated from Europe 34 874 bodies to the United-States. At the end of 1948, a total of 62 000 U.S. fallen soldiers from Europe had arrived out of a World total of 114 715 repatriations.

---

[22] The number is different to that given previously. It can be explained by the number of bodies recovered after the conflict either on the beach or in the fields and buried thereafter in the temporary cemetery at Saint-Laurent-sur-Mer.

Coffins unloaded on their arrival in the port of New-York City.
Edward Steere, Thayer Boardman.

Remains loaded aboard a mortuary wagon destined for a distribution center. *Edward Steere, Thayer Boardman.*

At the end of August 1949, the ports of Anvers and of Cherbourg were no longer used but the family responses continued to arrive in dribs and drabs. A port unit was established in Bremerhaven (Germany) to achieve the repatriation of the remaining bodies. Between November 1947 and June 1949, 18 896 bodies were transported via Cherbourg. The activity officially ceased on 31st December 1951.

The quality of the work of the AGRC finally allowed the repatriation of 113 834 soldiers from Europe to the port of New-York being 55% of the 206 677 American soldiers killed in Europe. In total, 171 542 bodies were repatriated to the United-States by the AGRC. We can estimate that 59.5% of the bodies previously buried in the temporary cemeteries of Blosville, Sainte-Mère-Église Nos. 1 and 2, La cambe, Saint-Laurent-sur-Mer and Saint-André-de-l'Eure were repatriated to the United-states meaning a total of 13 000 soldiers were repatriated[23]. Thus we can establish that 40.5% of the soldiers buried in these temporary cemeteries were buried in the Normandy American Cemetery at Colleville-sur-Mer.

The success of the repatriations – more than half of the families chose this program – can be explained by the American mentality. For many American families, it was insulting to be buried in foreign soil. During the First World War, the repatriations were favored by commercial enterprises and American entrepreneurs who did not doubt the superiority of America over Europe. Furthermore, important publicity campaigns in favor of repatriations had been started by the American funeral industry. Had there been a resurgence of this phenomenon after the

---

[23] The calculation has been made based on information provided in the book *United States Temporary Military Cemeteries European Theater Area*. However, we used the figure of 3 808 soldiers buried in the temporary cemetery of Saint-Laurent-sur-Mer and not that contained in the book quoted.

Second World War? The question remains. However, another more simple reason can be raised: it was no doubt easier for a family to commune with and to honor their dearest in a cemetery in his/her village rather than 3 700 miles away.

THE FINAL BURIALS

The preparations

The American Congress started from 1946 to enact the first laws permitting the permanent burials of soldiers of the Second World War. While the AGRC and the office of the Quartermaster-General experienced significant pressures for completion of the repatriation and reburial operations, the ABMC had to in turn provide as soon as possible the plans of the future permanent cemeteries. It was expected that the final burials commence immediately upon the arrival of the family responses.

With the death of Paul D. Cret, consultant architect for the American Battle Monuments Commission in September 1945, the Fine Arts Commission, at the request of the ABMC, recommended three eminent architects, from which one was chosen as consultant architect. The commission selected John Harbeson in July 1946. He was a former Professor of Design at the school of architecture at Pennsylvania University. He was also recognized and respected in his profession and would play a determining role in the architecture of the new cemetery at Colleville-sur-Mer. Harbeson prepared a list of architects of which all nominees were American. It was agreed with the commission that there would be a different architect per permanent cemetery so that the cemeteries would not all look alike.

Work sketches started quickly for the four priority cemeteries: Henri-Chapelle, Colleville-sur-Mer, Épinal and Draguignan. Projects were undertaken in accordance with Public Law 368 of 5th August 1947 which gave official architectural responsibility of the cemeteries to the ABMC and assigned the purchase of the necessary lands to the War Secretary. The work of the architects was difficult in spite of the topographical data and the photographs which they had received. Furthermore, they did not yet know the exact number of soldiers who would be buried in the cemeteries under their control since not all of the families had expressed their wishes. The general design had to therefore be flexible and they took as a benchmark data from the First World War: 40% of the soldiers killed had been buried in the First World War cemeteries.

Each plan proposed by the architects had to be approved by the ABMC and by the Fine Arts Commission; the ABMC fortunately did not have to submit the plans to the foreign governments, thereby accelerating the work. The firm Harbeson, Hough, Livingston and Larson of Philadelphia was chosen to realize the final sketches and finished its work in February 1948, well after the original deadline but in sufficient time to allow the engineers of the AGRC to prepare detailed plans of the rows of graves. Once validated by the ABMC, the projects were submitted for tender to several French companies. The company that won the bid was not able to start operations before June 1948 because of a delay in receiving entry rights from the French Government. During the summer, detailed cost preparations were undertaken in Paris. The sum of 37 million dollars was estimated as being required to complete the fourteen cemeteries but a budget office spokesman noted this estimate at 50 million dollars. Despite procrastination, all was ready at the start of November 1948 to allow the first permanent burials.

The conduct of the funerals

The final burial provisions abroad of American soldiers killed during the Second World War were considered part of the demobilization plan. The choice of Colleville-sur-Mer as permanent cemetery required the concentration of the 9 300 non-repatriated remaining bodies from the provisional cemeteries of Blosville, Sainte-Mère-Église Nos. 1 and 2, La Cambe, Saint-Laurent-sur-Mer and Saint-André-de-l'Eure.

The European permanent cemeteries were divided into different operational zones to facilitate their future organization. The first zone included the cemeteries of Henri-chapelle, Margraten and Neuville-en-Condroz while the second included Draguignan, Colleville-sur-Mer and Saint-James. Of these last three cemeteries, Draguignan was the one which received the first permanent burials on 11th July 1948. The operations were completed on the 15th February 1949 with the erection of the 853rd grave, making it the smallest American military cemetery in France.

Preparations for the Colleville-sur-Mer cemetery started very early. During the initial work starting in 1947, the double valley that surrounded the cemetery was filled and levelled about 0.6 mile in length to obtain the current regularity of the site. It was not before the 4th November 1948 that the first grave was dug. On the day before, the first grave of the St. James permanent cemetery had been realized.

The delays of between six and eighteen months[24] which separated the exhumations of the final burials in the cemeteries of Colleville-sur-Mer, Saint-James, Hamm, Henri-Chapelle or Margraten, were very unsatisfactory. They obliged the AGRC to

---

[24] Because of these problems, the AGRC decided that henceforth, no further permanent cemetery would be built on the location of a temporary cemetery.

acquire additional land to store the bodies. Moreover, the burials realized during the remainder of the year had not been quick enough, according to the War Department, because of inadequate equipment and of the difficulty in modeling certain sites. This was the case for Colleville-sur-Mer: because of its location near the sea, the zone's drainage permanently soaked the clay soil. Thus, at the end of 1948, only 1 500 burials had been realized being about 15% of the total, whereas during the same period of time, 2 400 graves were dug in the Saint-James cemetery, being about half of the graves that it would finally contain.

The burials at the permanent Normandy American Cemetery were first undertaken on the side nearest the temporary cemetery of Saint-Laurent; the coffins were then placed as and when they arrived in their protective cases. No specific burial plan was respected and the bodies were buried in a totally random manner. However, the cemetery of Colleville-sur-Mer was divided into ten plots of graves starting with the letter A to the letter J, organized around a central path east-west, and on a total surface area of 1 800 000 square feet. Each row and each grave was numbered and a census of all the bodies was undertaken. The Army Secretary and the ABMC approved this project allowing the location of a soldier's body to be found. They allowed the Graves Registration Service to organize each plot of graves.

At the beginning of 1949, the employees at Colleville-sur-Mer were being provided with equipment of better quality and were finally able to speed up the work rate. It was hoped that the burials would be completed by the end of May 1949. The burials followed a regulatory protocol: each coffin/protective casing was draped in the colors of the United-States and escorted by a military platoon. After the blessing by a military chaplain, three volleys were fired and the bugle sounded. The flag was then regulatory folded and the body, lowered into the soil within its protective casing. The flag was eventually sent to the closest Next-of-Kin.

The coffins awaiting burial in the Colleville-sur-Mer cemetery.
Collection Alain Dupain.

A coffin just before the final burial. We can see its shipping/protective case situated in the background. *Collection Alain Dupain.*

In December 1949, a total of some 9 362 bodies had been finally buried in the Normandy American Cemetery. The work was then practically finished. When the program of the AGRC finished at the end of 1951, the service had realized the largest re-burial operation ever achieved to this day by the Americans. The cemetery of Colleville-sur-Mer became the largest military cemetery in Normandy with its surface area of 7 500 000 square feet. In comparison, twice as many bodies were interred in the German cemetery of La Cambe composed of a surface area of three times less[25].

The permanent American cemeteries of the Second World War and their number of graves today

Location	Identified soldiers	Unknowns	Total number of graves
Cambridge (England)	3 788	24	3 812
Carthage (Tunisia)	2 601	240	2 841
Colleville-sur-Mer (France)	9 080	307	9 387
Draguignan (France)	799	62	861
Épinal (France)	5 186	69	5 255
Florence (Italy)	4 189	213	4 402
Henri-Chapelle (Belgium)	7 898	94	7 992
Luxembourg	4 975	101	5 076
Manila (Republic of the Philippines)	13 462	3 744	17 206
Margraten (Netherlands)	8 195	106	8 301
Nettuno (Italy)	7 371	490	7 861
Neuville-en-Condroz (Belgium)	4 536	792	5 328
Saint-Avold (France)	10 338	151	10 489
Saint-James (France)	4 313	97	4 410
Suresnes (France)	-	24	24
Total	**86 731**	**6 514**	**93 245**

---

[25] This example shows us also the different treatments vis-à-vis other nations and in particular between winners and losers.

The dug trenches to receive the thousands of coffins and protective cases ready to be buried in the cemetery of Colleville-sur-Mer.
Collection Alain Dupain.

Excavator used to dig trenches at the permanent cemetery of Colleville-sur-Mer.
Collection Alain Dupain.

French employees lower a body into the ground: they use mechanized equipment to help them in their task.
Collection Alain Dupain.

The fifteen cemeteries in the preceding table bring together the essential numbers of American soldiers killed during the Second World War and buried abroad: 93 245 men. It also shows us that by the end of the burial process, the AGRC grouped in a rectangle of about 1 500 feet by 650 feet, 9 387 graves of American soldiers at Colleville-sur-Mer. 4 410 bodies were buried at Saint-James giving a total of 13 797 American burials in Normandy, representing 15% of the total of American bodies buried abroad.

Families with specific requests

During the course of the burial operations, specific requests were made to the War Department on behalf of families. If none of the options proposed by the Government suited them, then the families had the possibility of submitting their requests to the Quartermaster's Office on the questionnaire response they had received.

The families sometimes requested that their buried loved one was not moved. If the body was buried in an isolated grave, the request was generally accepted by the Quartermaster General on condition that this family renounced all their rights for an eventual subsequent repatriation at Government expense. In those cases, responsibility for the grave was borne by the family releasing the Government of all future responsibility. It was nevertheless necessary that the family obtained authorization of the Government of the host country together with the land owner where the body was found. Obviously, this request was impossible for the bodies moved meantime into a temporary cemetery.

Thus, in addition to repatriations and the creation of fourteen new cemeteries, certain soldiers were left in isolated burials by family request: General North reported forty-one bodies – including Quentin Roosevelt who will be referred to later – left to the upkeep of the families. The ABMC, in its general register lists today ninety-four isolated graves of which only two are in France: First Lieutenant Burton W. Gross of 478th Anti-Submarine Group, buried in the military cemetery of Saint-Désir and First Lieutenant John G. Rahill of the 45th Infantry division buried at Hochfelden in the Lower-Rhine department.

Sometimes it also happened that families requested that a body already buried in a temporary American cemetery was not to be moved. However, if the temporary cemetery had not been retained as part of the permanent cemeteries, the request was systematically rejected. Others requested participation in the funeral services organized abroad and for that, the express authorization of the Quartermaster General had to be obtained.

The bodies might also be incinerated by request of the closest legal relative. The latter had the possibility of burying the ashes abroad or of having them repatriated. Sometimes, the instructions ordered that the requests of the relatives be ignored. However, those who made such requests were being informed that the decisions of families at the funeral were final.

The most sensitive cases were those of bodies mixed and buried together. Indeed, sometimes the bodies were unable to be separated for temporary burial: it was often the case for the airmen or the tank crew… During the repatriation operations the mixed remains were buried in the United-States in a National cemetery. Certain bodies were identified and the families preferred that they remained buried in a permanent cemetery abroad. The War Department generally accepted this request and authorized the installation of bronze plates to mark the burials of bodies buried together. There is no burial of this type at the Normandy American Cemetery, but there are several in other sites such as that of Neuville-en-Condroz.

Many families regretted their choices: they regretted that the remains of their relatives were not buried in an ABMC cemetery when they saw what had become of the permanent cemeteries abroad. The ABMC received and continue to receive many families who regret their original choices. Others, on the contrary, have sent requests to the ABMC to have the body of their relative exhumed and repatriated to the United-States. The commission has always been opposed to these late repatriations considering that the families had time beforehand to make their choice. Furthermore, the laws authorizing repatriations has now become obsolete. Other objection criteria could support these refusals, in that the ABMC personnel had never received training for the exhumations. Moreover, the ABMC has always expressed its fear that incomplete rows of graves would denature the beauty of the locations. In July 1993, for example, a man requested that his brother's body be moved from the Normandy American Cemetery to be repatriated to New Jersey and his request was, like the others, denied.

MAKING SHIPSHAPE

The handover of power between the Graves Registration Service and the ABMC

With time and thanks to the good management of the permanent American cemeteries of the First World War, the prerogatives of the ABMC amplified gradually: a Presidential order signed on 4th March 1946 extended the functions of the commission to cemeteries of the Second World War and notably to Colleville-sur-Mer. Following the excellent work undertaken in the First World War cemeteries, the ABMC also received the burden to achieve the architectural program of these new sites. The transfer of responsibility would become effective once the final burials be completed. The power of the commission was further expanded when in 1947, an Executive order gave it the responsibility and the maintenance for the Mexico-City cemetery previously borne by the Department of the Army. The maintenance of this cemetery was given to the ABMC on the principle that the commission should become responsible for all of the military cemeteries abroad. The commission saw confirmed its new status: originally created to symbolize the participation of the United-States in the First World War, its role was henceforth to take charge of the future burials of soldiers killed outside of American soil and to perpetuate their memory.

In spring 1948, the operations had advanced sufficiently to allow the Quartermaster General and the AGRC to plan the transfer of power of certain permanent cemeteries in Europe. This transfer would be carried out as to the completion of burials in each cemetery. The first site transferred would be that of Draguignan on 1st September 1948, followed by that of Cambridge on 1st December 1948, then Henri-Chapelle and Épinal on 1st January 1949, Saint-James on 1st February, Colleville-sur-Mer on 1st May, Saint-Avold on 1st July and Margraten as well as Hamm on 1st January 1950. But the provisions proved optimistic as proved the example of Saint-James: this cemetery was assigned to the ABMC administration only on 15th September 1949. Other cemeteries were completed only in 1951, for example that of Neuville-en-Condroz.

The handover of power at Colleville-sur-Mer was realized on 28th December 1949 during a ceremony organized at the foot of the great flagpole and in the presence of the American Vice-Consul in Cherbourg, the Sub-Prefect of Bayeux and the mayors of the three communities of Omaha-Beach. On that occasion, the site was officially handed to the ABMC and particularly to Major Gibbs, director of the ABMC Europe, representing General Marshall. The ABMC could now assume full responsibility for the general organization, the development of the cemetery and the work layouts. Major Collman, the new and first

Superintendent of the Normandy American Cemetery, stated that day that the work should continue for five more years.

Compensation for affected farmers

The construction of the temporary cemeteries, the burials and then the constitution of the permanent cemeteries were made possible thanks to the purchase of the necessary land by the American Army. For many of the inhabitants, these requisitions proved difficult and deprived them of income. Very early on, compensation files were constituted. Thanks to documents provided by Mr. Hamel we are able to better understand the roll out of these expropriations.

From the month of June 1944, the American troops needed land to accommodate the different temporary cemeteries. Consequently, one of Mr. Hamel's plots, today adjacent to the permanent cemetery of Colleville-sur-Mer was requisitioned for temporary use. In September 1948, once the American authorities had completed drawing up plans for the new permanent cemetery, Mr. Hamel was contacted once again for new land. However, unlike the first requisition, the Army asked him to give land to be transferred on a permanent basis. Mr. Boivin, agricultural engineer specializing in judicial business in Bayeux was instructed by the French Quartermaster to prepare the expropriation files necessary for the construction of the cemetery even if, at this period, the limits were still not clearly defined. He then contacted Mr. Hamel for the expropriation operations. Every owner would receive restitution of 120 000 francs for every two acres.

The farmers, whose lands were requisitioned for the construction and the various works necessary for the Colleville-sur-Mer cemetery, had the opportunity to claim for damage occupation. Mr. Hamel decided to establish a claim in 1950 for the property he had conceded in 1944 to the Americans. After the course of the final burials, the aggrieved owners had the possibility to recover the possession of their domains henceforth useless to the American Army. Thus, on 15th October 1949, the American authorities gave back to him his land after having transformed it into a coffin depot for the final burials some months before, on 1st July. The nine acres occupied by this coffin depot also belonged to Mr. Angers who himself also established a file for damage occupancy. We have already mentioned above that the Americans tried wherever possible, to return the occupied lands in their original condition. Nevertheless, this had not always been possible and it explains why in the specialist report given to Mr. Angers and Mr. Hamel, they were granted a sum of over 500 000 francs in order to allow them to undertake the necessary repairs. They also received a sum of 17 000 francs to compensate for the loss of use.

These examples demonstrate that the local owners generally were treated with respect and were compensated. The expropriations were made under the auspices of French law and it endeavored to settle these claims rapidly to allow the laying out of the new permanent cemetery of Colleville-sur-Mer as soon as possible.

The architecture of the cemetery

ORGANIZATION OF THE BURIALS

The choice of the final markers

Once the bodies were buried in the permanent Normandy cemetery, it was anticipated that the wooden markers be replaced by dedicated stelae to commemorate their memory in the long term. Before the arrival of the new markers, it was necessary to delineate the location of the bodies. The Graves Registration Service re-utilized the wooden crosses and the Stars of David from the temporary cemeteries carefully restored for their second use.

The history of the crosses dated back to the First World War. This type of marker can still be seen today at Colleville-sur-Mer. At the end of the Great War, the Americans were impressed by the white wooden crosses from temporary cemeteries marking the graves of Allied soldiers. The ABMC asked the Secretary of War to adopt the cross as a symbol of permanent burial. However, the resistors were many because these crosses were more costly and because the American Army had already utilized the old style markers called slab-shaped headstones (as those in the Arlington National Cemetery). Moreover, families could eventually have asked to dispose of similar crosses for their repatriated relatives. This would have resulted in disfiguring the harmony of the slab-shaped stelae in the National cemeteries. Finally, the Secretary of War approved the request of the ABMC and asked that all the graves in the permanent cemeteries abroad be henceforth marked by the Latin cross, except for persons of the Jewish confession for which was proposed the Star of David. Taking into account the possibility that certain soldiers were Muslim or Buddhist, research was undertaken to determine an appropriate symbol. However, these religions did not have a universally known sign and the project was therefore abandoned.

Thus, the idea that spreads the existence of graves in crescent form for the Muslims is absolutely wrong.

Two sorts of materials were proposed: granite and marble. Finally, the commission's choice was focused on white marble whose quality/price ratio was more advantageous and whose life turned out to be superior to that of granite. The white marble from Italy was chosen because it was less expensive than that of the United-States marble: it cost between 12.5 to 15 dollars for the engraving and dispatch of an Italian marker.

Initially, the commission examined the wish formulated by certain families to include a maximum of fifty letters to the back of the marker of their relative, as was the custom amongst the British. The trials were not conclusive. The commission then chose to retain exactly the same markers with the same engraving already in place in the First World War cemeteries to represent the graves in the permanent cemeteries of the Second World War. With the need for crosses or stars in marble beckoning, the commission established an office in Rome: the Mediterranean office. This office was responsible both for the work execution in the cemeteries of Florence, Nettuno and Carthage and for ordering and for the supervision of the production of the markers. The factories of Lasa and of Carrare competed for the supply of the necessary marble. The first factory was retained since it offered prices for a Latin cross inferior to that of its competitor: from 26.95 to 29.15 dollars for Lasa against 46 dollars for Carrare.

The first stage in the preparation of the markers was to obtain complete data on the soldiers. The ABMC therefore allied itself with the Quartermaster General and with the Navy office of surgeons and doctors[26]. The commission followed the format of inscriptions on crosses and Stars of David in cemeteries of

---

[26] NORTH, *op. cit.*

It is, to our knowledge, the oldest photograph of the cemetery taken on 5th June 1951: we note the perfect alignment of the wooden crosses. *Ouest France.*

View of the permanent cemetery of Colleville-sur-Mer, of its wooden markers and of the remnants of the Omaha-Beach artificial harbor. *Life Magazine.*

the First World War, namely: Christian name, initial of second Christian name and family surname. Below, the rank, the division and on the last line the State in which the soldier had enlisted and the date of death. On the rear face, at the base of the marker, was written the serial number and on the front face, also at the base, was written the number of the grave. It should be noted that the date of birth was never written on the markers of American soldiers buried in a permanent cemetery abroad. According to "legend" the American authorities have refused because they did not wish to reveal the age of the soldier so that visitors did not gather solely on the graves of the youngest. In fact, it seems that this choice was dictated primarily for practical reasons: because on numerous crosses or stars, there was simply not enough space[27].

The biggest difference between the inscriptions of the First World War and those of cemeteries of the Second World War like Colleville-sur-Mer concerned the markers of the unknown soldiers. After the Great War, the ABMC had chosen to indicate the same inscription as that in Arlington cemetery: *"Here rests in honored glory an American soldier known but to God"*. This time, the important proportion of airmen, of coast-guards, of sailors, of women auxiliaries etc. rendered obsolete the term soldier. The commission therefore chose to inscribe the term *"comrade in arms"* which it judged more representative of the conflict scarcely finished: *"Here rests in honored glory a comrade in arms known but to God"*. All the markers of the unknowns by default were in Latin crosses[28].

---

[27] Some might say that it would have required to diminish the size of the engraving. However, it was necessary that the inscription be readable by all.

[28] There is an example in the Suresnes cemetery indicating a star of David above an unknown grave. It was possible that the AGRC could not determine the identity of a body but noticed his religion through some cult objects on his person.

The flowered grave of an unknown buried in Plot A. Moist sand has been placed in the inscription so that the engraved sentence in marble stands out.
Photo C. Lebastard.

Photograph of the cemetery dated November 1960. The alignment of the crosses and Stars of David is perfect. Pointe-de-la-Percée can be seen in the background and marks the extreme western part of Omaha-Beach.
Life Magazine.

SECOND PART 135

The installation of the grave markers

Once the definitive markers were completed, they were sent to the corresponding cemeteries. The Épinal cemetery was the first served with crosses and stars from Lasa. In most cemeteries, the Graves Registration Service decided to utilize the marker sketches as planned for the First World War sites: a grave every seven to ten feet, except for the circular cemeteries – that of Manila for example. Once the marble markers arrived at their destination, the wooden crosses were taken down; the inscriptions were erased and the wood was made available to the local population or destroyed.

At the end of 1949, substantially all of the soldiers had been buried in the Colleville-sur-Mer cemetery and it remained only to place the final markers. The major concern of the American technicians was that of the stability of the new markers. The AGRC had to ensure that no sagging would occur. This problem existed in the First World War cemeteries: the markers tended to sag preventing the maintenance of the level alignment.

In 1950, a Parisian company of public works embarked on a huge project in the cemetery to dig trenches of 20 inch depth and the same width at the head of the graves throughout the cemetery. At the bottom of the trenches, piles in reinforced concrete were placed some eight inches in diameter, equidistant from 20 feet each, to enable the fixing of the grave markers. In total, 3 500 piles were implanted, over which, reinforced concrete beams, as long as the row of graves, twelve inches in width by ten inches in height, were arranged over all the cemetery for a total length of 12 miles. The French company in charge of the project was also responsible for planting the marble crosses and Stars of David.

The alignment of the markers did not present any major difficulty since it was equidistant and parallel. But levelling made the task difficult back at Colleville-sur-Mer and in seven other American cemeteries of the Second World War. The position of the land did not facilitate the evaluation of altitudes, delaying the casting of the beams: plots B, D and F had a much steeper slope than the others. At the end of May 1950, the piling was well advanced and they were able to begin installing the beams[29]. The verification operations were performed by American Army and Navy engineers.

The markers were then fixed to the beams by means of bronze pegs and mortar then treated with chemical products to prevent the absorption of elements from the soil and of salt which could damage and stain them. The absence of laser, which did not exist at that time, forced the employees to align the markers by cord. The marble crosses were all installed between 1951 and 1952 and ready for the ceremony of the eighth anniversary of the Normandy invasion which included the presence of the American General Ridgway, on 6th June 1952.

THE BUILDINGS

Construction of the chapel and facilities

The real architectural work started in 1949 when the burials were almost completed and when the jurisdiction of the cemetery had been formally transferred to the commission. The architectural consistency initially planned was respected thanks to the good cooperation between the ABMC and the ARGC.

---

[29] MATHIEU (George), Author of mini conference "The American cemetery of Saint-Laurent-sur-Mer", testimony of a participant in the construction of the Normandy American Cemetery. [No date], 12p. His testimony is very valuable to us but unfortunately he did not participate in the planting of the beams or the crosses. His work consisted above all of measuring the different levels.

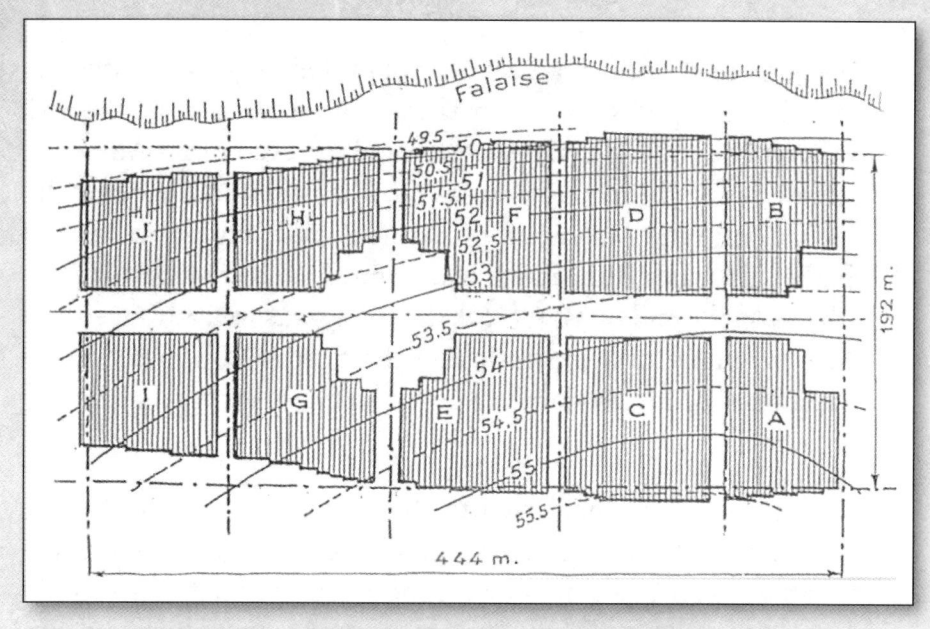

Representation of the reinforced concrete beams installed in the cemetery as well as the elevation curves of the site. *George Mathieu.*

Device used to maintain the alignment of the Stars of David and the Latin crosses in the cemetery of Colleville-sur-Mer. We can see the concrete beam which runs the entire row of graves. The cross is that of Gafford W. Sanders. *Photo ABMC.*

138

A water supply system was installed once the burials were terminated and once the system of reinforced beams to maintain the alignment of the markers was achieved. Barriers and a vehicle park were also constructed; a drainage system was installed; the electricity was provided to the site, etc. The ABMC constructed, in collaboration with the French administration of the *Ponts et Chaussées*, an access road about eight hundred and seventy five yards in length to allow access to the cemetery from the Departmental 514 road.

The first major difficulty the ABMC faced was to find qualified employees with professional experience and with knowledge of foreign languages. The work was undertaken most of the time by local workers who had to communicate with the American personnel, specifically designated and present on site. These American employees sent monthly reports to Washington to inform the head office of the ABMC of work progress.

Harbeson, with his company Harbeson, Hough, Livingston and Larson (the Philadelphia design firm), personally handled the architecture of the Colleville-sur-Mer cemetery and thought on the construction of new equipment placed under his responsibility: the future memorial, the chapel, the Visitor Center, the home of the Superintendent or again the pathways and the roads.

By its rectangular form, the Colleville-sur-Mer cemetery looked like the majority of the commission's cemeteries. The Harbeson architects planned from the start to conserve a central double driveway cut perpendicularly by another double driveway between the north and south squares of graves. A service road was also constructed to encircle all the graves.

The designers retained the neoclassical style for the different architectural works of the cemetery. It was the case for the chapel installed at the crossroads of the two principal driveways: the

ABMC earnestly wished for the presence of a shrine in all of its cemeteries abroad to give to these places and their visitors the benefit of spiritual recollection. The chapels designed by the ABMC were not dedicated to any religion in particular to enable them to serve Catholics, Protestants, Jews, Muslims or Buddhists.

The Normandy cemetery chapel was constructed in Vaurion limestone except for its steps conceived in granite according to the Harbeson plans. On the top of the building, he added a spherical armature in bronze serving as a lightning rod for the entire cemetery. Several inscriptions were inlaid in the chapel and its walls. A dedication on the exterior wall was written to recall the reason for the construction of this shrine by the United-States: *"This chapel has been erected by the United-States-of-America in grateful memory of her sons who gave their lives in the landings on the Normandy beaches and in the liberation of northern France. Their graves are the permanent and visible symbol of their heroic devotion and their sacrifice in the common cause of humanity".* The colonnades were designed to be a reminder of Greek temples. Above them can still be read these words: *"These endured all and gave all that justice among nations might prevail and that mankind might enjoy freedom and inherit peace".* In front of the chapel door was engraved a replica of the Medal of Honor – the highest military honor awarded by the United-States Congress – highlighting the bravery of its men. Today, the visitors entering the chapel can immediately notice the Grand Antique black marble altar from the French Hautes-Pyrénées department. This altar was surmounted by a large window where were engraved forty-eight stars representing the forty-eight American states during the Second World War. Flags were placed around the altar to symbolize some of the Allied nations who participated in the fighting during the battle of Normandy.

The multiconfessional chapel of the cemetery. *Photo C. Lebastard.*

The interior of the multiconfessional chapel. *Photo C. Lebastard.*

This first Visitor Center was closed and replaced by a new Visitor Center in 2007. It is now used as the Superintendent's office. *Photo C. Lebastard.*

The René Coty walkway leading to the memorial decorated by multiple flags on the occasion of the Memorial-Day ceremony on 29th May 2011. *Photo C. Lebastard.*

This chapel was erected on a multi-confessional basis, symbolized by the large Latin cross fixed on the glass above the altar and by the Star of David dominating this same glass. Peace was remembered by a dove situated in the center of the Star of David. Besides the chapel, the ABMC committed itself to the construction of a first Visitor Center to enable families to obtain the information which they desired. This building was constructed at the entrance to the René Coty driveway leading to the memorial.

The memorial

The commission made the choice not to construct large war memorials contrary to what had been done after the First World War. It envisaged rather the building of memorials in each cemetery which had to include a list of the missing and battle maps.

The construction of the memorials was planned after the overall conception of the cemeteries' general aspect was achieved. Each architect had to submit a minimum of two different plans accompanied by a budget. It was mentioned in each contract with the American architects that another architect of the memorial's home country had to be engaged to translate the American architectural plans. In France, these included: Auguste Perret, one of the pioneers of contemporary architecture, and Paul Branche who became responsible for establishing construction costing estimations. On 4th November 1949, the commission organized an exhibition at the Philadelphia Art Alliance to show the plans of the fourteen new war memorials planned in the permanent cemeteries.

One of the most sensitive questions was that of the use of materials. France offered an important variety of construction stones: granite, marble, sandstone. Burgundy limestone was eventually chosen for the Colleville-sur-Mer memorial. This limestone was also planned for the Henri-Chapelle memorial.

The Normandy final architectural project consisted of a semi-circular colonnade including two battle maps arranged in two loggias facing each other. In the center was envisaged the installation of a statue surrounded by pebbles from the landing beaches and welded together by mortar. On each memorial was engraved the same dedicatory inscription: *"In proud remembrance of the achievements of her sons and in humble tribute to their sacrifices this memorial has been erected by the United-States-of-America"*.

The commission called on scholars to draft the memorial inscriptions into suitable epitaphs. This was a difficult exercise and some of the texts proposed were refused because of double meanings, the risk of dislike by the families or lack of understanding. The ABMC therefore chose to write the texts itself. It was sometimes necessary to add explanations on the memorials so that visitors could better understand their purpose. This was the case at the Normandy cemetery where were engraved these few words *"This embattled shore, portal of freedom, is forever hallowed by the ideals, the valor and the sacrifices of our fellow countrymen"*. The commission called upon André Maurois a French writer bilingual in English, who was exiled to the United-States during the Second World War, in order to translate the English texts into French and to avoid errors.

Opposite the memorial, further west, was installed a reflecting pool which was designed as a reminder of Omaha-beach allowing the visitors to walk alongside before collecting their thoughts at the graves of the soldiers. An overlook made in Swedish black granite was erected further north in continuity with the memorial allowing contemplation of the beach and thus enabling a better understanding of the Allied sacrifices on D-Day. The ABMC - who desired to explain the Omaha-Beach landing – erected an orientation table at this overlook complementing the wall maps of the memorial. Two stairways were added to access

Stunning view on the memorial. We can observe the colonnades, the two loggias on each side and the perfect symmetry of the pool. *Photo ABMC.*

Memorial view from the reflecting pool side. *Roger D. Howlett.*

the beach and a second table was erected to explain the story of the artificial harbor built in 1944.

Construction of the Colleville-sur-Mer memorial ended in 1954 and the Great Seal of the United-States was engraved on the exterior side of the south façade of the memorial accompanied by the dedication date. The memorial was completed just in time for the tenth anniversary ceremony of the Normandy landing.

TO GLORIFY THE CEMETERY

A place of art

Architects, landscapers, sculptors and some American painters collaborated to design the commission's permanent cemeteries. However, no artist had the right to work on more than one necropolis and the artistic work was entrusted to local contributors and subject of separate contracts. 4% to 8% of the construction budget of a cemetery was on average intended for art works.

The circular mosaic decorating the ceiling of the chapel. Columbia is on the left and Marianne is on the right, recognizable by her Phrygian bonnet. *Photo C. Lebastard.*

Art can be found throughout the cemeteries whether at the memorials or the chapels. Leon Kroll (New-York) created an imposing mosaic adorning the ceiling of the Colleville-sur-Mer site symbolizing the freedom brought by the young American soldiers and representing a time loop: America blessing its sons leaving by sea or by air to fight for freedom. France grateful, symbolized by Marianne, lays a wreath of laurels on a dead soldier. The return to peacetime was remembered by the angel, the dove and the famous Homeward Bound Ships, ships which repatriated the soldiers to the United-States. At the center of this mosaic, Leon Kroll added thirteen stars which represent the first thirteen American states liberated from British oppression at the time of the War of Independence.

The installation of memorials was motivated by the need to commemorate the deeds of the Armed Forces during the war. This explains why loggias were installed on the memorial in the Normandy cemetery. The military advances were described on each of the walls thanks to maps and to engraved legends in English and in French. The commission was inspired by the maps of the expansion of the Roman-Empire which Mussolini had realized and placed along the *Via dei Fori Imperiali* in Rome. They consisted of four maps in three stone colors black, grey and beige. The ceilings of the memorial's loggias in Colleville-sur-Mer were conceived in blue ceramic tiles and designed by Gentil and Bourdet (Paris). Robert Foster (New-York) designed the maps and also realized the orientation tables at Utah and at Omaha-Beach. The work on the maps was not executed by Robert Foster but by Maurice Schmit (Paris).

The two largest and impressive maps in the memorial's loggias were conceptualized to measure 32 feet wide by 20 feet high and had to give a rendering and a crafted presentation thanks to the use of a number of materials such as marble, ceramic or concrete.

They were etched directly into the limestone wall. The maritime zones were tinted ripples and the coast line was reduced in the stone and tinted to increase the shade. The military units were represented by symbols in enameled bronze and the military advances by red arrows in the same material.

The largest map of the south loggia was titled "*The landing on the Normandy Beaches and the development of the Beachhead*". The objectives of this map were to recall the landing of 6th June 1944, the establishment of the beachhead, the liberation of Cherbourg, of Saint-Lô and of Caen as well as the different breakthroughs which the Allies made to liberate the Normandy region. Two smaller maps were designed into the same loggia: one depicting the air operations necessary for the preparation of the landing and the other explaining the naval operations conducted on D-Day.

Inside the north coast loggia the larger map was entitled "*Military operations in Western Europe 6 June 1944 – 8 May 1945*". Additional to this map, six smaller maps were installed on the west and east walls of the loggia recalling the military operations in Europe and in the Pacific from the United-States entry into the war until the end of the conflict.

On the west and east walls of each loggia were written the legends of each of the two principal maps located in the memorial. Each legend has been written by the ABMC and particularly by Robert Foster thanks to historical data that the commission had. In fact, the War Department had not at that moment written the official history of operations of the Second World War. The commission composed then its own historical section directed by Lieutenant-Colonel Joseph F. Mitchell.

THE WORK OF DONALD DE LUE

The statue of the American youth

The most important artistic work undertaken in the cemetery of Colleville-sur-Mer was realized by Donald de Lue from Leonardo, New-Jersey, in collaboration with Lee Lawrie, consultant architect of the commission since 1951. De Lue was elected in 1940 to the National Society of Sculpture before becoming its head in 1945. In 1941, he was nominated Associate of the National Design Academy and he was recognized very early as a specialist in reliefs. Moreover, he won numerous awards including the Guggenheim award.

Donald de Lue proposed to the ABMC that the art works be carried out by American artists. He drew numerous sketches for the commission. In 1951, Harbeson supported his candidature as artist of the Colleville-sur-Mer cemetery. This site the ceiling of the Colleville-sur-Mer made him one of the most prominent monumental sculptors of the fifties and sixties. This project at Colleville-sur-Mer constituted the most important work of his career on a war memorial and the most ambitious artistic project implemented for a cemetery by the commission. He was given all the bronze work of the cemetery and notably the making of an imposing statue adorning the memorial today. The commission wished that the memorial's sculptures were intelligible and understandable by all and did not want "tortured" metal statues held so dear in contemporary sculptures. De Lue dreamed from the start of realizing the statue of a man armed with a large sword. But after having drawn 179 different sketches, he sculpted a reduced size model of the future *"Statue of the American Youth Rising from the Waves"*. The model represented a young man emerging from the waves arms outstretched. The sculpture's movement recalled at the same time a flight over water and a hymn to the resurrection.

The first sketches of the memorial's statue realized by Donald de Lue. *Roger D. Howlett.*

Reduced model of the final statue designed by Donald de Lue. *Roger D. Howlett.*

Donald de Lue works on the model in plaster (full-size) of the future statue of "*The spirit of American youth rising from the waves*". *Roger D. Howlett.*

The arrival of the urns at the Normandy American Cemetery. *Roger D. Howlett.*

The ABMC decided to retain this project.

The artist worked on a full-size model of 22 feet during the spring of 1953. The statue in plaster was completed for the month of August and it was published in the New-York Times on 6th August. The statue was eventually cast in bronze in a foundry in Milan and installed in the memorial in 1955. It was posed on a rectangular pedestal of Ploumanac'h granite arrayed by the first verse of the *Battle Hymn of the Republic* written by Julia Ward Howe in November 1861: *"Mine eyes have seen the glory of the coming of the Lord"*. Two copies of the statue were subsequently realized: a first one at half-scale, in bronze, placed at the entrance of the visitors pavilion at Brookgreen garden (South-Carolina) and an identical model placed at the MacCormick museum in Cantigny (Illinois) to honor the men of the First Infantry Division.

The memorial urns

Donald de Lue undertook simultaneously the realization of four decorative urns for the openings in the memorial's loggias. He revealed his final project at the end of 1952 and the urns were cast in the Marinelli foundry of Florence. Meantime, he received the visit of a delegation of Swedish-Americans in New-York who ordered from him a fifth urn at half-scale to be presented to Stockholm to honor their countrymen who took part in the Normandy campaign. On 7th June 1953, this urn was sent to Stockholm on the occasion of the 700th anniversary of the town. The other four urns arrived at the Normandy American Cemetery only in May 1955.

Each one was composed of two distinct scenes in relief for a total of four different engravings. The four scenes of the urns in the loggia's northern side were intended to be identical to the four in the southern loggia. It was planned that each urn showed a different engraving when someone looked at them in the loggias. On the first engraving, de Lue depicted a kneeling woman holding her child to her, behind a cross decorated by a wreath and a brilliant star representing eternal life. He designed an allegory of the immense sacrifice of women and children bereaved by war. The laurel wreath surrounding the urn was added to symbolize victory and honor. The artist represented a dying warrior astride a horse charging the enemy (symbolic of war) on the second engraving and an angel receiving his valorous spirit. On the third one, he wished to reveal God in Genesis (Chapter 1): *"The spirit of the Lord moved on the face of the waters"*. A spray of laurel was engraved on the surface of the water recalling those who lost their lives at sea and a rainbow symbolizing hope and peace from the divine figure. An angel pushing away a stone was represented on the last engraving, symbolic of the Resurrection and Eternal Life.

The statues of the United-States and of France

An opening to the west of the chapel still offers today a breathtaking view over the Ruquet valley and of the church of Vierville-sur-Mer perfectly aligned in the axis east/west of the cemetery. This opening was created as a reminder of the existence of the temporary cemetery of Saint-Laurent-sur-Mer as well as a remainder of the location of the American airfield established after the landing.

However, the west end of the cemetery was empty, with no real boundaries and the openness did not close the site as the commission desired. The ABMC then asked Donald de Lue to further develop this frontage and to prepare sketches of two statues to symbolize France and the United-States. He prepared the models in the mid 1950's. The works were made in 1957-1958 by A. Cinla & Figlio before being finally sent to Colleville-sur-Mer. The two 9-foot high statues in granite from Baveno (Italy) were intended to represent the allegories of the two nations: Marianne for France holding a sword and the French rooster, and Columbia, for the United-States, draped in the colors of the United-States and armed with a sword on which was perched the symbolic eagle.

Ultimately, Donald de Lue's projects were the most expensive of all the artistic work realized by the commission. The artwork of the Normandy cemetery was the most developed among the other American cemeteries of the Second World War. On a large scale, the artistic program of the ABMC constituted the most important esthetic project ever undertaken by the United-States abroad.

Many critics have called the ABMC sculptures in its cemeteries naïve or bad elements. It must however be noted and admitted that the commission engaged four great artists each one decorated with the Henry Hering medal of the U.S. National Sculpture Society for their work in the cemeteries of Colleville-sur-Mer, Nettuno, Honolulu and at the West-Coast memorial. The most important aspect in the eyes of the ABMC has always been that it has never received negative comments from the families.

The setting designed by the landscaper

The ABMC's ambition was to make its cemeteries havens of peace. It imagined numerous projects for the realization of a landscape worthy of remembrance left by Omaha-Beach. The idea of a "green necropolis" created by Jean-Didier Urbain may be taken up here[30]. The Normandy American Cemetery was effectively transformed into a cemetery/garden essentially because of the romanticism of the Anglo-Saxon people – and by the way of the American people – with the idea that there was a link between nature and the symbol of eternal recommencement. The American people usually compare the concept of the garden to that of the Garden of Eden and of Paradise. American Protestantism identifies God to the World and therefore tries to connect them.

---

[30] URBAIN (Jean-Didier), *L'Archipel des morts*, Payot & Rivages, Paris, 2005, 411 p.

The symbolism of the cemeteries changed during the eighteenth century: the cemeteries that received the dead henceforth also received the living, coming to pay their respects under the best possible conditions. Western society had and still has a tendency to reject the idea of death. Thus the cemetery/garden (park or forest) born in the nineteenth century sought above all to hide death and tried to play on concealment. In its cemeteries, the ABMC attempted to appeal to visitors and relatives: it thought that the location should in no way become a visit of reluctance. Sometimes visitors and especially European visitors visiting the ABMC cemeteries gained the impression of not being in a cemetery: death had been sanitized to a significant extent for them. In fact, the idea of creating a cemetery/garden can sometimes become a trap as we will have the opportunity to discuss later.

The landscape plans of the different permanent cemeteries were submitted to Washington and then sent to the ABMC offices abroad. Their implementation was undertaken by contracts supervised by specialists of the commission. Plantations were assigned to a landscape architect named Markley Stevenson of Philadelphia, who eventually became the consultant landscaper of the commission in 1947. He was replaced after his death in 1960 by Gilmore D. Clarke.

Once the principal installations were implemented, the commission sought to beautify the site of Colleville-sur-Mer following the idea that the vegetation should be used to fence the cemetery making it a separate territory. On the 170 acres of the site, only 37 acres were utilized for the cemetery itself and the major part of the space was dedicated to service areas and to the abundant vegetation. The Colleville-sur-Mer site had to face a number of problems essentially related to sand and wind: many imported young shoots did not support the ground and the climate. After two trials many trees were replaced by oncoming species better adapted to the conditions of the area. The commission finally opted for a thick vegetation of pine, white alders, Bohemian olive trees, sea buckthorn, Japanese roses and tamarisks to fence the cemetery in the east, south and west. The entrance to the cemetery on the memorial side was flanked by cypress emphasizing the solemnity of the site and the pathways were planted with green oak. The whole site was enclosed by bushes. The French Government authorized the planting of a large band of hedges, resembling those found in the heart of the hedgerow country, to border the route leading to the site and to remind also of the famous battle of the hedgerows.

Additionally to this abundant vegetation, irregular spaces were kept between the graves during the permanent burials allowing the development of square planting consisting of trees, shrubs and roses. According to the cemetery statistics of 1973, sixty flowering bushes were incorporated in the middle of the grave plots on a surface of more than 22 600 square feet. Rumor has it that each planting square between the graves represented an American bomb crater created by the D-Day landing, no document confirming this hypothesis has been found.

The importance accorded by Americans to vegetation can be found in the immaculate lawn which covers the whole of the graves and which reveals the profound attachment of these people to the greenery. The grass is particularly well-groomed thanks to some specific measures implemented by the ABMC: the maintenance of the green spaces required and still requires constant attention as well as large quantities of water furnished by a wellbore situated on the site. The ABMC installed in the memorial two squares of vegetation just behind the statue to complete this real cemetery/garden and planted two olive trees in remembrance of a restored peace.

The two statues guarding the cemetery's boundaries are impassive even under the snow. *Roger D. Howlett.*

Old postcard of the cemetery. *Photo ABMC.*

The soldiers of the Normandy American Cemetery

MISSING IN ACTION AND BURIED SOLDIERS

General figures

Until 1955, 9 385 soldiers were buried in the permanent cemetery of Colleville-sur-Mer being 40.5% of the 23 193 bodies previously buried in the provisional cemeteries of Saint-Laurent-sur-Mer, Sainte-Mère-Église Nos. 1 and 2, Blosville, Saint-André-de-l'Eure and La Cambe. In comparison, 43.2% of bodies buried in the temporary cemeteries of Saint-James, Le Chêne-Guérin, Gorron, Saint-Corneille and Villeneuve-sur-Auvers were buried in the permanent cemetery of Saint-James[31]. The percentage was almost identical to that of the FIrst World War: 60% of the bodies were repatriated to the United-States while 40% were buried in the permanent cemeteries abroad.

The grave plots in the cemetery of Colleville-sur-Mer were constituted with an average of 938 bodies: plot I being the smallest with 804 graves and plot C, the largest, with 1 176 graves. 307 unknowns were buried among the other soldiers, representing 3.3% of the soldiers buried in Colleville-sur-Mer (being an identical proportion to the number of unknown American soldiers of the Second World War). In comparison, "only" 97 unknown soldiers were buried in the cemetery of Saint-James, representing 2.1% of the 4 410 graves. As in all the ABMC cemeteries, all soldiers, whether known or unknown, were buried randomly. This was also the case for the 149 soldiers of the Jewish confession buried under Stars of David in the Normandy cemetery.

---

[31] Figures issued by: *United States Temporary Military Cemeteries European Theater Area, American Graves Registration Command, op. cit.*

The cemetery of Colleville-sur-Mer was not only designed and built as a cemetery of the Normandy landing. In fact, many soldiers killed before the landing and initially buried by the Germans or the Norman civilians were reburied in the Normandy necropolis. These were essentially bomber crews who crashed during their bombing operations on French soil from 1943. Otherwise, many soldiers killed after September 1944 and who lost their lives in the area after the operations of the battle of Normandy were also interred at Colleville-sur-Mer. Most of them were not killed in action: they lost their lives notably because of accidents.

In fact, 842 soldiers, being less than 1% of the total, lost their lives on the 6th June 1944. Amongst them, 165 belonged to the 29th Infantry Division and 104 to the First Infantry Division. These two divisions were in the front line at the time of the landing on Omaha-Beach, which explains why they represent nearly one third of the soldiers killed on 6th June. The Airborne units parachuted in the night of 5th to 6th June behind enemy lines also suffered many casualties on D-Day: 135 soldiers of the 101st Airborne Division and 72 soldiers of the 82nd Airborne Division killed on that first day of battle were inhumed in the cemetery. The U.S. Army suffered fewer casualties on Utah-Beach than on Omaha-Beach on D-Day which explained the small number of soldiers of the 4th Infantry Division killed on that day and buried in the cemetery: twenty-nine graves. The small unit of the 2nd Battalion of Rangers is on the other hand represented by a high number of thirty soldiers who encountered fierce German resistance when some climbed the cliff at Pointe-du-Hoc and others landed on Omaha-Beach.

The 29th Infantry Division is the most represented unit on the site with 853 graves, being 9.1% of the total graves. Amongst them, 370 soldiers belonged to the 116th Infantry Regiment of this division. This regiment was sent in the first assault wave at Omaha-Beach on D-Day. The 4th Infantry Division follows the

29th Infantry Division in second place with 812 graves. The table below gives figures of the principal American units which participated in the landing and in the battle of Normandy and their number of graves in the cemetery.

The graves of the principal units following the landing and the battle of Normandy	
29th Infantry Division	853
4th Infantry Division	812
90th Infantry Division	671
83rd Infantry Division	543
2nd Infantry Division	475
101st Airborne Division	419
1st Infantry Division	225
82nd Airborne Division	212
U.S. Navy Reserve	112
2nd Rangers Battalion	34

The soldiers in the Colleville-sur-Mer cemetery were all American citizens. It is interesting to note that five of them joined the U.S. Forces in Canada, one in Mexico, one in England and one in Scotland. These men seemed to all have been American citizens but visitors can still see today written on their graves the different countries where they enlisted.

The fifty American States are represented, but not all in the same way: 1 071 soldiers, more than 10% came from Pennsylvania while only two of them originated from Alaska. Here are the principal States represented outside of Pennsylvania: the State of New-York (968 individuals), Ohio (524), Illinois (499), New Jersey (405) followed by Michigan (362). Conversely, the less represented states outside of Alaska are Hawaii (4 individuals), Nevada (8), Utah (12), Delaware (15), District of Columbia (25), Idaho (25) and Vermont (25).

The AGRC and the ABMC attempted, as soon as practicable to assemble soldiers from the same family. They also wished to bring close friends killed together, as for example bombing crews or tank crews. It was the case notably for a group of airmen still buried in Plot B of the cemetery. However, the Graves Registration Service at the time of the burials lacked data enabling them to bring together efficiently the pairs of brothers explaining why many sets were buried separately. Furthermore, the re-burials were performed rapidly. However, more than 250 cases of brothers buried side by side are registered in the military cemeteries managed by the ABMC. The AGRC also buried a father and son side by side in the cemetery of Colleville-sur-Mer.

The Normandy American Cemetery counts thirty pairs of brothers and half-brothers buried side by side and fifteen other pairs inscribed on the Wall of the Missing or buried separately making a total of 45 pairs of brothers and half-brothers according to the latest research undertaken. The Nilands are among the most well-known brothers in the cemetery as their story was adapted by a certain Steven Spielberg in his film *Saving Private Ryan*. If fiction took some genuine liberties, their tragedy was nonetheless real. The mother of the four Niland brothers gone to war received a first telegram on 6th June 1944 telling her that one of her sons, Technical-Sergeant Edward F. Niland, radio operator and gunner aboard a bomber, was reported missing since 20th May 1944 in Burma. During this time, the three other brothers were preparing for the landing in Normandy. On 21st June, a second telegram brought the news of the loss of Second-Lieutenant Preston T. Niland, of the 4th Infantry Division. He was reported missing since 7th June. The same week, their mother received a third telegram about Robert, also reported missing since his parachute drop on D-Day with his division: the 82nd Airborne Division. The family hoped for a time that the three brothers had simply been taken prisoner but, at the end of July, Mrs. Niland received confirmation of the death of Preston and at the start of August, that of Robert.

The Niland brothers. From left to right: Edward, Preston, Robert and Frederick. *Photo ABMC.*

The graves of Preston and Robert Niland, the real "Ryan brothers" situated in Plot F, Row 15, Graves 11 and 12. *Photo C. Lebastard.*

Sergeant Frederick Niland, parachutist in the 101st Airborne Division, was the only son which the mother had not yet received a telegram for. Since the tragedy of the five Sullivan brothers – those brothers who, died in 1942 after the torpedoing of their ship in the Pacific – the Government provided that in the case of multiple deaths in the same family the last member(s) would be sent home. It explained why Father Francis L. Sampson, Chaplain of the 101st Airborne Division sought out Frederick. No military detachment was sent on special mission to bring him back contrary to the film scenario *Saving Private Ryan*. The chaplain simply tried to convince him to return home and this is where our certainties stop.

According to Frederick's own daughter, there exist two distinct theories for the end of the story: the first indicates that he was soon evacuated to England then to the United-States. The second, which seems more plausible because it relies on a photograph of Frederick dated July 1944 at Lambourne in England, tells that he refused the repatriation and that he continued the fight in Normandy. His return would take place in July 1944, when part of the 101st Airborne Division was evacuated from the battlefield. However, a third hypothesis arose after research conducted by Brian Siddall. According to him, Frederick was not repatriated until October 1944 after having been parachuted over the Netherlands and having fought there for one month. Mr. Siddall based his account on elements of the H Company 501st Parachute Infantry Regiment Morning Report.

Edward, the first of the three brothers reported missing, was finally found: he was made prisoner by the Japanese in Burma from 20th May 1944. Freed by British troops, his parents were informed in early May 1945. If Frederick and Edward survived the conflict, Preston and Robert are today buried side by side in Plot F of the Normandy American Cemetery.

Decorated soldiers and generals

Soldiers killed in combat all received the Purple Heart which is the badge of military merit created by George Washington on 7th August 1782. This decoration was originally awarded in recognition of an act of bravery outside the common. The injuries received in combat were considered as the result of such an act. This medal presents itself in the form of a medal in bronze with an enamel heart shape and purple in color, bearing the features of George Washington. It is the oldest decoration awarded in the United-States.

The highest American distinction, the Medal of Honor, was awarded to only three men buried in Colleville-sur-Mer. Created in 1862; it is the only decoration which is worn around the neck. It presents itself under the form of a five pointed star in gold-plated silver and is based on a laurel wreath. A gold disc on which is represented the Goddess Minerve, symbolizing wisdom and war, can be seen in the center of the star. This medal is only awarded by Congress to reward a particularly heroic act.

Each recipient of this distinction, killed in combat and buried in a permanent cemetery abroad managed by the ABMC, received a different grave. The inscriptions on the crosses or stars in marble were engraved in gold letters to allow them to be easily recognizable while crossing the rows of graves in the cemetery. In the same way, the inscription "Medal of Honor" was also added below their name in the vertical axis of the grave and a gold star was engraved above their name. This highlighting of the Medal of Honor recipients can be explained by the difficulty of obtaining this reward and by its value: since its creation in 1862 and up to today, this distinction has only been given to 3 500 soldiers. Many of them received it posthumously and only for acts judged by Congress to be of extraordinary heroism.

The three soldiers in the Colleville-sur-Mer cemetery are good examples of heroism[32].

The first one, First-Lieutenant Jimmie W. Monteith, obtained his citation posthumously after recommendations by Generals Eisenhower and Bradley for his heroic acts on 6th June 1944 at Omaha-Beach. This young lieutenant of twenty seven years old landed with the first assault wave of the 1st Infantry Division. A minefield blocked the exit on the beach. Seeing that two tanks were immobilized under intense enemy fire, he began to climb onto one of them and asked the men to head towards one of the German strongpoints. He then advanced towards a machine gun nest which he reduced to nothing with a grenade. He did the same to the other places. However, he paid the ultimate price for his boldness and was killed on the beach that same day.

The second Medal of Honor recipient is without doubt more well-known and particularly by the inhabitants of Grandcamp, a small village a few miles from Pointe-du-Hoc. This soldier was named Frank D. Peregory. He was a young Technical-Sergeant of 29 years of age in the 116th Regiment of the 29th Infantry Division. He was one of the men who landed on Omaha-Beach on 6th June and one of the lucky ones who survived that first day of bloodshed. He then headed in the direction of Grandcamp and on his own initiative he advanced towards a German fortified position despite heavy fire. He found the entrance to a system of trenches and without hesitation, stormed inside and progressed therein. He met a German platoon who he charged with his bayonet whilst throwing some grenades. Eight Germans were killed and three surrendered. In view of this success, he continued his advance and forced the surrender of thirty-two other German soldiers as well as the MG42's machine gun crews.

---

[32] Today, visitors can see an example of this medal as well as that of the Purple Heart in the interior of the new Visitor Center of the Normandy American Cemetery.

The Purple Heart.

The Medal of Honor.

First-Lieutenant Jimmie Monteith is one of three Medal of Honor recipients buried in the Colleville-sur-Mer cemetery. His grave can be found in Plot I, Row 20 Grave 12. *Photos ABMC and C. Lebastard.*

SECOND PART 165

This feat of arms allowed the soldiers of his unit to liberate the village of Grandcamp. Unfortunately, Peregory was killed some days later, on 14th June, during an engagement. A small garden and a monument were erected to his memory in June 1994 in Grandcamp, in the presence of General Matthews and veterans of the 29th Infantry Division, at the exact emplacement of one of the German machine gun nests still visible today.

The last Medal of Honor recipient is without doubt the most well-known soldier interred in the cemetery: Brigadier-General Theodore Roosevelt Jr. Teddy, as he was nicknamed, was born in 1887 of a father who was to become President of the United-States between 1901 and 1909. Teddy took part in the First World War in the 1st Infantry Division and was wounded at Soissons during the summer of 1918. He was one of the founders of the soldiers' organization which would become the American Legion. He refused to be its President so as not to bring politics into the organization. Indeed, he ran for the post of Governor of New-York and became Assistant Secretary of the Navy between 1929 and 1932, then Governor of Porto Rico and Governor General of the Philippines in 1932. His political career stopped abruptly when in 1941, his cousin, President Franklin D. Roosevelt, took the country into the second World conflict. Teddy preferred to return to active service and was promoted to Brigadier-General. Between 1943 and February 1944, he was second in command of the 1st Infantry Division. He was then appointed Assistant Commander of the 4th Infantry Division, the unit he chose to disembark with on D-Day at Utah-Beach. Teddy was one of the very first to touch the sand of this beach and the only general on that day to land in the very first assault wave. He had to fight with his superior, General Barton, who reluctantly agreed to let him go. He declared on this beach his famous words relayed in the film *The Longest Day* in 1962: "We'll

Technical-Sergeant Frank D. Peregory buried in Plot G, Row 21, Grave 7. *Photos ABMC and C. Lebastard.*

Brigadier-General Theodore Roosevelt Jr. is today buried in Plot D, Row 28, Grave 45. *Photos ABMC and C. Lebastard.*

start the war from right here!³³" when he realized that his men had disembarked 1.2 miles too far south.

Despite his great strength of character, Teddy suffered serious health problems and in particular arthritis which required him to get around with a stick. He also suffered with heart problems. A heart attack struck him down one month after the landing, on 12th July 1944. He was buried in the temporary cemetery of Sainte-Mère-Église No. 2, on 14th July, 1944, in the presence of Generals Bradley, Patton, Collins, Hedges, Huebner as well as Barton. This sad day was also the anniversary date of the death of his brother Quentin. At the time of Teddy's death, Eisenhower had chosen him to become the new Major-General of the 90th Infantry Division. This nomination explains why the ABMC made the choice not to indicate any division on his marble cross, only the inscriptions "U.S. Army". The Medal of Honor was awarded to him for his fearlessness and his courage before and after 6th June.

Theodore Roosevelt Jr. is without doubt the most well-known general buried in the cemetery but he is not the only one. One other general with the same grade (One-star General) also rests in the cemetery of Colleville-sur-Mer: Nelson M. Walker, born in 1891 in Massachusetts. Walker participated in the First World War with the 47th Infantry Regiment and fought at the Aisne-Marne, Saint-Mihiel and Meuse-Argonne offensives. Wounded in combat some months before the end of the war, on 5th July 1918, he was then stationed in Germany until 1919. Promoted Brigadier-General on 11th September 1942, he became the Assistant Commander of the 8th Infantry Division in November 1943. His unit arrived too late in Normandy to participate in the landing

---

[33] There is an interesting anecdote to note relating to the Roosevelts: Theodore Roosevelt Sr. participated in the Spanish-American War. At the same time, the father of the Nilands was also in the same conflict. It is surprising to see the two men together on a photograph dating from the Spanish-American War; two men who both lost, two sons during the World Wars and who were buried a few feet from one another.

The Distinguished Service Cross and the *U.S.A.T. General Nelson M. Walker* photographed during the Vietnam War. *Source: VietnamGraffiti.com.*

The grave of Brigadier-General Nelson M. Walker decorated by an unknown person. The general is buried in Plot B, Row 23, Grave 47.
Photo C. Lebastard.

SECOND PART 169

but it took part in fierce fighting south of La Haye-du-Puits. Their first objective was to cross l'Ay, a river extremely well defended by the Germans. General Walker, then at the front, was seriously injured on 9th July and died of his wounds on the next day. He was decorated with the Distinguished Service Cross posthumously for his courage. In 1946, the Army transport ship the *U.S.S. Admiral H. T. Mayo* was re-named the *U.S.A.T. General Nelson M. Walker* in his memory. The vessel remained in service for more than half a century, until 2005.

Generals Roosevelt and Walker are not the highest ranking officers in the cemetery. This title goes to General Lesley J. McNair. In 1944, he commanded the American Army Ground Forces and he was responsible for military training. He went to Europe to observe the GI's in combat and to judge the efficacy of their training. The command of the ghost army disposed in the south of England was entrusted to him in replacement of General Patton. This phantom army was destined to deceive the enemy on a landing in the Pas-de-Calais. On 25th July 1944, McNair was in Normandy accompanied by the 30th Infantry Division when he was killed during allied bombing which cost the lives as well of some one hundred American soldiers. This tragic error made him the first Lieutenant-General (Three-star General) to die in combat. He was promoted posthumously to Four-star General, on 19th July 1954, by act of congress (Public Law 83-508) which made him the highest ranking General killed during the Second World War, Patton having lost his life after the conflict. During his career, McNair trained around one half of the two hundred divisions which made up the American Army. He was buried in Plot F in the Colleville-sur-Mer cemetery. General McNair and General Patton (buried in Luxembourg American Cemetery) are the only Four-star Generals buried in ABMC cemeteries.

The grave of General Lesley J. McNair is located in Plot F, Row 28, Grave 48.
Photos Life Magazine and C. Lebastard.

The minorities

Two per cent of the American soldiers killed during the Second World War were African-Americans. They were nearly 700 000 African-American soldiers serving their country just before the landing in Normandy. Most of them were based in the United-States. Nevertheless, 500 African-Americans were present on 6th June at Omaha-Beach and around 1 200 on Utah-Beach. There was a section of the 3275th Quartermaster Service Company involved at Omaha-Beach in which two men were killed and buried at Colleville-sur-Mer. There was also a part of the 320th Antiaircraft Artillery Balloon Barrage Battalion in which four were buried in the Normandy cemetery. The other part of the 320th Antiaircraft Artillery Balloon Barrage Battalion was sent to Utah-Beach, accompanied by an Engineer Dump Truck Company, amongst which two soldiers were buried in Colleville-sur-Mer. The 385th Quartermaster Truck Company and the 490th Port Battalion complete this list. One soldier of this last unit can still be found today in the necropolis. A total of only three African-Americans killed on D-Day were buried in the cemetery out of a total of one hundred and forty-six African-American soldiers buried or engraved on the Wall of the Missing. In spite of segregation after the war, the African-American soldiers were buried amidst other soldiers in the ABMC cemeteries.

The reduced proportion of African-Americans buried at Colleville-sur-Mer (1.3% of the total of the soldiers) partly explains the belated recognition of the role of these men and women. It is important not to forget that segregation in the Armed Forces remained active until 1948 and that the interest of historians was much reduced. It can be explained by the fact that they occupied 75% of the non-combative service jobs (material handling, laundry, cooking…) and because their military exploits were few. The coastguards employed them as stewards and the Navy, principally as kitchen assistants. However, it existed of African-American Artillery and Armored units as well of two Infantry Divisions: the 92nd which fought in Italy and the 93rd which was opposed to the Japanese in the Pacific.

At the end of the war, this population represented one eighth of the American Armed Forces but it always remained as an "Army in the shadows". These men were seen as low key combatants, having been obliged to serve by conscription. Those who entered voluntarily in the army sought it as a means of recognition and as an improvement in their living standards.

One could easily link this renewed interest in African-American soldiers to the investiture of a colored American President: Barrack Obama. However, the recognition started a little before with the gesture of President Clinton who on 13th January 1997 handed seven Medals of Honor to seven African-American soldiers for their services during the Second World War. It was the first time that colored men received this distinction. French recognition was more recent: the first Legion of Honor was given sixty-five years after the landing to William G. Dabney who landed on 6th June 1944 with three comrades of the 320th Antiaircraft Artillery Balloon Barrage Battalion.

There are three singular stories surrounding African-American soldiers in the cemetery of Colleville-sur-Mer: three women who, besides the fact that they were colored soldiers in an army of white soldiers, were women in an army of men. All three were part of the Women's Army Corps or WAC: Sergeant Dolores M. Browne, Private-First-Class Mary J. Barlow and Private-First-Class Mary H. Bankston. All three were soldiers of the 6888th Central Postal Directory Battalion who sorted more than seven million letters of the American soldiers. This battalion was entirely composed of black women, which was very rare in the WAC since less than 6% of the personnel were constituted of African-American women. This battalion of 855 women was commanded by Lieutenant-Colonel Charity E. Adams, at the time Major (the highest ranking American colored lady of the Second World War). They took care to deliver mail at first in England. Then after the landing, they were based at Rouen (Upper-Normandy). Even if these women had to face two discriminations – color and sex – their work was vital: they boosted the morale of the soldiers when handing out family mail.

On 8th July 1945, Barlow, Browne and Bankston obtained permission to go to another military base but died in an accident near Saint-Valery-en-Caux. Bankston and Barlow were killed outright but Dolores M. Brown died of her injuries at the American Army Hospital in Rouen five days later. At first buried in the temporary cemetery of Saint-André-de-l'Eure, they were permanently buried in the Colleville-sur-Mer cemetery in 1948.

As a symbol of femininity and devotion, Elizabeth A. Richardson was the fourth and only other woman buried in the Normandy American Cemetery. She joined up in 1944 as a civilian employee (non-military personnel) in the American Red Cross and traveled to Great-Britain and to France in a club mobile, a bus which enabled, amongst others, to be able to offer coffee and doughnuts to soldiers stationed in their military camps. On 25th July 1945, she took a plane in Le-Havre to go to Paris, but it crashed accidentally near Rouen. She was at first buried in the temporary cemetery of Saint-André-de-l'Eure before being transferred to the Colleville-sur-Mer cemetery in July 1948. She is buried today in Plot A, near the pilot of her plane William R. Miller. Aged twenty-seven at her death, she was a recognized artist and today her name is given to an award in the Annual Wisconsin Salon of Art.

A team of African-American soldiers of the 320th Anti-Aircraft Artillery Balloon Barrage Battalion prepare one of their balloons whose goal is to protect the Allied units from enemy planes.
National Archives USA.

The burial place of Mary H. Bankston situated in Plot D, Row 20, Grave 46. The grave of Dolores M. Brown is located in Plot F, Row 13, Grave 19 and that of Mary J. Barlow is in Plot A, Row 19, Grave 30. *Photo C. Lebastard.*

Major Charity E. Adams and Captain Abbie N. Campbell inspect the 6888th Postal Battalion in England.
National Archives USA.

SECOND PART 175

Portrait of Elizabeth A. Richardson the *"doughnuts dolly"*. *Photo ABMC.*

Elizabeth (on the left with the hat) and Mary Haynsworth in discussion with some GI's delighted to talk with these young women in front of their "clubmobile". *National Archives USA.*

Elizabeth is today buried in Plot A, Row 21, Grave 5. Her pilot is resting in Plot A, Row 20, Grave 22. *Photo C. Lebastard.*

Boys too young to die

It is not uncommon nowadays, to see films on the Second World War with actors, aged sometimes in their thirties, indeed in their forties playing the role of soldiers, who at the time, were very much younger. They were thousands in the cemetery of Colleville-sur-Mer who never saw their thirtieth birthday. Some were just twenty years of age when they died, and others, unfortunately were much younger…

Private Roy U. Talhelm was one of them: a young boy killed during the battle of Normandy who never became eighteen. Roy grew up in Maryland and had above average intelligence. However, he had a difficult life: his mother died when he was only nine years old and his father took very little care of him. Roy only had one dream: to become a pilot. In order to get closer to it, he decided to join the Airborne, and more particularly Company G of the 506th Parachute Infantry Regiment of the 101st Airborne Division: the famous Screaming Eagles. He took part in the invasion on the night of 6th June 1944 jumping above Normandy but he was mortally wounded on 8th June 1944 when he attempted to secure a bridge near Carentan on the Douve River. He died of his wounds on 12th June while his comrades liberated Carentan that same day. Aged seventeen at his death, he changed his birth certificate in order to enroll in the army leaving his girlfriend and a baby, Donna, who he saw and took in his arms only once. This young girl grew up without knowing precisely who her father was. Donna remembered asking her mother numerous times where her father was and what did he look like. The answers were evasive and did not satisfy the young girl who, at the age of twenty-one began a search to know a little more about her father. In the 1990's she eventually discovered the first photograph of Roy, on the day of her forty-eighth birthday. After contacting the American WWII Orphans Network (AWON), she received a photograph of her father in his uniform of the 101st Airborne Division. Since then, Donna has visited the cemetery of

Colleville-sur-Mer twice. During her first visit, she received the Medal of Carentan in a ceremony in honor of her father.

The Wall of the Missing

The names of 94 132 men and women who served under the American flag were engraved on stone walls today maintained by the ABMC in order to symbolize their loss. These walls are located in the First World War and Second World War cemeteries as well as in three memorials in the United-States. The names of the missing were carried over to walls in cemeteries which corresponded to the geographical area of their disappearance. Cambridge's Wall of the Missing was one of the first of the Second World War to have been constructed and commemorates the names of 5 125 soldiers missing.

The missing in action during the battle of Normandy were much less numerous than during the fighting in North-Africa or in the Pacific. Nevertheless, special memorials were realized to receive the names of some 2 000 missing in the region: two walls had been built and engraved for this purpose in the two cemeteries of Saint-James and of Colleville-sur-Mer. A total of 498 names were engraved on the Wall of the Missing in Saint-James and 1 557 names were enrolled on the wall of the Colleville-sur-Mer necropolis. The latter, in semi-circular form, contains the names of men from forty-nine out of the fifty American states. Amongst them, the wall includes the names of 168 soldiers missing on the 6th June 1944. Contrary to the buried soldiers, the men were listed in alphabetical order and the rows of names were separated by large sculptures of laurel leaves.

For each soldier, was indicated his surname, Christian name, his rank, unit and the state in which he enrolled in the Armed Forces. No date of death was inscribed contrary to the soldiers buried in the cemetery. However, the United-States wanted absolutely to

We can see on this photograph the youthful face of Roy. He is amongst the youngest soldiers to be buried in a cemetery administered by the commission.
Photo ABMC.

The grave of Roy Upton Talhelm is located in Plot C, Row 9, Grave 32. Roy was only 17 years old...
Photo C. Lebastard.

French workmen engraving names of soldiers on one of ABMC's Wall of the Missing. *Photo ABMC.*

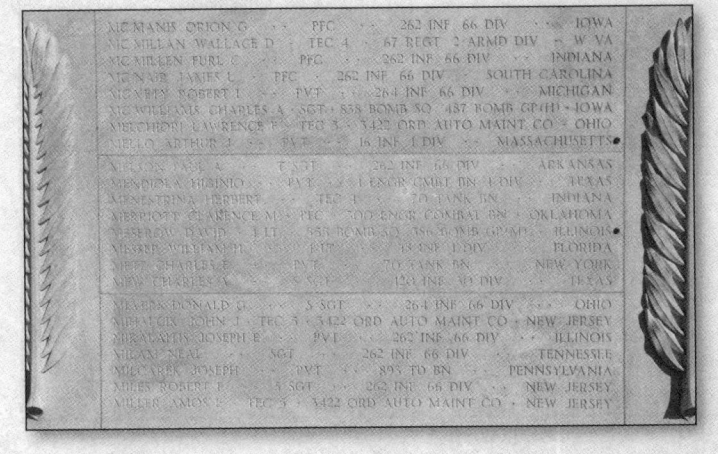

One of the panels on the wall of the Missing in Colleville-sur-Mer.
Photo C. Lebastard.

SECOND PART 179

formalize the death of all the missing. In order to do this, the ethics committee of the War Department determined (when nobody knew the date) that it would be set at one year and one day after the soldier had been reported as missing and presumed dead. The date of death can today be found on the databases of the buried soldiers designed by the ABMC. These bases are consultable on the internet at the address: www.abmc.gov. Neither civilians nor war reporters can be found listed on the Wall of the Missing at Colleville-sur-Mer contrary to the permanent cemetery graves found abroad. Law 871 of the 80th Congress made the choice to engrave only the names of members of the American Armed Forces.

The Wall of the Missing in Colleville-sur-Mer was divided into three parts. The first part groups the names of the Army, Armored units and of Aviation soldiers in alphabetical order. The second part lists the names of the U.S. Navy sailors also in alphabetical order. These sailors represent nearly 24% of the Wall of the Missing. This important percentage can be explained by the slaughter caused by loss at sea and the subsequent difficulty in finding the bodies. Finally in the last part was engraved the name of the only missing Coastguard.

Some units represented on the Wall of the Missing	
66th Infantry Division	489
U.S. Navy Reserve	305
300th Engineer Combat Battalion	69
U.S. Navy	66
101st Airborne Division	40
4th Infantry Division	37
29th Infantry Division	32
1st Infantry Division	24
2nd Infantry Division	14
90th Infantry Division	12
83rd Infantry Division	10
82nd Airborne Division	4

This table shows the number of Missing in Action registered on the wall in the cemetery for some units and notably for the more well known of the landing. 31.4% of the names registered on the wall are those of men who belonged to the 66th Infantry Division. This division had ten times more missing than the 4th Division, the second infantry division represented in the table. The 101st Airborne Division also had ten times more Missing in Action than its counterpart, the 82nd Airborne Division.

The *Leopoldville*

The number of soldiers of the 66th Infantry Division inscribed on the Wall of the Missing regularly intrigues the visitors when they remark that one name in three relates to a soldier of this division.

On Christmas Eve 1944, the *S.S. Leopoldville*, a Belgian ship, was part of a convoy which transported aboard 2 235 men of the 262nd and the 264th regiments of the 66th Infantry Division and which was crossing the Channel to join the front. At nightfall, the ship was torpedoed by *U-Boat 486* commanded by Lieutenant Gerhard Meyer[34]. Many men were killed instantly, but most of them assembled on the bridge to leave the ship in an emergency to avoid sinking with her. The rescue was difficult because of bad weather conditions. The other ships in the convoy continued on their way for fear of receiving a torpedo in their own turn. Nevertheless, several ships embarked in pursuit of the German submarine including the *U.S.S. Anthony*. During this time, some of the Leopoldville's lifeboats were put into the water. Unfortunately, there was not enough room for everybody: only eight hundred men were able to get aboard. One of the ships of the convoy, the *H.M.S Brilliant* – a British vessel - tried to give help to the drowning. However, because of the bad weather, she

---

[34] This submarine was sunk on 12th April 1945 by the British submarine *Tapir*.

had to stand off from the *Leopoldville* and could not recover the soldiers fallen into the sea. The next morning, on 25th December, a thousand men still waited to be rescued.

A veteran recalled this event: *"A soldier standing behind me started to sing our National Anthem The Star Spangled Banner in a fine and clear voice. Others joined in, then all the side where I was were in turn singing. The instinctive patriotism of these young infantrymen clasped my throat and prevented me from singing. I was one of the lucky ones who were able to climb on board the British destroyer which came alongside our ship before she sank. We learned some days later of the heroic efforts of those who perished attempting to save men in the water".*[35]

Many men drowned as they did not know how to use their life jacket. Others were crushed between the hulls of the *Brilliant* and the *Leopoldville* having missed their jump from one bridge to the other during the transfer. A few days later, the Division was sent to Rennes to be reorganized. The first news of this tragedy did not reach the allied newspapers until 7th January 1945 but without any confirmation by the Army certifying the event. In 1996, some documents came into the public domain. A memorial was built at the National Infantry Museum in Fort Benning, Georgia to commemorate the tragedy.

The torpedoing of this ship was the biggest American disaster at sea of the Second World War in the European theater of operations. According to the official list of the shipwreck in the American National Archives, 763 soldiers perished by drowning or by explosion: 493 bodies were never found, and among them, four names were engraved on the Wall of the Missing in Cambridge whereas 489 names were engraved on the Wall of

---

[35] 13D: *The Leopoldville*, testimony of Corporal Reitz, veteran of the 66th Infantry Division. Testimony collected during his visit at the Normandy American cemetery in 2003.

The *SS Leopolldville* was a Belgian ship used as a troop carrier during the Second World War. *Photo ABMC.*

the Missing at Colleville-sur-Mer. The state of New-York alone lost eighty soldiers of whom thirty-nine of them originated from New-York City. In addition to the Missing in Action, seventy-six soldiers from the 66th Infantry Division were buried in Colleville-sur-Mer, which brings the total number of members of this unit to 565 at the cemetery (463 from 262nd regiment of which 426 are missing and 102 from 264th regiment of which 63 are missing). Twin brothers Glenn and Jack Lowry and twins Carl and Clarence Carlson were among the losses. Their names were engraved on the cemetery's Wall of the Missing.

The Bedford Boys

There are countless tragedies in the cemetery but that of the Bedford Boys is among the most poignant. Today, eleven soldiers originating from the little town of Bedford, Virginia are buried or engraved on the Wall of the Missing in Colleville-sur-Mer; amongst them are Raymond and his brother Bedford.

Bedford joined Company A of the 116th Infantry Regiment, 29th Infantry Division in February 1937. His brother Raymond left school very early to earn some money and was hired to build the New-Deal roads. In 1940, he finally decided to join his brother in Company A. Once war was declared, the 29th Division was sent to England in 1942 for training which lasted twenty months. During this time Raymond fell in love with a young English girl who he began to court as was witnessed in the letters of his brother to their sister Mabel. Their parents were terrified at the idea of Raymond wishing to decide to stay in Great-Britain after the war in order to wed this young lady. In May 1944, one month before the landing, Raymond was struck with heavy nose bleeds which compelled him to stay in hospital. He was offered an exemption from the Army but he refused in order to stay with his friends and his brother. This exemption would have saved his life…

At 6.36 am on 6th June 1944, Raymond and Bedford, accompanied by some thirty soldiers from the small town of Bedford, Virginia landed with A Company, 116th regiment in the first assault wave on Omaha-Beach. Raymond was one of the first soldiers killed during the assault that morning. Bedford was hit a first time and remained injured on the beach at the side of a Czech hedgehog. Suddenly, he was hit by a shell which killed him instantly, as remembered Harold Baumgarten of Company B. Nineteen soldiers from Bedford lost their lives this 6th June and five others were injured. This small town of 3 200 inhabitants was shaken by this tragedy as was the rest of the United-States.

According to the town sheriff, John and Macey Hoback learned only on the 16th July 1944 that their eldest son Bedford had been killed on the beach on 6th June. The next day, they were told that their second son, Raymond was reported missing in the same spot. The body of Bedford Hoback was recovered but that

Raymond Hoback on the left and his brother Bedford on the right. Their photographs can be seen in the Visitor Center of the Normandy American Cemetery. Bedford is today buried in Plot G, Row 10, Grave 28. *Photo ABMC.*

The National D-Day Memorial in Bedford, Virginia commemorating the sacrifice of 4 000 Allied soldiers who lost their lives during the D-Day landing in Normandy.

Second Part 185

of his brother Raymond never was; only his Bible was found[36]. The Hoback family decided to leave the remains of Bedford in Colleville-sur-Mer while his brother's name was inscribed on the Wall of the Missing. This example demonstrates that it was sometimes not possible for the American Government to gather together close relatives killed in combat.

At the end of the war, the town of Bedford established that it had lost a total of twenty-one men who were in the same A Company, ten of whom were repatriated and buried in the United-States. The losses so marked the spirit of the township that an important memorial was inaugurated on 6th June 2001 by President Bush in the presence of sixteen thousand people. This memorial cost eight million dollars and extends over twelve acres to commemorate the sacrifice of these men. A "twinning" association exists also since 1999 between Omaha-Beach and Bedford. The objective of this association is to maintain the relationship between these two communities by means of exchanges and of receiving Americans in Normandy.

THE NEW BURIALS

Quentin Roosevelt

Until 1955, 9 385 soldiers were buried in the Colleville-sur-Mer cemetery. Things changed with the arrival of Quentin Roosevelt. Quentin was the younger brother of Theodore Roosevelt Jr. and he was part of the 95th Aeroplane Squadron, 1st Pursuit Group in the U.S. Army Air Service during the First World War. He was sent to France as a pilot in July 1917 onto Nieuport 28. One year later, on 14th July 1918, he was shot by a German airplane and buried in the first place, not by the Americans but by the Germans with full military honors. When his family faced the choice of repatriation or not of Quentin's body after the First World War, his father decided

---

[36] KERSHAW (Robert), *The Bedford Boys*, Da Capo Press, 2004, 274 p.

that he would remain where he was buried. The family maintained the grave during several years and also constructed a fountain at Chamery in his memory whose realization was given over to the architect Paul Cret, future Consultant Architect to the ABMC.

After the death of Theodore Roosevelt Jr., the family decided that it would be better to bury Quentin at the side of his brother in the Colleville-sur-Mer cemetery. In fact, the family was no longer able to find people locally to maintain the grave and its surroundings. Their brother Archibald as well as one of their sisters wrote a letter requesting the displacement of Quentin's body. As a general rule, the ABMC refused all requests to displace a body, indicating that the family has had enough time to make its choice. Requests had been made by certain families to obtain a new law authorizing the exhumation of bodies buried in isolated graves in order to re-bury them in military cemeteries at Government expense. The ABMC always opposed these requests. Even if the details remain unknown, the commission finally made an exception for the Roosevelt family and the body of Quentin was exhumed from his isolated grave to be brought to Normandy. On 22nd September 1955, he was re-buried in the Normandy cemetery alongside his brother. The crash site was marked by two memorials at Chamery. Quentin is still today the only soldier from the First World War to be buried in the Colleville-sur-Mer cemetery.

Gafford Sanders

Between 1955 and 1994, 9 386 soldiers were resting in the vast cemetery of Colleville-sur-Mer whose peace, as we will see later, was only "troubled" by ceremonies in their honor. But during the following year, in 1955, a 9 387th and last burial was realized: that of Technical-Sergeant Gafford W. Sanders. Gafford joined the 180th Infantry Regiment, 45th Infantry Division a unit of the National Guard in September 1940 and participated in campaigns in Africa, in Sicily and in the Italian Peninsula. It is there that he was reported missing on 28th May 1944. The confirmation of his death arrived to his family on 5th July. His brother, Sam E. Sanders, Sergeant in the 535th Anti-Aircraft Artillery Automatic Weapon Battalion was killed on 9th June 1944 in Normandy.

Gafford was at first buried in the cemetery of Nettuno (Italy) and Sam at Colleville-sur-Mer until their sister, in 1995, wished to have Gafford's remains moved so that he was buried with his brother in Normandy. She proposed to fully support the operation of re-internment. The ABMC accepted the special request of this sister as it did not concern a new burial. It was considered to be a transfer request by a close relative from one ABMC cemetery to another. The sister therefore received a positive answer in February 1995. The work started quickly because the family intended to go to the Colleville-sur-Mer site on the following 30th and 31st May. The body was exhumed in April from the Nettuno cemetery and repatriated to France from Italy by plane. The Funeral Agency of Freedom took in charge the body and drove it to the Colleville-sur-Mer cemetery, where the burial was effected on 24th May 1995 in collaboration with the American Mortuary Affairs (successor of the Graves Registration Service).

In this type of situation, the body of Gafford would normally have been buried alongside that of Sam. However, Sam was located in the middle of Plot D and it was impossible to authorize the exhumation of neighboring bodies to allow Gafford to be buried alongside him. The ABMC tried nevertheless to bury Gafford as near as possible to his brother, in the same plot, not too far from the Roosevelt brothers.

A cemetery closed to burials for families, veterans and recovered soldiers

No new burial could be realized once the new permanent cemeteries abroad were finished except for the remains

The provisional grave of Quentin Roosevelt. *Photo ABMC.*

Quentin Roosevelt was shot at the age of 20. This photograph was taken in 1917. *Photo ABMC.*

Quentin's grave at Chamery maintained by the Roosevelt family. *Photo ABMC.*

Gafford is buried in Plot D, Row 25, Grave 46. It is interesting to note that these two brothers were Native-Americans. Currently, 14 Native-Americans have been identified by employees of the Normandy American Cemetery. *Photo C. Lebastard.*

Quentin Roosevelt was buried in Plot D, Row 28, Grave 46 by the side of his brother Teddy. *Photo C. Lebastard.*

SECOND PART 189

found on battlefields and only in certain specific cemeteries. No family member or veteran could be buried in the commission's cemeteries. Some people, and in particular some veterans of the D-Day landing made the request. Jacques L. See, President of the Honeycomb Panels Patent Association went so far as to go to the headquarters of the ABMC in Europe, at Garches, in September 1985 to try to reach a compromise with the commission. He proposed a mortuary project to allow new burials, which the ABMC refused because it did not wish to alter the architecture of its cemeteries. He then proposed, subsequently the construction of shrines to enable the families of veterans who wished to be cremated, to deposit their ashes in the cemeteries, which again the ABMC refused[37].

After the end of the burial and repatriation operations, the American Government became conscience of the probability of finding missing soldiers on the battlefield. It was decided to retain a service charged with undertaking exhumations in the field; to embalm, to identify and to bury bodies found. However, the Colleville-sur-Mer site was officially closed to new burials on 31st December 1951 in order to preserve the general appearance of the site. The commission preferred the Ardennes cemetery to bury any new soldier found. From 1952 to 1997, the site received the remains of 164 soldiers of the Second World War. One of the very last burials at Colleville-sur-Mer before that of Quentin Roosevelt and Gafford Sanders – took place in May 1951 for a soldier found by a French company[38].

---

[37] 8D Mortuary Affairs: Letter of Brigadier-General John W. Donaldson to the Secretary of the ABMC dated 18th September 1985, Normandy American cemetery.

[38] *Ouest France* Monday 24th and Tuesday 25th December 1951, *"The remains of an American soldier were discovered near the shore at Colleville-sur-Mer"*. Original title of the article: *"Près de la grève, on découvre à Colleville-sur-Mer les restes d'un soldat américain"*.

Numerous bodies of American soldiers have thus been and are again found in Normandy. In March 1979, for example, the remains of a pilot were discovered at Octeville in the Manche department. The United-States rushed a team of four representatives accompanied by an official of the American Embassy. The Superintendent of the Normandy American Cemetery took care of the remains and sent them to Germany to undergo the necessary medical examinations to reveal his identity. Indeed, an agreement had been signed on 1st July 1955 between France and the United-States to allow American troops based in Frankfurt to be able to travel freely and to transport the bodies unhindered to the German military base before undergoing medical examinations there.

Three similar affairs to that of Octeville occurred in only eighteen months. Only one of them could be elucidated and the body sent to the family. The other two bodies remained unknown and were sent to the Ardennes cemetery. Such cases have been repeated since and the Colleville-sur-Mer cemetery is always informed of such discoveries by the French authorities[39].

The names of Missing in Action soldiers in Normandy had been engraved on the Colleville-sur-Mer and Saint-James Walls of the Missing. The ABMC always refused to erase the name of a soldier subsequently found. It chose instead to fix a small bronze rosette at the side of the soldier's name in question. Today, there are fifteen such rosettes on the cemetery wall at Colleville-sur-Mer.

---

[39] On 17th February 1983, the ABMC received a call from a councilor of Colombelles informing them of the discovery of a soldier's remains of the Second World War by council workers of the commune whilst digging a trench. Another example: in July 1985, the remains of an American soldier were found in the Manche department at Plessis-Lastelle near Mont-Castre. The Gendarmerie contacted the Normandy American Cemetery to request an intervention by the American Government. These examples are not exhaustive. Other bodies have been found since. 8D Mortuary Affairs: Exhumation of remains at Octeville, Normandy American Cemetery.

One of the last rosette was posed for a soldier named John R. Simonetti found and formally identified on 10th November 2009. Among the fifteen rosettes, four were affixed at the same time. These concerned four members of the same bomber crew who crashed on 22nd June 1944 above Mondrainville (Calvados). The four bodies were found in 1986 by a French civilian. It took some years after their exhumation to discover their identity. These four men were Lieutenant-Colonel Weiss, First-Lieutenant Meserow, First-Lieutenant Slustrop and First-Lieutenant Hazlett, being the four members at the front of the bomber. The three members serving at the back of the plane remained missing. Only one coffin was used for the four comrades in arms subsequently buried in Arlington National Cemetery.

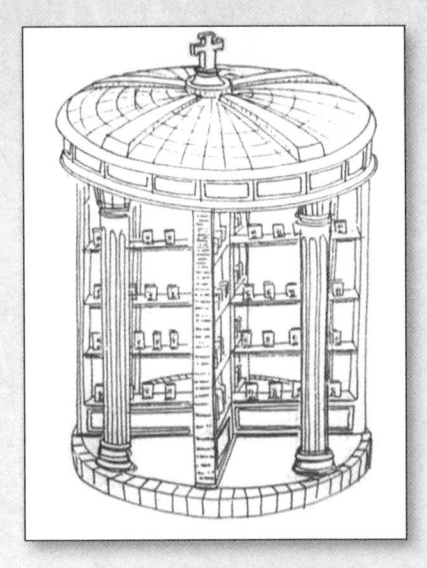

The mausoleum project proposed by Jacques L. See at the ABMC for the Colleville-sur-Mer cemetery. *Photo ABMC.*

Staff-Sergeant John R. Simonetti of the 2nd Infantry Division died on 16th June 1944. *Photo ABMC.*

The bomber crew of the "Incendiary Mary" which crashed at Mondrainville in 1944. *Photo ABMC.*

SECOND PART 193

Tribute to buried soldiers at the Colleville-sur-Mer cemetery during Memorial Day on 29th May 2011. *Photo C. Lebastard.*

THIRD PART

A VITAL MISSION: TO PERPETUATE THE MEMORY
OF THE BURIED SOLDIERS

The Ceremonies

THE FIRST COMMEMORATIVE CEREMONIES

The commemorations of the D-Day landing before the inauguration of the cemetery

The commemorative ceremonies paying homage to the American soldiers started from 1944. They took place on the sites of the temporary cemeteries. Then, progressively they were held at the permanent cemetery of Colleville-sur-Mer.

The most important ceremonies have always been those re-calling the events that occurred on 6th June 1944 on the Normandy beaches. These were inevitable as they could mark peoples' minds and allow the witnesses to recall the memories of their experiences. From 6th June 1945 until today, each anniversary has been marked by ceremonies more or less important according to the years or the times. In the Colleville-sur-Mer cemetery, the ceremony on every 6th June has above all as its objective the remembrance of the sacrifices of the American soldiers fallen in the liberation of France and the rest of Europe. This theme can be found each year during the major events that gradually emerged.

The anniversary ceremonies were officially authorized by the French Government through the law of 21st May 1947 and their organization was entrusted to the D-day Commemoration Committee created by Raymond Triboulet, first Prefect of Bayeux after liberation of the town. The communes remained nevertheless free to organize their own ceremonies as well as the cemetery of Colleville-sur-Mer where the events were borne by the Americans, for whom it was essential that each anniversary of the landing be marked by a ceremony at the cemetery. The ABMC organized its ceremonies in partnership with the committee who put into place the commemorations in the American sector every two years, including most often the American cemetery[40].

During the early years, the ceremonies of the D-Day Commemoration Committee in the American sector took place on the beach: at Vierville-sur-Mer, Saint-Laurent or Colleville-sur-Mer. It was notably the case when the President of the French Republic, Vincent Auriol, went to Omaha-Beach before joining Port-en-Bessin on 6th June 1948. In 1950, Vierville-sur-Mer was chosen to be for the first time the framework of the principal events of the D-Day anniversary. The guests, including General Koenig, the French Minister of Veterans and the French Minister of Commerce and Industry, visited the location of the first temporary cemetery on the beach. The following year, a ceremony was organized during the visit of General Eisenhower in the permanent cemetery still under construction. It was the first time that the permanent cemetery hosted an official commemorative D-Day ceremony. In 1952, another illustrious guest was invited to participate in the 6th June ceremonies: the NATO Supreme Allied Commander, Europe: General Ridgway who was commanding the 82nd Airborne Division in 1944. In view of his presence, the official procession made a detour to the cemetery of Colleville-sur-Mer for a ceremony.

Many felt that the enthusiasm towards the anniversaries of the landing would fade after the initial ceremonies. However, many articles were written in the newspaper *Ouest-France* (best-selling French daily newspaper) describing the growing fervor

---

[40] The D-day Commemoration Committee was created on 22nd May 1945. The Allied countries like the United-States, Great-Britain and Canada quickly joined it. The committee then started to organize the anniversary commemorations and the memorial buildings. They decided to separate the commemorations of the British and the American sectors because it was unthinkable and unmanageable that all the ceremonies take place at the same time.

Ceremony of 6th June 1951 in the presence of General Eisenhower at the Colleville-sur-Mer cemetery. *Ouest-France.*

Ceremony of 6th June 1952 in the presence of General Ridgway. *Ouest-France.*

Ceremony of the tenth anniversary of the landing in the presence of the President of the French Republic René Coty. He was the first acting Head of State to visit Colleville-sur-Mer. *Life Magazine.*

of the population and of the communities marking this event. This enthusiasm could be seen during the first major occasion: the tenth anniversary of the landing. On that day, the President of the French Republic, René Coty and his President of the Council, Joseph Laniel made the trip to Normandy and in particular to the Normandy American Cemetery. Important military detachments and officials were present accompanied by a huge crowd. It was the first time that the newly finished memorial was utilized to commemorate the American landing.

The cemetery's inauguration ceremony

The site turned a page of its history when the burials and the architectural works ended, with its opening to the public. It was now time to think about commemoration, remembrance and the welcome of the soldiers' relatives as well as those individuals wishing to pay their respects.

The ABMC decided to organize official ceremonies of inauguration in all its Second World War cemeteries to formalize this transition. It followed the pattern of the First World War cemeteries inaugurated after the Great Depression during the summer of 1937. In 1952, the enlarged memorial of the Suresnes cemetery was the venue for a ceremony presided by General Marshall. The dedication was made by General Ridgway in the presence of the United-States Ambassador in France Clement Dunn, of the Marshal of France Juin and of the French Prime Minister Pinay.

The ABMC was so occupied with the end of the works in the different cemeteries that it was incapable of recruiting more than two or three temporary assistants to prepare for the ceremonies. It had to call upon for help from the State Department and from the Armed Forces services who furbished equipment and the necessary personnel. The work of these men was considerable: they had to draw up the guest list, take note of the responses, install the

The cemetery's inauguration ceremony on 19th July 1956. *Photo ABMC.*

Mrs. Roosevelt pays her respects on the graves of her husband and her brother-in-law on the day of the cemetery's inauguration. We can see the flags placed in front of each grave. *Photo ABMC.*

seating places, arrange with the parties who were going to make speeches, prepare the programs, print them, construct the podiums, communicate information to the Press, reserve buses and hotels... The commission also had to ask for help from protocol experts so as not to make an error in the allocation of the seating places.

Finally, the cemetery of Cambridge was inaugurated on 16th July 1956 and that of Colleville-sur-Mer on 19th July 1956 and not on the 18th July as many assert[41]. Contrary to another accepted idea, the French President René Coty and the American President Eisenhower did not take part in the ceremony. However, many hundreds of French and Americans were present during this event which took place under the presidency of the American Navy Admiral Thomas Kinkaid and of the Deputy Secretary of the ABMC. General Ganeval represented the President of the French Republic and the Minister of Veterans Tanguy Prigent represented the French Government. The Prefect of Calvados, the Sub-Prefect of Bayeux and the President of the General Council were also invited. Military honors were rendered by American and French troops in parade dress and especially by the Special Military School of Saint-Cyr and by the musicians of the 38th French Signal Regiment from Laval. The five principal American patriotic organizations were present that day: the Veterans of Foreign War of the U.S., the American War Mothers, the American Legion, the Disabled American Veterans and the AMVET (the American Veterans of World War II). Each grave was decorated with two flags: one French and one American giving a total of nearly 19 000 flags. This tradition has continued in all following Memorial Day ceremonies and during the significant D-Day ceremonies.

---

[41] It has always been said that the cemetery was inaugurated on the 18th July because the official speeches were written on this date. However, the archive documents and the newspapers confirm that the cemetery was inaugurated on the next day, the 19th July 1956.

After the rising of the colors, Admiral Kinkaid greeted the personalities present and notably the wife of Theodore Roosevelt Jr., who wished to pay her respects at the graves of her husband and her brother-in-law. Major-General Donovan read after the message from President Eisenhower and then that of President René Coty. The inaugural speech was made by the U.S. Secretary of the Army. After the last post and the honor salvos, the ceremony ended on the National Anthems and with a wreath laying on behalf of the two absent Presidents, of the ABMC, the Prefect and the Commonwealth War Graves Commission. If the evocation of the ceremony program may seem trivial, it may be noted however that all the major ceremonies, thereafter, were organized around this scheme.

The day after, on 20th July 1956, the cemetery of Saint-James was inaugurated in the presence of the French Minister of Foreign Affairs. The ABMC concentrated many other inaugurations during the same period of time: the commission organized the official ceremony of inauguration of Épinal cemetery on 23rd July, the one of Draguignan on 26th July and the one of Nettuno in Italy on 30th July.

The cemeteries of Luxembourg, Margraten, Henri-Chapelle, Neuville-en-Condroz, Saint-Avold, Florence, Carthage, Manila and the West-Coast memorial were only inaugurated in 1960. The East-Coast Memorial was in turn inaugurated by President Kennedy in 1963.

A degree of public disinterest in the D-Day ceremonies

Following the major events of the tenth landing and of the cemetery's inauguration, many thought that the location would become an essential site of commemoration. However until 1960, the ceremonies were very discreet, reuniting only some veterans as in 1955 or some personalities as Marshal of France Juin and the wife of Marshal of France Leclerc during the ceremony of 6th June 1958. During this period, the principal ceremonies relayed by the media were organized by Raymond Triboulet, President of the D-day Commemoration Committee. It was thanks to his efforts that the commemorations in the Normandy cemetery were so lavish. In 1959, Triboulet as Minister of Veteran Affairs chaired the ceremonies of 6th June one of which was held at Colleville-sur-Mer. However, the commemorations suffered from a certain public disinterest as they did not attend in the same numbers as before[42].

1960 was an exception. The D-day Commemoration Committee started the initial stages of the landing commemorations in the American sector with a ceremony in the Colleville-sur-Mer cemetery in the presence of the French Minister of Foreign Affairs M. Couve de Murville, Raymond Triboulet likewise Minister, and the Ambassador of the United-States in Paris. This was a major event that involved four warships off the coast. However, until 1964, the cemetery was neglected by the major official events. The 6th June 1963 was eclipsed by the death of the Pope John XXIII which occurred on 3rd June.

For the twentieth anniversary, preparations for the commemorative ceremonies started from May and an official ceremony at the cemetery of Colleville-sur-Mer was planned. The event was important: thousands of veterans made the journey in the region and the enthusiasm was of such importance that the entire world's media headed for the Normandy coast. It was also the first time that the newspaper *Ouest-France* mobilized so much for the 6th June ceremonies. This fervor was linked to the cinematic release of the Hollywood film *The Longest Day*

---

[42] *Ouest-France* of Monday 8th June 1959, « L'anniversaire du débarquement sur les côtes normandes », "The anniversary of the landing on the Norman coast".

The twentieth anniversary ceremony of the landing in the presence of General Bradley. *Ouest France.*

in 1962[43]. Numerous personalities attended the event: General Bradley and nearly twenty other generals or admirals including Taylor, Collins and Ridgway as well as the British and American ambassadors. Nevertheless, no Head of state was present. France was only represented by the Minister of Veterans and by Raymond Triboulet who was at that time the Minister of Cooperation.

After the pageant of the twentieth anniversary, the cemetery remained for three years without major events. Naturally, the death of Robert F. Kennedy made all the headlines and gathered the Americans around the site of Colleville-sur-Mer on 6th June 1968. However, the ceremonies of 1968 for the French were overtaken by the social tensions which followed the public unrest from the month of May.

---

[43] We can measure the impact of this film by the number of posters existing linking the blockbuster and the ceremonies planned for 6th June 1964. Cornelius Ryan, author of the *Longest Day* even travelled to the Colleville-sur-Mer cemetery to decorate the grave of one of his comrades fallen during the battle of Normandy.

For the ten years up to 1978, the British and American sectors shared the commemorations but there were few references in the newspapers regarding the ceremonies in Colleville-sur-Mer. However, in 1972, the cemetery was the center of official events in Calvados on the occasion of the twenty-eighth anniversary, in the presence of dozens of veterans.

A large-scale event was in preparation which would fail to re-launch the interest around the Colleville-sur-Mer cemetery: the thirtieth anniversary of the landing on 6th June 1974. This ceremony was one of the most important commemorations ever realized by the D-day Commemoration Committee. However, the impact on the American cemetery was minimal as the major part of the ceremonies took place in the British sector. The only memorable ceremony in the American sector took place at Pointe-du-Hoc: a unit of Rangers climbed up the cliff loaded up with flowers which they offered to the officials present and notably to the ambassadors of the five principal Allied countries involved in the 1944 events.

THE MAJOR COMMEMORATIVE EVENTS OF THE D-DAY LANDING

The starting point of the presidential ceremonies

On 5th January 1978, a curious event broke the daily routine of the cemetery: Jimmy Carter, President of the United-States, paid a visit to the site accompanied by the French President Valéry Giscard-d'Estaing, the Minister of Foreign Affairs, the Minister of Defense, the Secretary of State for Veterans and General Donaldson. A major ceremony was organized during which the two Heads of State made a speech. It was the first time that an American incumbent President came to the Normandy cemetery.

This event marked the start of a new trend which was confirmed during the next thirty years[44]: the Normandy American Cemetery has to be considered as a must location for remembrance. Jimmy Carter's visit did not take place within the framework of the 6th June commemorations but he initiated the tradition of international ceremonies in the presence of American Presidents on the site. Many of his successors imitated his gesture and paid tribute to the soldiers in the American cemetery. Nevertheless, the immediate impact of his visit was not felt during the ceremony of 6th June 1978.

On 6th June 1982, the visit of Mrs. Nancy Reagan, wife of American President, confirmed the interest brought to the cemetery and to the commemorations of 6th June. She arrived by helicopter accompanied by the Ambassador of the United-States in France. She took part in a ceremony organized in the margins of the official ceremonies commemorating the thirty-eighth anniversary of the landing. This event made newspaper headlines. Mrs. Reagan took advantage of this occasion to lay a wreath in front of the grave of Elizabeth Richardson, one of the many feminine victims of the war. President Regan meanwhile was present at a summit of the most industrialized countries in Versailles, thus explaining the presence of his wife in Normandy.

The fortieth anniversary of the D-Day landing made an impact on everybody's minds. The commemorations mainly took place in the American sector. Never before, on the Omaha battlefield were welcomed as many Heads of State, Queens and Kings: François Mitterrand, Ronald Reagan, Baudouin Ist of Belgium, Elizabeth II

---

[44] A comparison may be made with the work of Delphine Leneveu who showed clearly that between the years of 1980 and 2004, the importance of the commemorations was unparalleled: she took as an example the monument inaugurations and observed that nearly 80% of them took place during this period. See LENEVEU (Delphine), *Les Monuments commémoratifs américains du débarquement et de la bataille de Normandie dans le Calvados*, op. cit.

Presidents Jimmy Carter and Valéry Giscard-d'Estaing in the American cemetery on 5th January 1978. *Ouest France.*

The American First Lady, Mrs. Reagan, places a bouquet of flowers in front of the grave of Elizabeth Richardson on the occasion of the thirty-eight anniversary of the landing.
Ouest France.

Presidents Ronald Reagan and François Mitterrand crossing the René Coty walkway towards the American cemetery's memorial on 6th June 1984.
Ouest France.

of Great-Britain, Olaf V of Norway, Beatrix I of Netherlands, the Grand Duke Jean of Luxembourg, Elliot Trudeau, Head of the Canadian Government and Prince Charles of Great-Britain. This was the first time that the French and American Presidents honored together the operations of 6th June 1944 on the anniversary date in the Normandy American Cemetery. The speech of the American President recalled the losses on Omaha-Beach and the importance of remembrance incumbent on each person to remember these acts. The different ceremonies were marked by great attention from the officials *"to the fighters in the shadows"* which Reagan also made allusion to in the cemetery: the French resistance. He wished to erase the mistrust of Roosevelt and to officially pay tribute to them. This ceremony was one of the most impressive it had ever known at that time and can still be considered as the real starting point of the 6th June presidential ceremonies at the Normandy American Cemetery. However, this was not the culmination of the commemorations of 1984: all the Heads of State met at Utah-Beach for the international ceremony.

The changes of the 1980's

In the 1980's and in particular because of the forthcoming fortieth anniversary, the importance of recent history through the landing commemorations started to occupy a more prominent place amongst the public. More widely, the 1980's were the years for an accrued public interest in history which was accompanied by a deep wish to remember the past and by a new term in France: *"devoir de mémoire"* which can be globally translated as "duty of remembrance". A new philosophy emerged: those who forget the past are condemned to repeat it. At the same time, many Anglo-Saxon historians had the conviction that it was necessary to learn from history: *"The places of remembrance are born and live out of a sentiment that there is no spontaneous remembrance, that we must create the archives, maintain the archives, maintain the anniversaries, organize commemorations, pronounce funeral eulogies, notarize acts, because these operations do not happen naturally*"[45].

It is not the objective of this book to study this notion of "*devoir de mémoire*". However, we can observe that the veterans and survivors of the 1944 events felt themselves responsible for the remembrance of their comrades. Their effort to tell their life story, to talk with people… often took the form of homages paid to their fallen comrades in arms in particular at the Colleville-sur-Mer cemetery. The way they considered remembrance towards the dead soldiers no longer engaged them only in a simple act of respect.

With the 1980's and the approach of the fortieth anniversary, the population started to become aware of the near disappearance of those witnesses to the landing. The commemoration organizers really started to bring together the generations and invited school children to participate in ceremonies with veterans. The number of schools and children coming to lay wreaths on the soldiers' graves markedly increased at the Normandy American Cemetery. A new exchange tended to be established between the veterans and the population through the testimonies of these witnesses. This did not exclude the former German soldiers: Governments, organizations, even individuals also attempted to bring together the enemies of yesterday. *Ouest-France* reported in 1978 for example the arrival of German tourists to the cemetery; a simple visit which would have been frowned upon a few years before by locals and veterans. "*This is proof that remembrance has no frontier or nationality*"[46].

---

[45] Quote taken from NORA (Pierre) (dir.), *Les Lieux de mémoire*, Gallimard, Paris, 1997, 3 vol., 451 p. See also the work of B. H. Liddell Hart, *Why don't we learn from History?*, Hawthorn Books, New York, 1971, p. 115.

[46] *Ouest-France* of Wednesday 7th June 1978, « Du cimetière américain de Colleville à la Pointe du Hoc, la commémoration du débarquement allié en Normandie », "From the American cemetery of Colleville to the Pointe du Hoc, the commemoration of the Allied landing in Normandy".

These changes could be observed thanks to the media and through the multiplication of articles, of reports, of numerous specials… Initiated during the 1964 commemorations, this trend was truly confirmed in the 1980's. The role of the media became prevalent: the French newspaper *Le Figaro* dated 4th June 2004 provided evidence that only one in three British students knew the location of the landing and that the essential knowledge of the conflict came from the media of television. In fact, the media gradually monopolized the ceremonies and transformed them into major events and contributed to the internationalization of the 6th June commemoration.

Moreover, the politicians and in particular the Heads of State started to exploit these commemorations to register them in a social and political context. The meeting between President Carter and President Giscard-d'Estaing in 1978 at Colleville-sur-Mer as such was difficult because of its sensitive political context: the recent American withdrawal from Vietnam (1975) and the desire for a French-American rapprochement opposing the Eastern Block in the middle of the Cold War. In 1984, Reagan opposed the communist world. The objective of his visit at Colleville-sur-Mer was essentially to re-affirm the American commitment to defend Europe against the policy of the U.S.S.R. The ceremonies took on real political importance with the fortieth anniversary as if the American President *"was giving to his nation ravaged by the Vietnam War faith in its values".* This commemoration was for many witnesses and media considered as an occasion for the United-States to celebrate its leadership and its moral superiority and for France, to express its partnership: *"In 1964, De Gaulle had refused to go to the landing commemorations, which caused uproar among the Allies. In 1984 Mitterrand, on the other hand, welcomed the crowned heads and the year before, he had approved the installation of the Pershing missiles in Europe. The message is clear: France is on the side of the Free World. Mitterrand recognized what was evident for each American at that time-there. The defense of the Western World against communism started on 6th June 1944"*[47].

The 6th June has become regarded as an opportunity to witness joint success: that of a United Europe against its aggressor. The story of the Normandy landing became henceforth the starting point of Europe. The ceremonies also enabled to further justify actual conflicts by comparing them to the Second World War: for example the war against terrorism. The political parties tried to appropriate the commemorations and criticism gradually formed around the anniversaries such as those organized at the cemetery of Colleville-sur-Mer. Many critics were angered to see men parading with decorations, to see flags of Nations and to hear National anthems resonating… Some historians in France - notably those of the left parties (social liberals…) – considered these events as meeting places of right wing nationalists.

The ceremonies until 2008

The change initiated in the 1980's materialized in the succeeding years. Population and Governments were more and more interested by the D-Day commemorations: on 6th June 1988, the President of the French Republic came to inaugurate the new Memorial of Caen surrounded by the delegations from sixteen nations! In 1990, the 6th June ceremony, took place in the presence of General John S.-D. Eisenhower (son of Dwight D. Eisenhower) bringing together a large assembly to the Normandy American Cemetery. The son of the former American President also came that day to pay his respects on the occasion of the hundredth birthday of his father and of de Gaulle. Delegations from seven nations accompanied him during this ceremony which was the highlight of the forty-sixth anniversary.

---

[47] *Ouest-France* edition of Wednesday 2nd June 2004, « Jour J : entre mémoire et diplomatie », "D-Day: between remembrance and diplomacy".

The son of former President Eisenhower during a ceremony at the American cemetery of Colleville-sur-Mer on the occasion of the forty-sixth anniversary of the landing.
Ouest France.

Presidents George W. Bush and Jacques Chirac on the occasion of the sixtieth anniversary of the landing on 6th June 2004 at the Colleville-sur-Mer cemetery.
Photo ABMC.

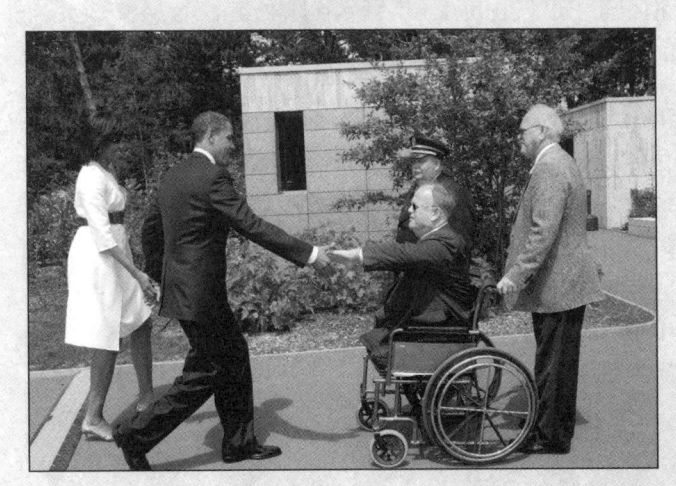

The American President and his wife welcomed by Max Cleland, Secretary of the ABMC and Daniel Neese, Superintendent of the Normandy American Cemetery, on the occasion of the ceremony of 6th June 2009. *Source: acclaimimages.com.*

THIRD PART 213

Everybody agreed just before 1994 that the fiftieth anniversary would mark the peak of the landing remembrance. There was an explosion in publications around this event, which Jean Quellien estimated at an increase of some 900%. It marked well the regional, national and even international focalization around this commemoration.

The calm of the 1992 and 1993 ceremonies contrasted with the pomp of 1994. As the years had passed, the number of visitors to the Normandy region had increased considerably to the point of exceeding the bar of ten million visitors annually and causing traffic jams on the normally calm roads. The fiftieth was named the "Jubilee of Liberty" and concentrated all the momentum of Normandy tourism.

The first negotiations to choose the principal commemoration sites had already started one year before the 50th anniversary events. Important work amenities were undertaken to welcome the important expected crowds: roads, vehicle parks and museums, amongst others, were arranged or constructed to cope with the influx expected. Twenty-seven sites took part in the anniversary events and twenty-five to thirty thousand veterans travelled to Normandy for the ceremonies attended by the Heads of States of the countries involved in the 1944 operations: Bill Clinton, Elizabeth II, François Mitterrand, Ramon John Hnatyshyn (Governor General of Canada)...

A first American ceremony headed the festivities at Cherbourg on 5th June 1994. After a journey to the Nettuno cemetery, then to the Cambridge cemetery, President Bill Clinton chose the cemetery of Colleville-sur-Mer to honor the sacrifice of the American soldiers in Normandy. Besides the considerably reinforced security, the media peaked: the ceremonies were re-transmitted on the three principal French television channels[48].

[48] Mirage 2000, radar, ships, 7 000 gendarmes and numerous soldiers assured the security of the 70 miles of road leading to the sites of the major ceremonies.

Nevertheless, no direct transmission of the ceremony at Colleville-sur-Mer was realized while the location was the theater of one of the largest commemorations which the place had ever experienced since its creation. Phil Rivers, the Superintendent at that time, confirmed to the media that this ceremony could not be compared with the previous ceremonies and notably with that of the fortieth anniversary. One of the cemetery employee testified: *"It was the biggest event that the cemetery had known with thousands of veterans present and an imposing security. The guests were handpicked"*[49].

Marquees, giant tents, artificial roads and a camp hospital were installed as well as an immense wooden floor the length of the central walkway in the cemetery. However, the French President did not take part in the ceremony: Pierre Méhaignerie, Keeper of the Seals, represented the French Government. The French-American meeting between Mitterrand and Clinton took place on Utah-Beach, a little before the ceremony at Colleville-sur-Mer. The big international ceremony took place at Saint Laurent-sur-Mer, a few miles from the cemetery.

The 6th June 1994 marked a break for the employees of the cemetery. The major ceremonies in the past as that of the fortieth anniversary were much more intimate. There was also much more exchange and coordination between Washington and the cemetery. With the fiftieth anniversary, the White house would take a major hand in the organization of the big events leaving little margin for maneuver to the ABMC and to the cemetery.

Following this event, the official commemoration retinue has made a stop every year at the site of Colleville-sur-Mer which has really become a must-site for commemorations. The promotion of the landing and by extension that of the cemetery intensified: the cemetery attracted the crowds during the 6th June 1999

---

[49] Testimony of Maryvonne Guidon, Interpretive Guide at the Colleville-sur-Mer cemetery since 1st November 1993.

ceremony. This was an outcome of the Steven Spielberg film *Saving Private Ryan*. The fifty-seventh anniversary also had a significant impact: the HBO series *Band of Brothers* relating the story of company E of the 506th Infantry Regiment of the 101st Airborne Division was presented during a ceremony at Utah-Beach. We can note however that the logic was somewhat modified compared to the fiftieth anniversary as explained by Delphine Leneveu: *"Stone became obsolete to the benefit of new material: films, shows, exhibitions, meetings with veterans and witnesses of the conflict"*.

This new logic was confirmed during the sixtieth anniversary in 2004. The organization of the 6th June ceremony at Colleville-sur-Mer was identical to that of 6th June 1994: the same logistic was reused, the same measures of security, etc. The entire device was based on that of the fiftieth and the media were again very present: serials, reports, special issues… However, the thematic were different.

The welcome of Presidents George Bush Jr. and Jacques Chirac fitted into a double thematic. The first was that of the renewed interest of the American and French population in the Second World War very likely initiated by Hollywood. Some days before, in May 2004, President Bush had inaugurated the Washington World War II Memorial. In the same way, the French Prime Minister Jean-Pierre Raffarin had made the journey the year before in the company of the Ambassador of the United-States to the Colleville-sur-Mer cemetery. The second thematic was more pragmatic and mostly played on diplomatic relations: the year 2004 was marked by the French-German rapprochement, the Iraq question, the war against terrorism… George Bush wished above all to improve the international image of the United-States with the difficult Iraq War. He attempted to get closer to France which had not supported the United-States during this conflict reminding them of their old friendship. The American President looked to draw a parallel between the Second World War against the Axis perceived as legitimate and the war against Al-Qaida and the Iraq War. The hazards of international politics played henceforth a leading role in the magnitude of the commemorations.

From 2005 to 2008, the cemetery was at the heart of the ceremonies, albeit they were smaller, but which brought together numerous personalities: the French Minister of Veterans Hamlaoui Mékachéra in 2005; the American Secretary of Defense Robert M. Gates, the French Minister of Defense Hervé Morin and the daughter of Eisenhower in 2007. Finally, the Governor of Texas was accompanied by the American General Wilson during the 2008 commemoration at Colleville-sur-Mer.

The 6th June 2009: the ultimate major ceremony?

A new theme was developed from the fiftieth anniversary of the landing: to share with the veterans memories of the events that occurred in Normandy before they passed away. This idea was related to the progressive loss of the last soldiers of the First World War and to the fear that this conflict could be forgotten. During the organization of the fiftieth anniversary, this commemoration was spoken of as the last "major" anniversary. Many were those who thought that the veterans would not be able to undertake the journey to Normandy. This fear also explained the important number of media covering the event.

The 1994 festivities, rather than bury with dignity the landing remembrance, produced the opposite effect. In fact, besides the numerous publications they had captivated the attention of the population and of other media including the cinema industry or television by the production of documentaries, of video-games, etc. All an economy was structured around the D-Day landing and explained the new appointment fixed ten years later for the sixtieth anniversary.

In 2004, the fear that the witnesses would disappear in a few years was taken up. People then spoke of the event as the last "major" anniversary. The media exposure was even more consequential. The cinema industry led the way with numerous youngsters marked by the story of the film *Saving Private Ryan*. All these elements created a real "remembrance tourism" around the event.

Many had evoked the end of the major commemorations with the fiftieth anniversary or again with the sixtieth anniversary of the landing. But the frequency of the major ceremonies of 6th June intensified rather than conversely running out of steam. The ceremony of the sixty-fifth anniversary at the Colleville-sur-Mer cemetery was a good example. Until then, the habit was to organize the major events every ten years. However, with the age of the veterans marching on, it was decided to accelerate the rhythm of the ceremonies. President Barack Obama wished to start his mandate by a visit to the Normandy American Cemetery. He also perpetuated the tradition established by Jimmy Carter. Usually, the major ceremonies were prepared at least one year in advance. In 2009, the cemetery was warned only three weeks before the Presidential visit but the ABMC was less solicited about the organization of the major commemoration.

The same provisions as realized for the fiftieth and sixtieth anniversaries were installed in three weeks. It was not only envisaged to organize a French-American diplomatic meeting but the objective was to prepare the major international ceremony of the sixty-fifth anniversary. Besides Nicolas Sarkozy and Barack Obama, the Prime Minister of Great-Britain Gordon Brown, his Canadian counterpart Stephen Harper as well as Prince Charles of Great-Britain were invited. A hundred veterans again made the journey and four amongst them were decorated with the Legion of Honor by the President of the French Republic. This event, of significant international standing was re-transmitted on the televisions of numerous countries and was followed by hundreds of journalists from the World over.

The example of this ceremony of the sixty-fifth anniversary of the D-Day landing shows us that far from ending this page of history, it marked the acceleration of the major events and in particular regarding the cemetery of Colleville-sur-Mer. The enthusiasm provoked by the seventieth anniversary and that, in spite of the gradual disappearance of the last witnesses, underlines the important interest also of the people and of their leadership towards the liberators of 1944.

COMMEMORATIONS THROUGHOUT THE YEAR

Memorial Day

No special ceremony was ever organized by the American cemetery to commemorate the end of the war in Europe. However, each year the Normandy American Cemetery celebrates a Federal holiday at the end of the month of May: Memorial Day also known as Decoration Day. In 1868, General John A. Logan, former Commander in Chief of the Army of the Northern States, published an order designating this day to decorate with flowers the graves of the fallen soldiers. This National holiday was at first destined to honor the memory of soldiers fallen during the Civil War but it has since been consecrated to the memory of all the American soldiers fallen during all the wars.

The first celebration after the Second World War was organized on 30th May 1945, being just three weeks after the capitulation of the Third Reich. It was celebrated in all the temporary cemeteries of the Second World War and in all the cemeteries of the First World War managed by the ABMC. The American Graves registration Service headquarters organized the different commemorations and invited the local population to participate. After the establishment of the permanent cemeteries, including Colleville-sur-Mer, the Memorial Day ceremonies continued to be organized each year.

Initially, the ceremonies occurred each 30th May. Then, the Normandy American Cemetery progressively organized its ceremonies on each last Sunday of May in order to allow the inhabitants to come to pay their respects outside of work hours.

The American forces generally supplied the military music but were sometimes accompanied by French military orchestras. The course of the ceremonies was very similar to those of the 6th June ceremonies except that the religious office was much more important. These ceremonies were and are still organized, sponsored and financed by the American Overseas Memorial Day Association (AOMDA), an association founded in 1920 which has as its mission, in France, to decorate the graves and monuments of all American soldiers.

Besides the principal ceremony organized in the enclosure of the cemetery, the Americans have tried to share this celebration in paying homage to the dead of other nations, and in particular to the British: a ceremony was organized in the Bayeux Commonwealth cemetery in 1965, then in 1966, 1982 and 1996 to quote just some examples.

There has always been a correlation between the major anniversaries of the D-Day landing and the organization of the Memorial Day major ceremonies. Thus, in 1954, year of the tenth anniversary of the landing, the Memorial Day ceremony was held at Colleville-sur-Mer in the presence of General Bradley accompanied by numerous French officials. In the same way, more recently, the Memorial Day ceremony of 2009 was undertaken in the presence of three American Senators and numerous high ranking American and French personnel.

In 1958, an event disturbed the traditional Memorial Day ceremonies in France. In view of political and ministerial troubles of the French IV Republic which led De Gaulle to power, all the ceremonies were cancelled. A state of emergency having been declared, gatherings were forbidden: the event at Colleville-sur-Mer was de-programed. Nevertheless, a small improvised American ceremony was held at the feet of Donald de Lue's statue, organized by the AOMDA and the ceremony of 6th June 1958 was not disturbed.

In 1987, during the Memorial Day ceremony, a carillon system was offered to the Superintendent of the Normandy American Cemetery by Morgan S. Ruph, Director of the American Veterans of World War II, Korea and Vietnam wars (AMVETS). *Taps* also called *Butterfield's Lullaby* has been played every day during the descent of the colors since this carillon arrived at the cemetery. The story of this project goes back to 1948. The association was looking for the best way to pay tribute to the American soldiers killed during the Second World War. After some thought, the AMVETS opted for what it called a "living monument"; a carillon whose bells would sound as a constant reminder of their acts. The first carillon system was installed in Arlington National Cemetery. Then, others were progressively put into place. There are today a total of forty-three carillons in addition to that of Colleville-sur-Mer: one was given to the Harry S. Truman Library and another one to the Hoover Library at West-Branch, Iowa[50].

The most important Memorial Day ever celebrated in the Colleville-sur-Mer cemetery was without doubt that of 2002. For the first time in the history of the United-States, an American

---

[50] During the 52nd anniversary of the cemetery, a new carillon was given by the veterans of the AMVETS association and its founder Robert L. Willbraham to replace the first which was defective. Source: *Ouest-France* Bayeux edition of Friday 7th June 1996, « Un carillon souvenir de la mémoire vivante », "Remembrance chimes keeping alive the memory".

President was going to celebrate this Federal Holiday outside of American territory. After a visit to Sainte-Mère-Église, George W. Bush Jr. went with his French counterpart, Jacques Chirac to the Normandy cemetery to celebrate the event. During their speeches, the parallels with the recent events of 11th September 2001 were numerous. The American President linked his policy against terrorism in the furrow of what his country had undertaken during the Second World War. He introduced also the theme that he would take up again during his visit two years later, for the sixtieth anniversary of the landing. The ceremony was broadcast live by the American media. He is for the time being, the only American President who has visited the Normandy cemetery twice during the course of his term of office.

The "private" ceremonies

Numerous "private" ceremonies were and are still organized around official commemorations. These ones are generally realized in collaboration with veteran associations, dignitaries or with excursion groups wishing to pay their respects to the cemetery's soldiers. The number of ceremonies varies according to the years and in particular according to the major anniversaries. However, these low key commemorations are counted in their dozens each year.

Here is a description of the proceedings of such events: the ceremonies are still today organized by one or several cemetery employees according to very precise procedures. The employee greets the participants and introduces them to the cemetery and also to the procedure which they will follow. Then, the American National Anthem is played on the carillon offered by the AMVETS. A wreath is then placed at the foot of the statue gracing the memorial and the Taps sounds. The ceremony ends generally with a minute of silence and with some suitable words spoken in conclusion. These ceremonies are by their nature very brief, never exceeding more than twenty minutes.

It sometimes happened, that the celebration required more preparation: for example, during the visit of General James L. Collins in 1997, during the reception of large groups like those of the one hundred and ten young choristers received in June 2004, or again with the one hundred and fifty members of the Ancient and Honorable Artillery Company received in October 2009.

Ceremonies are often offered to dignitaries who wish to pay homage to the American soldiers. On occasion, personalities may wish to be received outside the formal framework as happened with the former American President George Bush Sr. on 28th April 1995 or once more, during the impromptu visit of the United-States Ambassador in 2006.

The most numerous ceremonies have always been those undertaken for the excursion groups such as the People to People association and the Grand Circle Travel foundation. The first is a non-profit association founded in 1956 by President Dwight D. Eisenhower to promote peace and understanding between nations. Since 1963, it has organized trips to Europe orientated to cultural and intellectual enrichment for young Americans between eleven and eighteen years of age. The second, Grand Circle Travel, was established in 1992 and proposes journeys throughout the world. These two organizations offer excursions to the landing beaches and notably to the Colleville-sur-Mer cemetery. These two associations represented nearly fifty per cent of the ceremonies organized in the cemetery in 2009 and 2010. The other ceremonies undertaken during this same period were: military groups (10%), school groups (10%), personalities or families of soldiers buried in Colleville-sur-Mer (3.5%), or once more for diverse and varied association such as the Lions Club or the Flowers of Memory (*Les Fleurs de la Mémoire*).

The achievements of the ABMC after the founding of the cemetery

THE PROJECTS IN COLLABORATION WITH THE CEMETERY OF COLLEVILLE-SUR-MER

The management of certain monuments

In July 1924, the French Government authorized the building of commemorative monuments by American sponsors having obtained the approval of the ABMC. Shortly after the Second World War in 1945, several generals including General Eisenhower reported that units were already building war monuments as it had been the case after the First World War. They insisted on the urgency there was to put into place a system regulating these constructions. The ABMC was given the responsibility of authorizing or not the implementation of American monuments and the maintenance responsibility for certain monuments: in 1957, for example, a law transferred the maintenance of the Santiago Surrender tree near Santiago de Cuba, from the American Army to the commission's responsibility.

Even before obtaining the prerogative of the cemeteries, the commission had received the task of erecting and maintaining monuments dedicated not to units but to the entire Nation. After the Second World War, the ABMC decided to continue this policy and to extend the numbers of memorials. A budget had been anticipated in 1948 of a little over thirty million dollars to build the new cemeteries but in 1966, once the work in the cemeteries was achieved, the ABMC realized that there remained a sum of six million dollars. It decided on the construction in New-York, of a monument in honor of those that lost their lives in the American waters of the Atlantic and another in San-Francisco, for those who perished in the American waters of the Pacific. The Honolulu memorial and the re-construction of the Brest monument were part of these supplementary monuments constructed after obtaining the approval of the Budget Office and of

Congress. Besides the twenty-four permanent cemeteries directed by the ABMC, as well as the Clark Veterans Cemetery, the commission maintains today a total of twenty-six monuments and memorials.

The role of the Normandy American Cemetery gradually expanded. This movement was linked to the political extension of the prerogatives of the commission. In the 1980's, the ABMC decided on the creation of the Utah-Beach monument to commemorate the achievements of the American forces of the VII Army Corps who fought from 6th June to 1st July 1944 to liberate the Cotentin Peninsula. Situated some 3.7 miles north-east of the commune of Sainte-Marie-du-Mont, the Utah-Beach monument was the largest monument erected by the commission related to the Normandy landing. It was inaugurated on 5th June 1984 on the occasion of the fortieth anniversary of D-Day. It was designed in red granite surrounded by a small park overlooking the dunes on the beach. This monument was fully financed by the ABMC and realized in collaboration with the French Government. The work was delegated to a French construction company at a cost to the ABMC of a total of 291 700 francs (around 60 000 dollars). Since then, the ABMC has always employed a gardener affiliated to the Colleville-sur-Mer cemetery to maintain the monument as well as the lawn which encircles it.

Besides the construction in strict terms, the commission received the supervision of several monuments in Normandy including that of the 1st Infantry Division which is still visible to the east of the Colleville-sur-Mer cemetery. The Society of the First Division was at the origin of its construction and benefited from the presence of the ABMC in Normandy to entrust to it its supervision. This monument was made of a soaring pyramid setting out the list of the 1st Infantry Division fallen soldiers during the fighting of 6th June to 24th July 1944. The ABMC maintained the monument until 1988 but that same year, the commune of Colleville-sur-Mer became responsible for the maintenance of the land. In fact, the French *Conservatoire*

National du littoral (responsible for the preservation of the French coastline) approved plans concerning improvements to give to monuments and their surroundings (re-organization of access, new plantings, soil reparations…). This new plan brought about a signed agreement between the ABMC and the commune of Colleville-sur-Mer. The commune received 10 000 francs (2000 dollars) annually coming from the funds of the Society of the First Division in compensation. The agreement was signed in 1989 by General Donaldson of the ABMC representing the Society of the First Division and the Mayor of Colleville-sur-Mer. However, the cemetery of Colleville-sur-Mer retained the right up to present time to inspect the monument and to alert the association about its condition.

Other monuments or stelas were realized in partnership with the ABMC and more particularly with the cemetery of Colleville-sur-Mer. This was the case with the installation of the time capsule still buried today near the former Visitor Center at the entrance to the René-Coty walkway in the cemetery. This capsule, covered in red granite from Ploumanac'h in Brittany was filled with reports said to be "new" on the Normandy landing. They were placed by journalists present during the 6th June 1969 ceremony. We will not know its exact content until the day of its opening planned for 6th June 2044 on the one hundredth anniversary of the landing.

When we observed the correspondence between the ABMC and Norman towns, we noted that the commission had served and still serves as a relay with French officials. Much of the correspondence studied has revealed the major role played by the cemetery. In general, the most obvious solution for the municipalities wishing to erect a monument, to maintain it or to realize a ceremony, is to refer to the ABMC and more specifically to the Colleville-sur-Mer cemetery. This major role endorsed by the American cemetery during the major ceremonies has made of it, a sort of a U.S. embassy in the region. Thus, during the construction of the monument dedicated to Major Howie

The Utah-Beach monument commemorates the achievements of the VII Corps of the U.S. Army. In the background to the right, the Utah-Beach Museum. *Photo A. Lebastard.*

The monument in honor of the Big Red One overlooking WN62, a fortified German position on Omaha-Beach not far from the American cemetery. *Photo C. Lebastard.*

The time capsule will be opened on the one hundredth anniversary of the landing. *Photo C. Lebastard.*

at Saint-Lô, the town asked the ABMC for numerous pieces of advice via the intermediary of the American cemetery. This monument was finally inaugurated on 6th June 1969 in the presence of Major Howie's wife and of General Bradley.

The ABMC's wish: to protect the cemetery and Omaha-beach

The cemetery of Colleville-sur-Mer owed a part of its renown to its proximity with Omaha-Beach: it was created to overlook the beach offering to families and visitors a stunning view over one of the best known battlefields of the Second World War.

The ABMC wished to best protect both its cemetery and the beach situated just opposite. This sector of Colleville-sur-Mer was the only sector, with Pointe du Hoc, to remain virtually intact since the landing, even if some changes had been necessary. The first work consisted of demining the whole of the beach, which remained after the end of the war a dangerous location for the tourists. Many articles in the *Ouest-France* bore witness to accidents sometimes mortal which occurred after the landing or even many years after the end of the war.

From 22nd October 1946, an order of the French Education Minister registered the Saint-Laurent-sur-Mer temporary cemetery and the Colleville-sur-Mer and Saint-Laurent-sur-Mer neighboring lands situated by the sea on the inventory of historic sites of Calvados. It was the first act of protection undertaken for the area and its maritime frontage. This decision went hand in hand with the tourist development of the *Conservatoire National du littoral*. It was even envisaged by the General Council of Calvados to build a national road that would serve the landing beaches.

The ABMC always wished to leave the beach opposite the cemetery near to its 1944 state which included the artificial harbor established by the American Army to facilitate the supply and the landing of reinforcing troops. However, it was envisaged to dismantle it for safety reasons despite the implementation of Governmental protection regarding the beach. The artificial harbor had been heavily damaged during the summer of 1944 and was completely abandoned since 22nd November 1944. By notifications dated 23rd December 1946 and 23rd January 1947, the United-States Ambassador in France informed the French Minister of foreign Affairs of the decision taken by the War Department and by the Navy Department regarding the donation to the French Government of the materials ships, tanks, guns and wrecks still lying on Omaha-Beach. This signified quite simply that the artificial harbor at Omaha-Beach found itself entrusted to French responsibility.

The D-Day Commemoration Committee, thanks to its many relationships with the allies, obtained from the French Government the possibility to use part of the funds from the sale of the harbor's wrecks to finance the projects linked to the commemoration of the landing and especially for the construction of the Arromanches museum[51]. The committee's first wish was to completely delimit the D-Day commemorative area and it aspired to make of the Arromanches harbor a permanent war memorial. Even if the D-Day Commemoration Committee asked for the funds generated by the sale of the wrecks, other projects were envisaged: amongst them was that of the construction of a reception house for the American families visiting the newly completed Colleville-sur-Mer cemetery. Despite this new project, the ABMC and the cemetery of Colleville-sur-Mer protested vigorously against the destruction of the artificial harbor which they considered as a visible testimony to the American deeds during the landing.

---

[51] The Arromanches Museum was built four years prior to the sale of the port in 1952 and as a result it could not receive the funds from the sale of the artificial port. It was finally inaugurated in 1954 by the French President René Coty.

Nevertheless, companies were chosen to clean the beach and were put to work. Numerous problems arose during this dismantling: some companies bought the wrecks as compensation for the time spent cleaning the sectors under their responsibility. Some of them only took the scrap metal they wanted, leaving the dangerous wrecks on the beach. In 1949, complaints started to arise as nobody seemed to worry about removing them. Finally, the remains of the artificial harbor at Omaha-Beach were all dismantled in 1956; the year of the inauguration of the cemetery.

The protection of the Omaha-Beach site was approved by local authorities and the Prefect of Calvados on 10th January 1980. It concerned the American cemetery, the neighboring lands situated by the sea, the location of the first temporary American cemetery within a radius of 160 feet around the existing monument, the site walkways as well as the beaches situated to the coastal boundary of the communes of Vierville-sur-Mer, Saint-Laurent-sur-Mer and Colleville-sur-Mer. The protection was re-enforced by a circular of the French Minister of the Interior and of the Minister of the Environment on 11th July 1980. The objective was to define the measures ensuring a better protection of the surroundings of military cemeteries. This circular recalled the Municipality code stating that no person should without authorization elevate any dwelling, nor dig any well, within 330 feet of a cemetery.

In 1979, a discussion was engaged regarding the *Conservatoire National du littoral* project concerning the landing beaches during a meeting of the D-day Commemoration Committee. The idea was to purchase around 1 000 acres of land to preserve the principal locations of the major battle sites and to give their management to the municipalities and to the D-day Commemoration Committee. This project included the 420 acres of the beach of Colleville-sur-Mer. It was envisaged to make space for recreation and walks: walking trails, seaside playgrounds… The goal clearly displayed was to promote tourism on the coastline. In 1990, an enquiry was

The remains of the artificial harbor at Omaha-Beach before their total disappearance in 1956. *Collection Alain Dupain.*

The protected beach of Omaha-Beach in front of the American cemetery.
Photo C. Lebastard.

opened to declare the site of Omaha-Beach as a state-approved site. It presented a project of acquisition of land adjacent to the cemetery along the beach by the *Conservatoire National du littoral*. The ABMC was of course entirely in favor of this project and even wished it to be realized as quickly as possible in order to maintain the beach in the state of 6th June 1944, which had always been one of its objectives.

The action of the *Conservatoire National du littoral* was decisive to ensure the preservation of these spaces. A focused management was put in place thanks to a Management Committee bringing together the *Conservatoire National du littoral* and the party stakeholders including territorial collectivities, the ABMC, the French National Forest Office… In July 2001, the decision of the inter-ministerial land development committee to launch an operation called *Great Sites Normandie 44* consecrated to the major locations of the battle of Normandy, aimed to determine the program of development to be implemented by communities, the French Government but also the ABMC. The work of the Management Committee was organized and officially started in this perspective in 2003.

A new project was recently initiated by the association *Normandie Mémoire*. This association was created in 2002, initially to prepare the sixtieth anniversary of the landing and to enhance tourism in the region. Besides the promotion of tourism, this association had and continues to have as its project to include the landing beaches and the sites of the battle of Normandy to the UNESCO World Heritage Site list. In 2006, the process of sites registration was prepared by the Lower-Normandy departments and the Regional Council, and in October 2008, the regional councilors voted unanimously to apply for the nomination. However, the procedure already underway risks to be very long despite the support of the ABMC as indicated by the Superintendent of the Normandy American Cemetery, Daniel L. Neese.

Welcoming Steven Spielberg and shooting the film

Besides the elevation and the maintenance of monuments and besides the protection of the cemetery and its surroundings, the ABMC accorded a significant importance to the image of its cemeteries. One of the largest promotions of the commission's work was the reception of Steven Spielberg in 1997 in the Normandy American Cemetery to shoot some scenes of his world renowned movie: *Saving Private Ryan.*

While working in collaboration with Stephen Ambrose, Stephen Spielberg discovered the tragic stories of the Niland brothers. Inspired at the time by their story, by the script of Robert Roda, the documentaries of Frank Capa and George Stevens and the photographs of Robert Capa, he decided to devote a film to the battle of Normandy. He wished in the beginning to shoot the film in France to get as close as possible to the historic reality. However, France required a 52% tax to shoot locally and the film's budget did not allow it. The director then chose Ireland which offered him more facilities. If the film had been shot in France, the budget would have passed from 65 to 95 million dollars. The first scenes were turned in some studios in London in January 1996.

Nevertheless, Spielberg wished that a part of the long footage be realized on Omaha-Beach. He contacted therefore the ABMC to obtain permission to film some scenes in the cemetery of Colleville-sur-Mer. An agreement was signed on 5th September 1997 between the ABMC and the production company which gave the necessary authorizations for the shooting in the cemetery of Colleville-sur-Mer and provided the necessary assistance around the production. The ABMC reserved a right to view the filmed elements and accepted to support the shooting on the basis of the script supplied by Ian Brice on 19th December 1996.

The production company requested the supply of several dummy graves on the site. Initially, the Meuse-Argonne cemetery was asked to supply three engraved crosses in Lasa marble. Once ready, they were to be forwarded to the Suresnes cemetery and finally retrieved by the Colleville-sur-Mer cemetery. At the beginning of September, not three but four marble crosses were ordered, one of which being a Star of David. Finally, because events were moving on, the company decided to use several crosses, not in marble but resin. On 11th September 1997, a part of the production team brought the necessary material to the Colleville-sur-Mer cemetery for the shooting. Five dummy crosses were quickly installed but in the opposite direction to all the others in the cemetery to prevent the reading of the actual names of the soldiers buried there. These crosses were arranged between grave plots D and F, Spielberg having remarked some time before the presence of an actual Miller in this spot.

The shooting started on the morning of 12th September 1997. Naturally, this event completely upset the daily operation of the American cemetery: the employees not only had to raise the French and American large ceremonial flags to the flag poles but also channel the public who came in large numbers to assist in the shooting. Spielberg's team was made up of about a hundred persons of whom some twenty extras were recruited among American residents in Normandy. Tom Hanks was present and even though he did not participate in the shooting, he took the opportunity to discover the site and the famous Omaha-Beach.

The date of the shooting had not been chosen at random. That same month, the last film of Steven Spielberg *The Lost World: Jurassic park* was presented at the Deauville American Film Festival, the director thus making of his journey in Normandy "two birds with one stone".

One of the dummy crosses was that of a certain John H. Miller who had never existed. He was supposed to have been a Captain in the 2nd Rangers Battalion during the Second World War who joined the Armed Forces in Pennsylvania and who died on 13th June 1944 in Normandy. At the start of the film, Harrison Young, the actor who was playing the role of the old Private Ryan, collected his thoughts and cried on the tomb of his friend. This scene was filmed in front of this dummy cross and nobody acted in front of a real grave.

Spielberg was inspired by many men to create this fictional character of Captain Miller. Many similarities can be found with Major Thomas D. Howie (mentioned before for the monument dedicated to him at Saint-Lô, in memory of his actions for the liberation of the town). Spielberg was inspired above all by his human qualities to create from scratch the character of his hero. Other similarities can also be found with Lieutenant John Spalding of the 16th Infantry Regiment, 1st Infantry Division who landed on Omaha-Beach on 6th June. Many replies given by Tom Hanks were relatively identical to certain passages of his account. Thus, for all of those still asking today for the location of the famous Captain Miller's grave – and they are many – they have the possibility to meditate at Major Howie's grave killed on 17th July 1944 or read the testimony of John Spalding.

A year after the filming, Spielberg and Hanks returned to the cemetery: *Saving Private Ryan* was going to be presented in the opening of the Deauville American Film Festival. The film has had subsequently a considerable impact on the popularity of the Normandy American cemetery. In fact, this movie was without doubt the most brutal and realistic war film ever made. The power and realism of the scenes were such that the office of the American Secretary of Defense even opened a special telephone contact line in order to psychologically support any shocked people.

Steven Spielberg during the shooting of his film *Saving Private Ryan* in the cemetery of Colleville-sur-Mer on 12th September 1997. *Ouest France.*

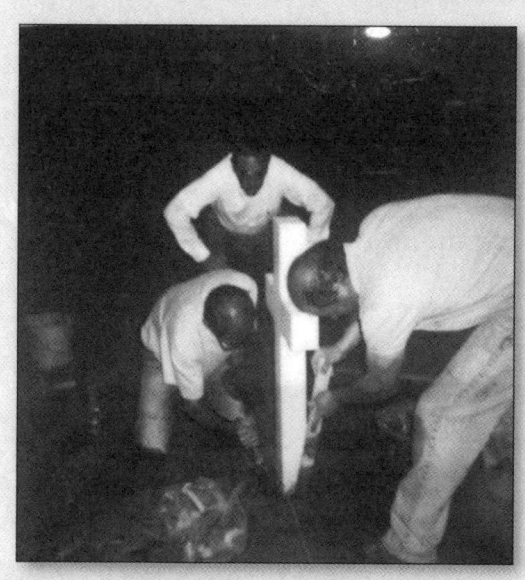

The installation of dummy crosses undertaken in the middle of the night for the film's shooting. *Photo ABMC.*

One of the dummy crosses utilized for the shooting of Spielberg's film. *Photo C. Lebastard.*

Major Howie was one of the principal figures in the battle for Saint-Lô. Unfortunately, he lost his life only one day before the town was liberated. At the request of General Gerhardt, his body was placed on the hood of a lead jeep so that he was, symbolically, the first American to enter the town.
Photo ABMC.

THOMAS D. HOWIE
MAJ 116 INF 29 DIV
VIRGINIA JULY 17 1944

The grave of Major Thomas D. Howie is found in Plot G, Row 14, Grave 12.
Photo C. Lebastard.

THE CONSTRUCTION OF THE NEW VISITOR CENTER

A congressional project

Since the construction of the cemetery, only a small Visitor Center had been built to welcome Next-of-Kin and to allow those who desired to seek information about the site. This building rapidly became too small to respond to the public demand. Superintendent Daniel L. Neese recalled that the cemetery employees were assaulted by questions and that it was necessary to correct this situation.

In June 2001, two members of the House of Representatives, David Obey and John Murtha, proposed to Congress to include in the budget of the United-States the financing of the construction of a new Welcome and Exhibition Center in the cemetery of Colleville-sur-Mer. The ABMC worked in close cooperation with the local authorities in order to ensure that the project was perfectly integrated into the Norman infrastructure renovation plan designed by the French Government. The project had three main objectives: the first one was to design an effective educational center complementing the cemetery with dignity. The second objective was to develop concepts allowing visitors to have a better appreciation of the importance of the 1944 operations in Normandy and the important sacrifices made for victory. The third and last goal was to improve the knowledge of the public regarding the ABMC services and objectives.

Tourism had long been based on past memories following traditional pilgrimage logic. The construction of a Visitor Center as imagined by the ABMC follows a very recent logic: interpret the past and teach the conflicts using new technologies. With the construction of this new Center, the commission decided to follow a more updated logic creating a parallel between the past and current society. This type of project is innovative in France. The interest of such a visit is obvious: give a best welcome to the visitors who benefit from an independent visit and without charge.

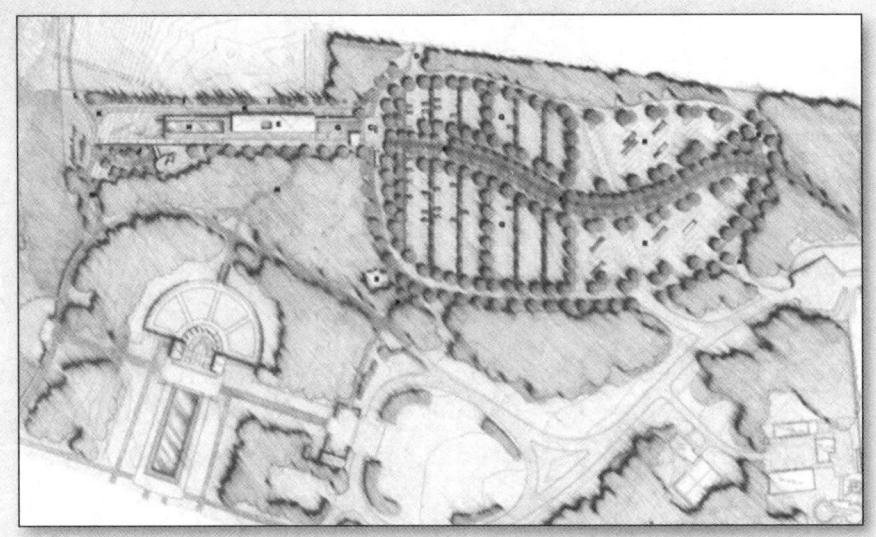

Plan of the Center and of the vehicle park conceived by *SmithGroup*.
Photo ABMC.

The inaugural ceremony of the Visitor Center on 6th June 2007. *Ouest France.*

In December 2002, the ABMC chose the architectural firm of *SmithGroup* based in Washington D.C. to conceive this new center at Colleville-sur-Mer. The *SmithGroup* firm was selected for its world fame in architecture and technology. Other companies were also contacted like *Gallagher & Associates* for the exhibition area and *Jacobs* for the technological services. The project financed by the American Government had to be completed by the middle of 2007 and it was planned that it would cost thirty million dollars.

The final plans were submitted by a young French-American architect: Nicolas Kelemen of SmithGroup. The Fine Arts Commission in Washington D.C. received the project presentation in mid-November 2004 and agreed to the general architectural plans. The documents were also submitted to local French officials. The ABMC then hoped to start work in February 2005.

The emplacement chosen for its construction was still very woody. Situated around 110 yards east of the memorial, the site offered the advantage of a sea view, a view of the cliffs and of the 1st Infantry Division monument. Furthermore, it was one of the last areas whose topography permitted the construction of a building and a large vehicle park landscaped for 480 vehicles.

The first stone of the center was posed on 28th August 2005 and work started in the following month. The building opened its doors less than two years after the start of the operations on 26th May 2007. The official inauguration occurred on 6th June 2007, on the occasion of the sixty-third anniversary of the landing. It was an exceptional event for the ABMC: since the establishment of the Second World War cemeteries, it had never designed such an important project. The inauguration attracted more than three thousand people and numerous officials including Robert M. Gates, American Secretary of Defense, Hervé Morin, French Minister of Defense, Craig R. Stapleton, United-States Ambassador in France and General Frederick M. Francks Jr., Chairman of the ABMC.

The architecture and the symbols

The center was constructed by Norman artisans using materials of high quality. The architect selected forms, materials and vegetation evoking the battles in Normandy which can be observed in the exterior thanks to large bay windows: the west side recalls the Caen plain where British and Canadian forces have fought. The east side evokes, by the presence of a hedge which borders the land, the Norman hedgerows and the battle of the hedgerows. An opening towards the sky, in the interior of the center, symbolizes the participation of the parachutists. The northern façade opens onto a pool prolonging the Channel Sea and re-calling also the landing of the troops onto the beach.

The architect also wished the visitors to identify symbols of the battle of Normandy through the materials chosen: the walls were composed of polished irregular concrete slabs inspired by mortar walls found throughout Normandy. Rather than using the region's limestone, the walls were constructed in grey irregular granite: their irregularity symbolizing the horror of war and the displaced earth caused by shooting and bombardments. The floor was covered in white granite coming from southern India sprinkled with rusted spots evoking the blood spilled by the soldiers in Normandy. In the interior, the wooden wall behind the information desk was added to recall the waves on the surface of the Channel.

Despite all these symbolic material elements, the ground floor was designed as an empty and open space destined to welcome the visitors and to show them the few necessary elements to be able to understand the exhibition mainly situated in the basement. Three panels were installed on the ground floor to introduce the three principal themes developed in the exhibition gallery: Competence, Courage and Sacrifice. Four touchscreen computers enabling visitors to search for the grave locations of the buried soldiers and maps outlining the work of the ABMC and its different functions completed the fitting of this first floor.

Of the 29 000 square feet within the building, only one third of the surface area was dedicated to the exhibition. The latter was willingly situated in the basement so as not to dominate the cemetery which had to remain of paramount importance to the visitor. The exhibition was imagined for a large public: for visitors having some overall knowledge of the conflict and to those closely aware of the Normandy liberation. However, it was also clearly designed for new generations discovering sometimes for the first time the 1944 Normandy operations.

Access to the exhibition is made by a stairway (and an elevator) which brings the visitors opposite the auditorium with a seating capacity of around 150 places. The film projected is called *Letters* and evokes the story of five soldiers killed during the battle of Normandy and buried in Colleville-sur-Mer. This scenario is around fifteen minutes, realized by Max Lewkowicz and it prepares the visitor for the remainder of the visit.

The first part of the gallery was oriented around the "Competence" necessary to undertake an invasion of Europe. Two films are offered (including one on the east wall of the building) as well as audio stories. The rigidity of the architecture in this first part recalls the rigor necessary in the planning and in the preparation of Operation Overlord.

The gallery of "Courage" is introduced by a short film telling of the difficulties for the Chiefs of Staff to establish such an invasion. The structures were arranged in an oblique way making reference to the variations and to the vagaries. This part finishes also by a short film projected by three video projectors which show the success and the advance of the troops in Normandy.

The ground floor of the Visitor Center is very luminous thanks to the numerous bay windows. *Photo C. Lebastard.*

Entrance to the Visitor Center. *Photo C. Lebastard.*

The signs "Competence", "Courage" and "Sacrifice" introduce the exhibition. *Photo C. Lebastard.*

View of the reflecting pool prolonging the English Channel. *Photo C. Lebastard.*

The theater with seating for 150 people in which the principal film of the exhibition is shown. *Photo C. Lebastard.*

"Competence", the first section of the exhibition. *Photo C. Lebastard.*

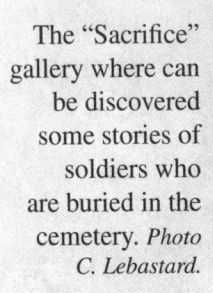

The "Sacrifice" gallery where can be discovered some stories of soldiers who are buried in the cemetery. *Photo C. Lebastard.*

A transition was designed to get into the last and no doubt most important part of the exhibition. The visitor crosses a corridor where a sound recording sets out the names of the soldiers and the civilians buried in the cemetery. He then enters an alcove recalling the memorial and the chapel. This room is in total contrast to the rest of the exhibition: there emerges a feeling of calm reinforced by the soundproofing created by the white plaster. The white floor in limestone and the translucent glass walls give a ghostly appearance to the room. In the center, a rusty colored cube refers to the vacuum caused by death symbolized by a helmet mounted on a rifle planted in the pebbles recalling also the temporary graves. Twenty soldiers' portraits were installed in this room enabling the establishment of a direct link with the cemetery towards which the visitor can make his way.

THE SPECIAL CASE OF POINTE-DU-HOC

The protection of Pointe-du-Hoc

It may seem strange to be interested in the case of the Pointe-du-Hoc in a study on the Colleville-sur-Mer cemetery. However, the relationships between the two places are important and the American cemetery plays a primary role regarding the management of the site.

This battlefield, located more to the west of Omaha-Beach and eight miles from the American cemetery was one of the fundamental objectives of the D-Day landing. After the end of the fighting, it was forbidden for the French to penetrate the perimeter of Pointe-du-Hoc. Despite the fact that German prisoners had cleared and demined the land, the site remained closed and waste until 1955.

On 30th June 1955, a study meeting took place under the leadership of the Grandcamp-les Bains tourist information office to rehabilitate the access road on the site and to create a vehicle park.

This new roadway was inaugurated on 15th July in the presence of French dignitaries. This rehabilitation was a first step to allow and encourage veterans, families and visitors to come to visit this battlefield.

Having to take into account the important tourist traffic to this site, officials decided on the creation of a Pointe-du-Hoc committee on 26th June 1956. This association gave itself as the objective to conserve, develop and maintain the site. It saw itself also entrusted with the task of erecting a monument in remembrance of the soldiers killed during the battle and the task of constructing the vehicle park. In parallel, the committee started to clear and to level many of the craters on the Pointe du Hoc. On 21st August 1960, the Pointe du Hoc committee erected the monument - still visible today - in memory of the 2nd Ranger Battalion on the renovated observation post. It was sculpted in a form of a Ranger dagger cut into grey granite accompanied by two tablets: one inscribed in English and the other in French.

The *Conservatoire National du littoral* gradually bought the Pointe du Hoc land and its twenty nine acres. On 13th January 1978, a first bill of sale was signed between the municipality of Cricqueville-en-Bessin and the Conservatory for a parcel of around four acres. A second bill of sale was signed on 9th June 1978 with five owners to obtain the last five plots of land representing a total of twenty five acres. This last purchase cost the Conservatory 10 000 francs for every two acres. The use of the land was given to the American Government and more particularly to the ABMC a little time after by collective agreement, on 11th January 1979. General Bradley came for a ceremony formalizing the transfer of power from the French to the Americans. However, the site remained French as the French Government only entrusted the responsibility and not the administration of Pointe-du-Hoc to the ABMC. The administration was organized around the Pointe-du-Hoc

The observation post at Pointe-du-Hoc surmounted by the monument in memory of the men of Lieutenant-Colonel Rudder. *Photo C. Lebastard.*

The signing of the Memorandum of Understanding between the ABMC and the Prefect of Calvados concerning the development of Pointe-du-Hoc on 6th June 2001. *Ouest France.*

committee of which the American cemetery Superintendent became one of its members.

The improvements realized on the site by the ABMC were numerous. During one of the Pointe-du-Hoc committee meetings, the Superintendent of the Colleville-sur-Mer cemetery advised for the installation of a 155 mm gun of the same type of those which had been in place on site in 1944. Signage panels were also installed to replace those stolen in 1992. Other disappearances also took place since and notably a small sign in sheet metal and a black cross which the committee had installed in remembrance of the German victims killed during the American assault on the Pointe du Hoc on 6th June 1944.

Pointe-du-Hoc: an important place for Americans

The importance of the Pointe-du-Hoc for the Americans and for the ABMC can be explained by 81 Rangers killed in assaulting this cliff: thirty of them were buried in Colleville-sur-Mer and nine names were engraved on the Wall of the Missing.

This importance was confirmed by the major ceremonies organized at the Pointe-du-Hoc in collaboration with the ABMC and the American cemetery of Colleville-sur-Mer: that of the twenty-seventh anniversary of the landing in 1971 or that of the thirty-fifth anniversary in 1979 for example. The ABMC was frequently responsible for organizing commemorations and undertaking the necessary procedures to obtain honor guards. These ceremonies were and are still generally held near the monument dedicated to the Rangers.

With the visit of President Regan in 1984, important efforts were undertaken in the management of the site: a roadway, a vehicle park, toilets, a telephone cabin as well as paths and a walkway enabling easier access to the bunkers and to the guns were constructed.

Three years later, the Pointe-du-Hoc committee and American officials met to study a significant museum project on the edge of the cliff to inform the important number of visitors coming to the site. However, the American administration always refused the idea. The former Mayor of Grandcamp Jean-Marc Lefranc, decided to travel to Washington D.C. in October 1989 to meet the officials and to convince them. He obtained authorization to open a museum but outside of the site. Thus, forty-six years after the D-Day landing, the museum in tribute to Colonel Rudder and his men was constructed not at Pointe-du-Hoc, but at Grandcamp. This museum was officially inaugurated on 6th June 1990.

Over time, the site welcomed more and more visitors. On the morning of 6th June 2001, a Memorandum of Understanding was signed between the Prefect of Calvados and William J. Leszczynsky of the ABMC with the aim of totally refurbishing the site which, according to *Ouest-France*, welcomed more than one million visitors per year. A budget of thirteen million dollars was provided for this project to allow the construction of a welcome and commemoration center parallel to the large driveway and the construction of a new vehicle park. Besides these new constructions, the twenty four defensive remnants had to be enhanced and secured. The work was undertaken by the ABMC in collaboration with the American cemetery of Colleville-sur-Mer and had to be completed for the sixtieth anniversary of the landing. Everything was organized around the operation "Great Sites Normandy 44". On 27th May 2004, the President of the Calvados General Council Anne d'Ornano, handed over the keys of the structure to the new managers of the building and of the site: the ABMC.

Recent works on the Pointe-du-Hoc site

Thanks to funds received by the municipality of Cricqueville-en-Bessin, by the United-States and by the French Government, the *Conservatoire National du littoral* and the Pointe-du-Hoc committee try annually to best meet the needs of hundreds of thousands of visitors.

One problem occurred in 2002: the old observation bunker on which had been erected the monument dedicated to the Rangers was closed to the public because of danger represented by the cliff erosion. Since 1944, the site has been submitted to the repeated assaults of the sea which has pushed back the cliff by more than thirty two feet. In 2002, the German bunker found itself no more than nine foot from the void. Enormous blocks of rock were coming away, risking the cliff to crumble and to be the cause possibly of deadly accidents: the site had become very dangerous. Already in 1974, a tourist had been victim of a fall off the 100-foot cliff onto the pebbles on the beach when he was alone on the cliff side. This fall caused him serious injuries.

By mutual agreement, the ABMC and the Pointe-du-Hoc committee decided from that moment on to give maximum attention to safety on site and envisaged substantial refurbishments. The American Government unblocked an envelope of six million dollars and entrusted to the ABMC the task of finding a solution. The titanic project retained by the ABMC started in February 2010: it consisted of entirely reinforcing the cliff and ensuring that the location regained the appearance it had in 1944. The works were completed in the space of one year and the observation post was officially reopened during a ceremony on 6th June 2011.

In parallel with the work improvements on the cliff, the ABMC initiated an enlargement project of the existing infrastructures:

a reorganization of the Pointe-du-Hoc small Visitor Center and also the installation of large informative signs, the length of the visit route. The first plans had been realized in January 2008 by *Gallagher & Associates*, the company elected for the design of the Colleville-sur-Mer Visitor Center. This new Welcome Center offers, besides information on the site, a short film of a few minutes duration. New projects undertaken or supported by the ABMC are still ongoing: the Pointe-du-Hoc smartphone application to give visitors' onsite information and the registration of the site to the UNESCO World Heritage Sites list.

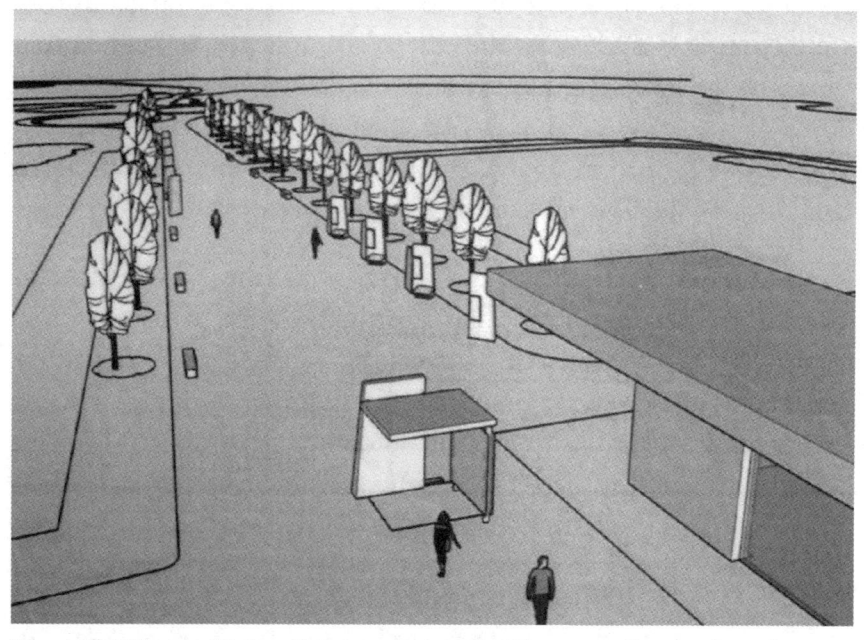

The ABMC's new Visitor Center at Pointe-du-Hoc according to plans drawn by Gallagher & Associates in 2008. *Photo ABMC.*

The Work of the Normandy American Cemetery

THE MANAGEMENT AND THE MAINTENANCE OF THE SITE

The administration

Since 1946, the governance of the commission was composed of eleven members nominated by the President of the United-States for an indeterminate time service and serving voluntarily. Today, these members lead a team of 400 full-time civilian employees. Only 75 among them are Americans. The remainder of the employees of the commission is composed of people of the countries in which the cemeteries are found. Each site has always been directed by a Superintendent supported by an assistant (except for small cemeteries such as that of Draguignan). All the Superintendents were specially selected for their administrative capacities, their knowledge of horticulture, of equipment maintenance, of vehicles, their knowledge of construction and their tact in respect of the public. All were by necessity American. The commission had constructed for their use staff housing to improve their expatriates living conditions.

No doubt that one of the greatest rewards for an ABMC employee is to be selected to manage the Colleville-sur-Mer cemetery. Its location, its exceptional number of visitors and its international renown has made the position of Superintendent a coveted appointment. Since its creation after the end of the Second World War, the cemetery has always been managed by a Superintendent: the first was Major Collman, a regular officer in the American Army who remained in place after the handover between the AGRC and the ABMC in 1949. Initially, the ABMC retained the Superintendents nominated and endorsed by the Graves Registration Service. Major Collman was subsequently replaced by Mr. Brasher and then successive Superintendents until more recently Messrs. Grove, Rivers in 1982, Dillinger in 1999, Neese in 2005, Hooker in 2010 and finally once again Mr. Neese in 2013.

The Superintendent of the Normandy American Cemetery is assisted in his task by a director of operations and since the erection of the new Visitor Center, by a director of the visitor services and his deputy. The Superintendent of Colleville-sur-Mer reports to the commission's office situated today in Garches near Paris. This Parisian office is the only step between the Superintendents and the commission's headquarters situated in the United-States in Arlington, Virginia[52].

The work teams

Since its inauguration, the cemetery has always been composed of French employees. Even before the handover to the ABMC on site, it was constantly under the responsibility of French guards to avoid intrusions. Jean Levillain, aged nineteen at the time, was one of them. He was responsible for looking after the graves during the night. His testimony would have been valuable but unfortunately, he committed suicide in the cemetery in November 1948.

Progressively, the number of employees considerably increased; the growing number of visitors making necessary an increasing workforce. The majority of the employees were taken on to help maintain the site but specifically the gardeners, whose remarkable daily work was and still is to maintain the lawns and the abundant vegetation. In the 1980's the cemetery was made up of some twenty employees of whom the majority were gardeners. In 1993, the team included twenty three employees including the gardener at Pointe-du-Hoc and the one at Utah-Beach.

---

[52] The Superintendents of the cemeteries of Mexico, Corozal and Manila report directly to the ABMC headquarters in Arlington, Virginia.

The major workforce evolution took place with the construction of the Visitor Center in 2007. *"Everything is different since the creation of the Center"* emphasized Sylvie Jean, Cemetery Associate at the cemetery. The expectations of visitors became so important that the ABMC decided to employ guides to inform the public. At the same time, a security team was added to protect the site. In five years, said Daniel L. Neese, the Normandy American Cemetery has gone from twenty-three to sixty employees.

Once or twice a year, part of the employee workforce gather together to decorate each grave with two small flags (one American and one French) on the occasion of Memorial Day ceremonies and for the main 6th June ceremonies. These flags were paid for by the AOMDA in the First World War cemeteries but in the others, like that of Colleville-sur-Mer, these flags were provided by the ABMC. Nearly 19 000 flags are planted on these occasions in the Colleville-sur-Mer necropolis by the gardeners helped today by several guides.

Besides the ceremonies that we have mentioned and for which today the guides have that responsibility, they also undertake daily free visits to answer visitors' questions. They have an important diplomatic role in welcoming each year numerous personalities, principally from the world of politics. The guided visits of the cemetery for the personalities may also include a visit to Pointe-du-Hoc, Omaha-Beach and sometimes to Utah-Beach.

Outside of these activities, the staff and principally the guides, research the stories of the buried soldiers in order to enable the visiting families to have better information on the story of their loved one(s). This work has led them sometimes to observe anomalies and enabled them to correct certain errors of the past. In 1999, for example, a clerical error was noticed for one of the buried soldiers in the cemetery. On his cross, was indicated that he fought in the 299th Engineer Combat Battalion when he was really part of the 229th Engineer Combat Battalion. Generally, when an error of this nature is found, the cross or the Star of David is replaced, as was the case on 20th May 2009 for the grave of Coxswain Amir Isbir whose date of death was incorrect. This procedure often takes considerable time: it is essential to confirm with certainty the error and then to send a request for a new marker. Many graves are changed every year but not necessarily because of errors: certain are replaced by the cemetery masons when damaged. Marble is a magnificent stone but nevertheless fragile.

The guides try also to link the different stories of fallen soldiers and sometimes have found family ties which were not evident before. Thus on 18th December 2009, one of the cemetery guides found trace of two brothers buried in the cemetery at Colleville-sur-Mer. Many reasons accounted for this discovery. The first brother was engraved on the Wall of the Missing whilst the second was buried in the cemetery. The family never had knowledge of the inscription of one of their sons on the Wall of the Missing. This research enabled the discovery of the family links between Radioman's Mate Second Class Ludwig J. W. Pieper and Radioman's Mate Second Class Julius H. O. Pieper. These two men, as well as being brothers were twins. Born in Esmond, South Dakota on 17th May 1925, they were both killed in the Atlantic on 19th June 1944 during operations in Normandy. The twins were cited for bravery and they received the Victory Medal. Julius' body was never recovered and Ludwig was initially buried in a field near Cherbourg before being buried in the Colleville-sur-Mer cemetery in Plot E, Row 15, Grave 39.

The budget of the ABMC and of the cemetery

For young nations such as the United-States, Canada, Australia or New Zealand, the two World Wars form an important part of their history. This historical backcloth enables a better understanding of their efforts, notably financial, which they have made to preserve the graves and the life stories of their citizens.

The ABMC obtains the funds necessary for the maintenance of the cemeteries and the monuments thanks to American taxes. Each year, it submits a budget to the Office of the President of the United-States and to Congress in order to be approved. The commission also receives the help of other organizations both public and private. The financial needs are obviously significant in order to maintain 130 000 graves and auxiliary structures on more than 1 600 acres. Furthermore, the 11 000 trees and the 3 000 000 square feet of plantation established in the different cemeteries also require considerable financial and technical means.

Before the establishment of the Second World War cemeteries, the budget allocated annually for the maintenance of the First World War sites was on average 140 000 dollars. During the Second World War, the funds attributed were derisory: only 51 000 dollars annually which was barely sufficient to maintain the cemeteries. The finances after the war were fortunately much more important: in 1947 for example, 207 000 dollars were attributed to the commission. However, it required several years to entirely compensate the lack of financing which the cemeteries had experienced.

With the establishment of the Second World War cemeteries, the commission received much more significant sums to maintain the twenty four sites[53]. Furthermore in 2004, 32.3 million dollars were attributed to the commission as well as an envelope of 9 million dollars destined to cover the construction charges for the Visitor Center at Colleville-sur-Mer. In 2005 and 2006, the commission received more than 55 million dollars for each financial year to compensate its expenses. In 2007, the funds available were 38.8 million dollars and in 2008 39.6 millions.

---

[53] Of course, we should not compare the dollar of the Second World War with the dollar of today. The values are not the same. Furthermore, new subsidies will no doubt be attributed to maintain the Clark Veterans Cemetery.

These last two budgets are without doubt the most significant concerning the resources available to the ABMC. The budgets of previous years were truncated by the construction of the Visitor Center.

More than sixty per cent of the finances, each year, are utilized to pay the commission's employees. The remainder is dedicated for the maintenance of the cemeteries and of the memorials but also for different work projects. The ABMC European office at Garches decides the funds to grant to the Normandy American Cemetery. Each year and depending on the projects undertaken, a precise budget is given to the cemetery which the Superintendent and his team are asked to respect. This budget remains unknown to us. Nevertheless, in view of the work undertaken on the site over recent years, we can easily estimate that the funds accorded vary between three and five million dollars per annum.

The money invested annually by the American Government in the cemetery of Colleville-sur-Mer galvanizes the regional economy: the cemetery contributes to local development even if it is exempt of taxation. This establishment employs some sixty people and uses French companies for the maintenance of installations or for the housekeeping of the Visitor Center.

THE DUTIES TOWARDS THE FAMILIES AND THE VETERANS

Frequent visits

All the military cemeteries either American or of other nationalities were prepared to welcome the bereaved families with as much dignity as possible. The Normandy American Cemetery was primarily created to give decent burials to the American soldiers in remembrance of their actions. Beyond its first objective it seemed obvious that the Colleville-sur-Mer cemetery would become a pilgrimage site for the families. The American Army and the ABMC had never lost sight of the considerable suffering of the families and the importance that the cemeteries would hold for them.

After the First World War, the United-States organized pilgrimages thanks to grants for the mothers or the widows whose relatives were buried in a permanent cemetery abroad. These trips were arranged by the Quartermaster Corps between 1930 and 1933, even if numerous private pilgrimages had already begun from the end of the war. The initiative was received with much enthusiasm by the Americans: 6 674 relatives were supported thanks to this program in the different permanent American cemeteries of the First World War abroad.

However, the initiative was not renewed after the events of the Second World War in spite of a declaration by the ABMC initiated by General Marshall, in favor of a sponsorship from the Government. Year after year, organized pilgrimage proposals were filed but never voted. Each family only received the necessary information for an eventual self-pilgrimage to the grave of their loved one(s), indicating the precise location of his or their burials. From the end of the war, the first families travelled to the temporary cemeteries and then to the American cemetery of Colleville-sur-Mer. After the inauguration of 1956, the work of the cemetery employees was orientated around the reception of the families who came in their hundreds to pay their respects each year.

With the passage of time, naturally fewer and fewer families came to visit the graves. A renewed interest by the families intervened after the release of Steven Spielberg's film. The employees noted a significant increase of some 35% in the number of families welcomed. It was no longer just wives or children but also grand-children or nephews who might have forgotten the events of the 6th June if they had not watched the film.

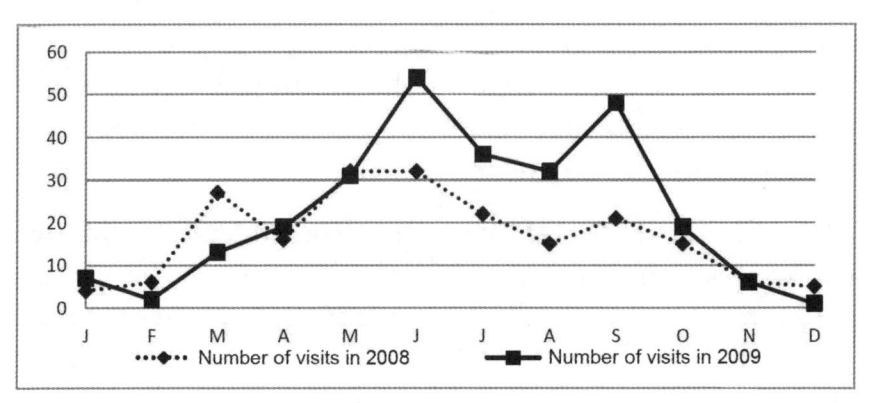

Family visits in 2008 and 2009.

Over time, the number of veterans welcomed by the team at the cemetery of Colleville-sur-Mer has considerably diminished as the employees have noted with regret.

As a consequence, the fathers and mothers of the soldiers have today passed away as have many of the wives. The American cemetery thus welcomes today a majority of distant relatives. Each year, the cemetery receives the visit of around two hundred families of which approximately 80% are distant relatives: nephews, great nephews, cousins or distant cousins. We can note thanks to the previous graph, the difference between say a "normal" year (2008) and a year with a major ceremony (2009) during which the families are more inclined to get about. In 2008, 201 families were welcomed, principally between March and September. In 2009, 299 visits were identified, 54 of which occurred in June. Naturally, we can draw the parallel between this increase and the sixty-fifth anniversary of the landing. The peak is September can be explained by the numerous holiday tours organized at the end of the high season.

The ABMC services

In 1956, Congressman George W. Andrews expressed a wish which was offered to each bereaved family a colored photograph of the relevant cemetery accompanied by a black and white photograph of the grave(s) of their relative(s) or of the name(s) engraved on the Wall of the Missing. Senator Lister Hill supported this idea, as well as the ABMC which was entirely in favor of this project. Unfortunately, the finances did not follow: the commission had to find around 50 000 dollars in additional funds to accomplish the project.

Finally, this idea named Andrews Project was taken up and approved sometime after but solely in the cemeteries and memorials of the Second World War[54]. The ABMC obtained the support of the U.S. Air Force cooperating to achieve the aerial photographs of the cemeteries. The office in Garches received instructions to photograph each grave in black and white with the exception of the unknowns. More than 30 000 photographs were thereby sent to the families. The ABMC received very favorable feedback as witnessed by the hundreds of letters from the families expressing their feeling of reassurance on the general state of the graves.

The commission still proposes to families today (at their expense) the offer to place flowers on the grave of their loved one(s) when they wish it. These flowers are bought locally by the Superintendents with funds provided by the family. When the flowers are placed at the foot of the grave, sand coming from Omaha-Beach is rubbed into the engraving so that the inscription stands out on the color photograph which will be sent to the family. The most flowered grave in the Normandy American Cemetery is that of First-Lieutenant Billie D. Harris. This P-51 Mustang pilot crashed on 17th July 1944 in the small township of Les Ventes in

---

[54] It was refused to do the same for the First World War cemeteries under the pretext that the wives had received the right of a sponsored pilgrimage and that in addition to this, their number had so diminished that it would not justify the photograph expenditure.

the Eure department. His grave is decorated several times during the year on behalf of his widow.

Families can also request that the ABMC provides a letter of authorization in order for them to obtain passports free of charge, so that close relatives may travel to the grave of their loved one. In view of the numerous requests received by the ABMC from Next-of-Kin wishing to know the grave location of their loved one(s), the commission realized a full listing of the Second World War and of the Korean War graves abroad. The list was composed of three volumes and identified more than 200 000 soldiers. It has today been replaced by a database which can be consulted on the commission's website: www.abmc.gov.

The families have always received the best of welcomes. Since the creation of the new Visitor Center and the employment of guides, families are invited to gather in the building to obtain more information on their relative(s). One of the prerogatives of the guides is to assist families by bringing to them all relevant information they have at their disposal. In welcoming them to the cemetery, they ask them to sign a guest book specially reserved for families, veterans and personalities. The importance granted to families by the ABMC can be found in a room which has been dedicated to them in the new center: the Next-of-Kin room.

When a family obtains from an employee confirmation that their relative(s) is buried in the cemetery, they are offered to be accompanied to the grave(s) and are taken by means of an electric car. Before that, they receive a folder containing all the essential information on the commission and on the different cemeteries which they manage, as well as all necessary forms to enable the graves to be flowered. Once at the foot of the grave, the employee rubs wet sand from Omaha-Beach into the grave's inscription to make the words stand out and also to mark the passage of the family. He also plants two flags in front of the grave marker: a French flag on the landward side and an American flag on the seaside. These flags are similar to the ones placed during the Memorial Day ceremonies and the major 6th June ceremonies and are then offered to the family as a personal keepsake.

Billie D. Harris and his wife. *Photo ABMC.*

The perception of the site by veterans and families

The presence of veterans and of families in the cemetery is always an emotional experience. Unfortunately, as the years pass, less and less are able to travel: in 2004, during the inauguration of the Washington Memorial, the American Government estimated that only 4 million American veterans of the Second World War remained alive out of the 16 million who served under the flag. Similarly, it was estimated that around 1 000 veterans died each day in the United-States.

The veterans and the families represent today only a small proportion of the visitors. They are counted in their low hundreds each year. The distance is obviously a major obstacle in their coming, as is their health. However, the motivation and the idea of making one final visit encourage many of them to make the journey. That explained, for example, the 9 115 chest insignia given to the veterans of all nationalities that travelled for the sixtieth anniversary.

But these explanations are not sufficient to understand their presence once more today in Normandy. In fact, in the United-States, veterans feel forgotten. Colleville-sur-Mer is a location where their acts are highlighted "to never forget". They do not perceive the same feelings in the United-States. In the cemetery, they express the feeling that they are listened to attentively and this is something which they do not find elsewhere. This explains why the cemetery continues to receive from the veterans and their families: donations of poems, veterans' photographs and family photographs. Many send documents which directly concern them: biographies, war testimonies… these documents often enabling employees to complete the stories of the buried soldiers.

A testimony collected in 2007 enables us to understand why certain veterans continue to make the journey. Floyd Ray Odess when asked his feelings of the cemetery replied: "*It is really sad. Perhaps one of these men could have found a cure for cancer. What would have happened if they had not died? We will never know. But we know how to honor their sacrifice today. They did not die for nothing. I am very honored and grateful for the huge appreciation that people have shown when we meet them. They march up to us and say: Thank you!*" For this veteran, the most important aspect is without doubt the recognition: the recognition of the Government, through the commission managing the cemetery; the recognition of the people who have not forgotten but above all the recognition for their deeds so that this does not reoccur: "*They walked on a magnificent site but I hope that they will never see something like that recommence. We must retain the lessons of the past*". The creation of the new Visitor Center is generally warmly welcomed as Floyd underlined: "*I think that it is a great idea. It is the only way to learn the lessons of the past especially for the young generations who have never known war. This can help educate the young.*"[55]

---

[55] Interview with Floyd Ray Odess collected on 5th May 2007 at the Normandy American Cemetery.

THE PROVISION OF INFORMATION TO THE MANY VISITORS

A popular tourism venue

The Normandy American Cemetery is today ranked among the top tourist sites of Normandy, neck and neck with Mont-Saint-Michel which welcomes according to sources between one and three million tourists annually. The American cemetery of Colleville-sur-Mer receives each year more than a million visitors. By comparison, the Caen Memorial welcomes 400 000 visitors per annum just like the Bayeux Tapestry and the Arromanches Museum has welcomed 330 000 tourists in 2009.

According to figures measured just after the fiftieth anniversary of the landing, the cemetery welcomed nearly a million visitors (1.25 million thereafter according to Major Holt). The last figures recorded by the American cemetery reported 1.5 million visitors in 2007, 1.25 million in 2008 and 1.7 million in 2009.

The following graph shows the strong correlation which exist between the visitor peaks and the major ceremonies. Thus in 2004, year of the sixtieth anniversary of the landing, more than 1.8 million visitors made the journey, principally between the months of May and September. It was the same trend in 2009 on the occasion of the sixty-fifth anniversary. Nevertheless, the two million visitors in 2001 are more difficult to explain: was it a resurgence of the phenomenon *Saving Private Ryan*, a consequence of the 9/11 events or only an "unforeseen event"? The question remains.

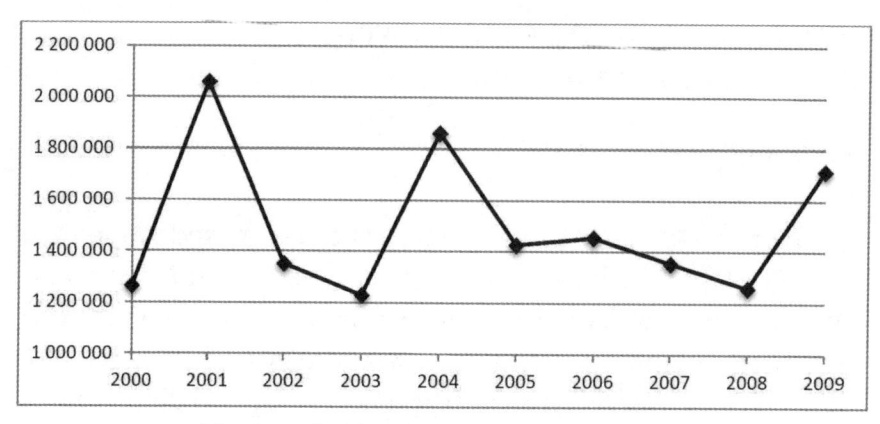

Number of visitors between 2000 and 2009.

The following graph shows that 80% of the visitors travel between the months of March to September. Conversely, during the months of December and January, the cemetery is much less frequented with only 20 to 30 000 visitors each month.

Of all the funeral sites maintained by the ABMC, the Normandy American Cemetery is by far the most visited. It brings to the region significant economic benefits. If these are difficult to quantify, we can nevertheless note the establishment of a hotel-restaurant at the entrance of the roadway leading to the cemetery and the multiplication of bed-and-breakfast establishments in the

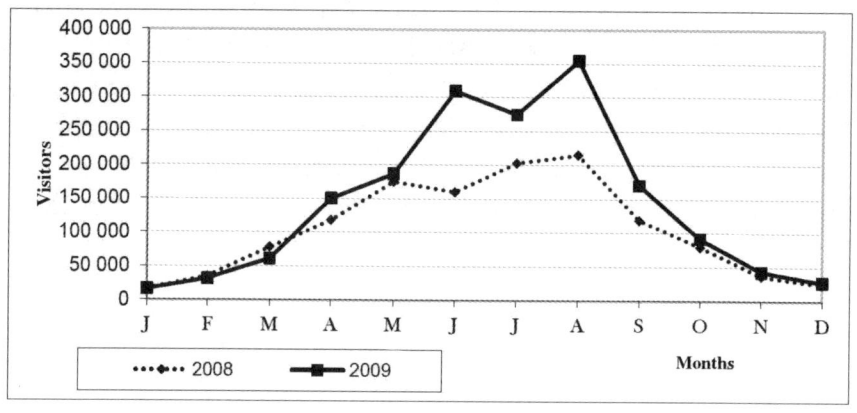

Number of visitors to the cemetery in 2008 and 2009.

surrounding villages. Moreover, visitors travelling to the cemetery of Colleville-sur-Mer, come often from a long way and stay several days in the region. Travelers take advantage to visit other tourist sites such as the Arromanches Museum, the Caen Memorial, Pointe-du-Hoc (which welcomes between 500 000 to 1 million visitors each year)... The impact of the cemetery is such that a new museum named Overlord Museum and directed by Jean-Christophe Lefranc opened in June 2013 on the outskirt of the American cemetery. Even if the American cemetery of Colleville-sur-Mer and the ABMC did not participate in the development of this project, this new museum confirms the importance of the cemetery and the impact that it can have on the local economy.

Numerous points may explain the influx of visitors to the cemetery. The first point is related to its access conditions: entry to the cemetery and to the Visitor Center is free of charge. Few tourist sites in Normandy can claim to offer such free services. The ABMC contents itself with the budget furnished by the American tax payers and from donations to ensure the maintenance of the cemeteries. As a consequence, no product whatsoever is sold on the ABMC sites. The second point is related to its location which plays a significant part by its situation on a plateau overlooking Omaha-Beach, ensuring a unique panorama and arousing significant passion amongst its visitors.

The incomparable publicity carried out, not by the ABMC, but by Hollywood is also one of the explanations. The release of Steven Spielberg's film created indirectly a sort of craze amongst the public in parallel with the fifty-fifth anniversary of the landing. Shortly after the film's release, the French newspaper *Notre-Vie* published an article with an evocative title "*Omaha-Beach, an in vogue pilgrimage*" proof if needed of the renewed interest created by this film. The hotels were fully booked: "*the release of* Saving Private Ryan *has visibly boosted the rush of pilgrims for the fifty-fifth anniversary of D-Day"* noted Ouest-France. All the press converged to the Colleville-sur-Mer cemetery which became the center point for the ceremonies of the fifty-fifth anniversary. The media started then to develop the idea of a "remembrance tourism" of which the cemetery became its heart.

Statistically, the number of visitors in the month of September 1998 increased by 36 000 relative to the same month in the previous year. The middle of autumn is usually a quiet period for Normandy tourism. But that year, the vehicle park was full and the hotels and restaurants of the coast were fully booked. As Phil Rivers, former Superintendent at Normandy American Cemetery noted: *"The cemetery had never known such a craze"*.

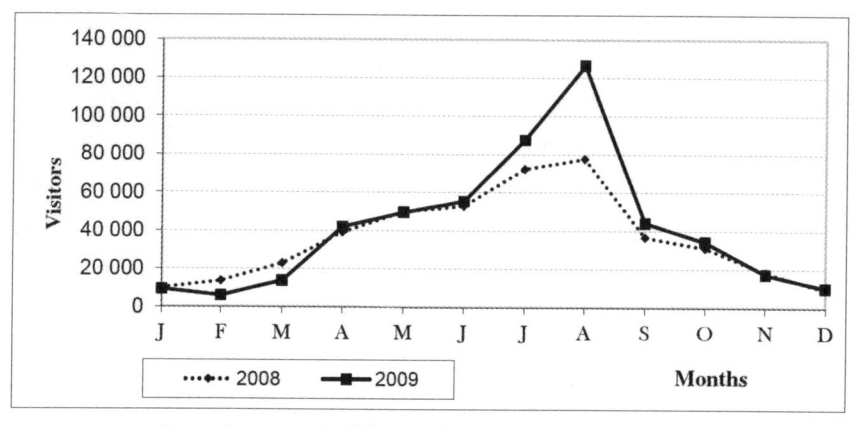

Attendance at the Visitor Center in 2008 and 2009.

The cemetery has become a real symbol of the landing in the American sector. In 2007, the creation of the new Visitor Center accentuated again the tourist phenomenon. Important publicity was relayed by the media during the construction and the inauguration of the center. Since June 2007, the center welcomes 400 000 visitors annually which represents about 30% of the visitors coming to the cemetery every year, a figure equivalent to that of the Caen Memorial.

Public guidelines and behavior

It was essential to write very strict rules of conduct to welcome as many visitors. For many tourists, it is only common sense. Nevertheless, in view of certain small problems encountered, these rules do not seem acquired by all. Animals for example are forbidden (except for guide dogs) to maintain the dignity and the cleanliness of the site. Similarly, any vehicle, whether motor or not is forbidden. Child pushchairs must remain in the walkways in order to avoid damaging the lawns and it is formally forbidden to eat on the site, to sit down or lie down on the grass. Any disrespectful conduct or improper attire leads to immediate expulsion from the site.

These rules did not prevent some problems of vandalism that the cemetery experienced such as the one which occurred on the night of 29th April 1985. An unidentified group penetrated the cemetery and vandalized the Wall of the Missing, the Memorial, the battle maps and the colonnades with painted graffiti. The ABMC attributed the action to the P.L.O. (Palestine Liberation Organization); the United-States having always supported the Israeli policy. Many of the inscriptions were written in French. The authors of this act of vandalism attempted to pass a political message to the United-States as indicated one of their inscriptions *"US go home"*. These degradations were quickly repaired but they had damaged some inscribed names on the Wall of the Missing requiring that they be newly engraved. Further acts of vandalism were experienced in 1991 against the American policy conducted in the Gulf but did not reach the magnitude of the acts of 1985. Fortunately, up until today, nobody has painted or damaged the graves of the soldiers. These acts of non-compliance are not specific to the Colleville-sur-Mer site. Identical acts were conducted against the sixtieth anniversary stelae as for example in Port-en-Bessin, Trévières, Bayeux, Caen, Caumont-L'Éventé or Tour-en-Bessin.

However, we should underline the good behavior of grateful visitors laying flowers for example on soldiers' graves during their visit to the cemetery. Many are doing so privately and others under associations such as French Will Never Forget. It realized, amongst other things, a major operation to decorate the American military graves in France on 4th July 2003. One other association, *Les Fleurs de la Mémoire* (Flowers of Memory) allows graves to be allocated to specific visitors at their request. It was created in 2000 by Frank Towers an American veteran, who was afraid that the graves of his friends would gradually be forgotten. The association consists of volunteers who wish to pay their respects to the fallen American soldiers in Normandy. Each member agrees to come to flower (if possible) once a year one or more graves attributed to them and preferably during Memorial Day. In 2004, the association comprised nearly 2000 members and in October 2013, it had a total of 4002 members flowering 10 282 American graves, 8 966 of which at Colleville-sur-Mer and 2 316 at Saint-James. Among its prerogatives, *Les Fleurs de la Mémoire* attempts to create links with new generations by accompanying school children to flower the soldiers' graves as in the case of the sixtieth anniversary of the landing in 2004 and regularly thereafter.

Sociological Inquiry

In order to have a better understanding of the thousands of individuals visiting the cemetery, we undertook to conduct an inquiry centered on visitors between the months of March and May 2010. This study was realized thanks to a sample of 105 persons sufficient to give us some behavioral tendencies. Certain trends from this study break with the conventional wisdom often accepted.

In accordance with the American cemetery statistics, we noted that the majority of visitors were not American. The French were by far the largest public welcomed and represented more than 50% of the visitors, the American tourists representing nearly 25% of them. *Ouest-France* confirms the importance of the site for the American tourists: *"Americans on holiday make a point of honor to come to Omaha-Beach even if it was not originally scheduled in their program"*. If we compare the visitor figures of 2009 with the ratio of American visitors, more than 400 000 Americans came to visit the cemetery that year.

The other visitors met during this enquiry came mainly from the European Union: Dutch, Italians, Belgians, Spanish, British, Irish, and Polish. The proportion of tourists coming from countries outside of the European Union is not to be neglected: it is not uncommon to meet Israelis, Australians, Canadians or Norwegians… as was the case during the realization of this survey. Some Germans also made the journey but their share still remains proportionally low. Only two of them were interviewed during this enquiry.

Nationality of visitors

	French	Americans	Other nationalities	Total
Number	58	25	22	105
Percentage	55,2	23,8	21,0	100,0

We have already mentioned that the witnesses to the events of 1944 are unfortunately reducing in numbers. This could be observed when we asked for the age of the visitors. The generations who experienced the landing are no longer those continuing to come to the American cemetery: individuals aged 70 years or more met during this inquiry did not represent the majority of visitors. Almost three quarters of them were under 65 years of age and so too young to have known the war.

70% of those interviewed came to the site with family composed of an average of 3 members. Less than 10% came in groups (school groups or tour operators). However, the cemetery team at Colleville-sur-Mer feels that a noticeable increase in the number of school visits has taken place thanks to the free entrance and also the publicity surrounding the cemetery.

Types of visits

	Individual visits	Family visits	Visits with friends	Groups	Total
Number	10	74	11	10	105
Percentage	9,5	70,5	10,5	9,5	100,0

Two thirds of the visitors declared during the inquiry that this was their first visit to the cemetery and that it was also their first journey to Normandy for most of them (70%).

Questioning the visitors to discover how they became aware of the cemetery's existence has always been a sensitive issue as the ABMC has never undertaken advertising campaigns of its sites: knowledge of these sites' existence by visitors has always been by indirect means. A quarter of the sample interviewed was informed of the existence of the Colleville-sur-Mer cemetery thanks to their families, friends or colleagues. Word of mouth therefore has been paramount in the location's reputation. Another quarter mentioned the history that they had learned in school or through books and documentaries: they knew the existence of the cemetery thanks to their education and/or culture.

Tourism also plays an important role: up to 15% of the visitors of this inquiry discovered the popular Normandy tourist spots and the cemetery thanks to explanatory leaflets on the battle of Normandy offered by museums and tourism offices. Some also discovered the Colleville-sur-Mer thanks to tour operators for which the cemetery is nearly a must stop. Contrary to what we might think, very few of them discovered the existence of the cemetery through ceremonies (5%), television (3%) or films (1%). However, it is important to note the comparative importance acquired by Internet (6%) which easily disseminates information. Some visitors referred to the geographic proximity of their home (5%), to the importance of the road signage (4%) or the work of commemorative associations (4%).

More than a half of the sample studied visiting Colleville-sur-Mer was also going on to visit other tourist places of the battle of Normandy during their stay in the region: the visit of the site is nowadays engraved in the landing beaches circuit.

The cemetery of Colleville-sur-Mer appears to be completely different from French cemeteries and is viewed by most of the European visitors as more a memorial than as a cemetery. 62% of the persons interviewed were convinced that all the soldiers were really buried under each cross or Star of David. However, it is interesting to note that 5% of them thought that all the remains were not necessarily buried in the cemetery and 8% had no idea on the question. One quarter of the visitors esteemed that the site is not a true necropolis and that the crosses are just figurative. For them, the cemetery is too well kept for it to be a real place of burial. When those visitors were informed that the Colleville-sur-Mer location was a real cemetery, these visitors did not understand the logic prevailing allowing people to walk directly on the grass and on the soldiers' graves. It should be noted that virtually all of these astonished visitors were French (86%) and are used to seeing a tombstone above the coffin.

During our survey, we also wished to observe whether the *Saving Private Ryan* effect had faded or if the phenomenon endured. Indeed, shortly after the film's release, *Ouest-France* in a June article in 1999 noted: "*The film hit on both sides of the Atlantic and not only among veterans. It motivates new generations to come to Normandy including young people born well after the war; and not all are descendants of veterans".*

This success was confirmed by those questioned of which 82% responded that they had already seen the film at least once in their life: being 4 visitors out of 5! Yet 78% of the visitors having already seen this blockbuster affirmed that *Saving Private Ryan* had absolutely nothing to do with their visit on site. However, 22% of them declared that it was one of the reasons even the main reason for their travel to Colleville-sur-Mer. These results can be interpreted in very different ways. However, the fact that practically one visitor in five travels to the cemetery following the viewing of a film more than fifteen years after its release, confirms the importance that this feature has had and that the phenomenon *Saving Private Ryan* is still ongoing.

Despite the construction of the Visitor Center, visitors sometimes fail to distinguish between fiction and reality. It is not surprising, therefore, to meet tourists who request to see Private Ryan's grave (who however does not die in the film!) or of Captain Miller as the *Washington-Post* noted on 21st October 1998: "*Many people ask to see the grave of John Miller and it is necessary to explain to everyone that he never existed*". Nearly half of the visitors who had seen the film (45%) were convinced of being able to find one of the heroes of the blockbuster in the cemetery. Barely 20% of them were aware of the true story of the Niland family who inspired Steven Spielberg.

It was also interesting to analyze the impact of the major commemorative ceremonies. To do this, we asked the visitors if they had heard of the last major ceremony namely that of 6th June 2009. More than 75% of them were aware of the visits of officials to the site. The impact of the media was considerable however, only 9 of these visitors stated to us that the ceremony was in part responsible for their visit to the site. Thus, the 6th June 2009 ceremony does not appear to have had the same impact that the fiftieth anniversary had on the cemetery which saw its attendance increase considerably during the years that followed.

Statistics undertaken by the American cemetery estimate that one third of its visitors go to the Visitor Center. We noted during our survey that this claim appears valid since 37% of the visitors questioned had effectively entered the building. Most of those who did not enter the building affirmed that they did not have enough time to do so and that the most important place for them was the cemetery.

Since the creation of the Visitor Center, the American cemetery offers free guided visits to the public. Despite the absence of advertising, one third of visitors interviewed had knowledge of the guided visits even before having arrived on site. It appears once more that word of mouth is very effective.

Finally, we were very interested in the visitors' vision of the cemetery. They are unanimous when we asked them what their feeling was about the general state of the site. All responded to us that the cemetery is *"very well maintained"*, *"very clean"* or just *"perfect"*. No negative opinions were voiced to us even if some visitors regretted (mainly European) the ability to walk directly over the graves or to take photographs. Conversely, others nearly forgot that they were in a cemetery and were disappointed by the "rigor" imposed on the site: *"The only things that I regret is the lack of a little refreshment stand!"* as one of the visitors emphasized to us. Anyway, we will quote another visitor interviewed whose vision summarizes and represents the large majority of persons interviewed who responded to us: *"The cemetery leaves us an impression of greatness but also of sadness. When we observe all the crosses of these young men who died in the region, we can only thank them for what they did. It is very important to still see today the respect people show towards them. It is true that we are less affected than our parents but it is important to continue to remember the 1944 events. That is why we must bring the children here. The cemetery is also very well kept and when we see the alignment of the crosses, we can say we could not have done better in their honor."*

CONCLUSION

The rich history of the American cemetery at Colleville-sur-Mer reflects the state of mind of the American Nation. Entered into the war two years after the outbreak of hostilities, it swung victory in favor of the Allies thanks to its economic and military power. Very quickly organized, it put in place an effective system to take care of the soldiers killed thanks to the action of the Graves Registration Service. This service undertook remarkable work and in particular in Normandy: the collection of bodies around specifically defined points, identification of 97% of the American soldiers killed, the establishment of temporary cemeteries well organized in the early days of the assault and the great attention paid to the burials and to the grave markers are good examples.

Conversely to what they had undertaken during the First World War, the Americans gathered the remains of soldiers in a dozen temporary cemeteries, dispersed across Normandy. The experiences in the European theater of operations showed rapidly the importance of having a reduced number of cemeteries in the same zone. One of the officers of the Graves Registration attached to the Third Army even put forward the idea that only one cemetery per army was required unless the evacuation line was located more than 100 miles away. The temporary burials were rapidly undertaken thanks to the employment of French laborers and to German prisoners. Besides the burial of American soldiers, the Graves Registration Service took care of the bodies of soldiers of other nations and notably those of German soldiers for whom were constituted specific cemeteries. The American Government, unlike the Commonwealth, offered families a choice for the future burial location of the soldiers' remains while preparing the construction of the permanent cemeteries.

The American Battle Monuments Commission played a primary role in the future of these fallen soldiers and in the selection of the future permanent cemeteries. It recommended the construction of a necropolis on the site of Omaha-Beach and this new cemetery of Colleville-sur-Mer became one of the fourteen permanent cemeteries constructed outside of American territory and subjected to the legislation of host countries. This concentration of bodies in only two cemeteries in Normandy (Saint-James and Colleville-sur-Mer) was the wish of the American Government and of the ABMC who would be responsible for them: they considered it easier to build, manage and to maintain two cemeteries rather than a dozen dispersed in the region, as the Commonwealth War Graves Commission chose to make.

The decision of the future locations of the fourteen new permanent cemeteries was difficult as the families had not yet responded to the requests concerning their loved ones. The commission therefore had no idea as to the numbers of soldiers to be buried there. Ultimately, around 40% of families wished that the bodies be transferred into the new permanent cemetery of Colleville-sur-Mer, whilst 60% of them preferred to repatriate the remains. 9 387 bodies were progressively buried at Colleville-sur-Mer, making it one of the largest military cemeteries in the region. Only the German cemeteries of La Cambe (21 222 buried), Huisnes-sur-Mer (11 956 buried), Marigny (11 169 buried) and Orglandes (10 152 buried) are of larger size. As a comparison, the largest British cemetery, that of Bayeux, shelters 4 648 graves.

The soldiers were mainly buried between 1948 and 1949. Each one received a Latin cross or a Star of David in marble similar to those of the First World War cemeteries administered by the ABMC. The commission undertook the construction of memorials, chapels and building annexes. These were decorated with remarkable artistic work entrusted to renowned artists in order to commemorate with dignity the sacrifice of these men. These places of remembrance also gradually became cemeteries/gardens with the implementation of various and luxuriant flora.

Inaugurated on 19th July 1956, more than ten years after the end of the Second World War, the Colleville-sur-Mer cemetery has evolved into a sort of United-States embassy in Normandy. Over the years, the site has hosted major international ceremonies commemorating the D-Day landing. From 1978, with the visit of President Carter, each American President – Reagan, Clinton, Bush father and son, as well as Obama – came to honor the memory of these soldiers, participating in the development of the popularity of the location and the growing influx of visitors.

This influx reached its peak during the ceremonies of the fiftieth and sixtieth anniversary of the landing. The cemetery's popularity was also relaunched by numerous Hollywood films and particularly that of Steven Spielberg. In the 1980's a new concept emerged: *"We should remember"* not to repeat the errors of the past. This *"devoir de mémoire"* was a real call for remembrance and brought many people to visit for the first time or indeed to visit once again the D-Day landing sites and cemeteries.

The visitors' statistics for 2009 (more than 1.7 million visitors being more than the Caen Memorial, the Arromanches Museum and the Bayeux Tapestry combined) made the cemetery of Colleville-sur-Mer the most visited site of the commission and the first "tourist site" of the battle of Normandy. The free entry to the cemetery is perhaps one of the explanations for this influx but we must also emphasize the remarkable work of the ABMC which was able to develop and evolve the location with time. Visitors directly linked to the cemetery are passing away: veterans, next-of-kin, friends of soldiers… The ABMC put in place both infrastructures (the new Visitor Center) and human resources (guides) to continue to make an impression and to challenge the younger generations. Following this success, the ABMC still continues to work on the realization of new projects in many of its sites, in order that the 125 000 buried soldiers for which it is responsible as well as the 94 000 unknowns will never be forgotten: smartphone applications, construction of a new Visitor Center in Cambridge American Cemetery, the new Visitor Center at Pointe-du-Hoc as well as that of the Sicily-Rome American cemetery at Nettuno in Italy…

CHRONOLOGY

17th July 1862: Establishment of the American National cemeteries.

1867: The Quartermaster Corps receives the mission to bury the dead.

6th April 1917: The United-States-of-America declares war on Germany.

7th August 1917: Creation of the Graves Registration Service (GRS).

4th July 1918: Death of Quentin Roosevelt.

1923: Establishment of the ABMC.

1928: Write up of the first ABMC brochure in order to make known the American battlefields of the First World War.

29th August 1929: Treaty signed with France concerning the concession of land used as military cemeteries on French territory.

1930-1933: Organization of pilgrimages by the American Army for families who wish to pay their respects on the graves of their loved ones buried in Europe.

21st May 1934: The military cemeteries abroad of the First World War are entrusted to the ABMC.

7th December 1941: The United-States-of-America enters the Second World War.

6th June 1944: The Allied landing in Normandy.

7th June 1944: Opening of the first provisional cemetery in the sands of Omaha-Beach and opening of the Blosville cemetery.

8th June 1944: Opening of the temporary cemetery at Utah-Beach.

9th June 1944: Opening of the temporary cemetery of Sainte-Mère-Église No. 1.

10th June 1944: Opening of a new temporary cemetery near the current cemetery of Colleville-sur-Mer. Closure of the provisional cemetery on Omaha-Beach. Opening of the temporary cemetery at La Cambe.

20th June 1944: Opening of the temporary cemetery of Orglandes originally for American soldiers then finally destined for German soldiers.

25th June 1944: Opening of the temporary cemetery of Sainte-Mère-Église No. 2.

1st July 1944: Opening of the temporary cemetery of Blosville.

31st July 1944: Opening of the temporary cemetery of Marigny.

5th August 1944: Opening of the temporary cemetery of Saint-James.

7th August 1944: Opening of Le Chêne-Guérin cemetery.

15th August 1944: Opening of the Gorron cemetery.

16th August 1944: Opening of the Saint-Corneille cemetery.

24th August 1944: Opening of the Saint-André-de-l'Eure cemetery.

25th August 1944: Opening of the Villeneuve-sur-Auvers cemetery.

24th December 1944: Sinking of the *Leopoldville*.

April 1945: 73 360 Americans rest in the twenty-four temporary cemeteries in France.

22nd May 1945: Establishment of the D-Day Commemoration committee by Raymond Triboulet.

30th May 1945: First official Memorial Day ceremony after the Second World War.

1st July 1945: The AGRS is replaced by the entirely autonomous AGRC.

8th July 1945: Accident of three African-American females buried in the Normandy cemetery.

25th July 1945: Plane accident in which Elizabeth Richardson perished.

8th September 1945: The repatriation plan is established by the War Department.

March 1946: Reorganization of the ABMC.

6th April 1946: the Quartermaster General's office lists a total of 359 temporary American cemeteries.

18th April 1946: Thomas North becomes Secretary of the ABMC.

29th July 1946: Agreement authorizing the Quartermaster General to choose the emplacement of the permanent cemeteries in the name of the Secretary of War.

Summer 1946: Visit to the potential permanent cemeteries in Europe.

22nd November 1946: The temporary cemetery of Saint-Laurent-sur-Mer is inscribed in the Inventory of historic sites of Calvados as well as the land bordering the sea.

Beginning of 1947: The first letters offering the possibility of repatriation are sent to the next-of-kin.

15th April 1947: Meeting at Washington; agreement for eight cemeteries abroad one of which being Colleville-sur-Mer.

22nd April 1947: The Secretary of War officially endorses the choice of fourteen new cemeteries but some potential sites are retained.

21st May 1947: New French law authorizing commemorative anniversary ceremonies within the territory.

27th July 1947: Beginning of the repatriation program in Europe.

5th August 1947: The architectural responsibility for the new permanent cemeteries is entrusted to the ABMC.

14th September 1947: Ceremony at the temporary cemetery of Saint-Laurent-sur-Mer which becomes the second cemetery to close in Europe.

16th September 1947: The first bodies at the temporary cemetery of Saint-Laurent-sur-Mer are exhumed to be repatriated.

Autumn 1947: The first repatriation vessel leaves from Anvers.

October 1947: French-American agreement concerning the permanent cemeteries.

20th October 1947: Officials at Washington confirm that there would finally only be two cemeteries in Normandy: Colleville-sur-Mer and Saint-James.

26th October 1947: A major ceremony is organized in Central-Park to honor the first of the fallen soldiers repatriated to the United-States.

27th October 1947: Beginning of the exhumation operations at the American cemetery of La Cambe.

30th October 1947: End of the exhumations at the temporary cemetery of Saint-Laurent-sur-Mer.

4th November 1947: The Robert F. Burns leaves Cherbourg with the first loading of coffins.

23rd November 1947: Beginning of the exhumation operations at Blosville cemetery.

8th January 1948: The ship *Joseph V. Connolly* sinks in the middle of the Atlantic with on board thousands of empty coffins.

Spring 1948: Exhumations in Sainte-Mère-Église No. 2 and Saint-James cemeteries.

9th July 1948: 34 874 bodies have been repatriated to the United-States.

End of August 1948: The ports of Cherbourg and of Anvers are no longer used.

4th November 1948: First final burial in the permanent cemetery of Colleville-sur-Mer.

Second quarter 1949: The permanent burials are nearly completed.

4th November 1949: Exhibition at the Philadelphia Art Alliance where the plans of the fourteen new memorials are exposed for the cemeteries of the Second World War.

December 1949: With more than 9 350 burials undertaken at the Colleville-sur-Mer cemetery, the work of the architect can begin.

28th December 1949: Management of the Colleville-sur-Mer cemetery passes to the ABMC after a ceremony.

31st December 1951: The activities of the AGRC are officially terminated. Closure of the last two body distribution centers. The laws regarding permanent burials (law 389 of the 66th Congress and law 368 of the 80th Congress) are henceforth obsolete.

1954: The memorial in the Normandy cemetery is completed.

1955: The family of Quentin Roosevelt request that his body be transferred to the cemetery of Colleville-sur-Mer. Installation of the statue of American youth in the memorial of the Normandy cemetery. The commune of Cricqueville-en-Bessin takes in hand responsibility for the maintenance of Pointe-du-Hoc which was until then abandoned.

1st January 1955: Agreement which regulates the procedure to be followed when a fallen American soldier is found in France.

May 1955: The urns of Donald de Lue arrive in the Colleville cemetery.

19th March 1956: Agreement between the United-States and France which replaces that of October 1947 relating to the concessionary lands required for the permanent military cemeteries.

19th July 1956: Inauguration of the Normandy American Cemetery.

25th July 1956: Law 792 of the 84th Congress institutes the establishment of a procedure similar to that followed for the Second World War in the event of a new war requiring the construction of military cemeteries abroad.

21st August 1960: The Pointe-du-Hoc committee erects a monument cut in granite in honor of the 2nd Ranger Battalion on the renovated former observation bunker.

6th June 1969: A time capsule is placed by journalists in the Normandy cemetery.

1971: Memorial Day is declared a National holiday to be celebrated on the last Monday of May.

11th January 1979: The maintenance of Pointe-du-Hoc is officially conceded in perpetuity to the American Government.

6th June 1979: The ABMC takes responsibility for the maintenance of Pointe-du-Hoc during a ceremony in the presence of General Omar Bradley.

11th January 1980: Circular of the Minister of the Interior and the Minister of the Environment regarding the protection of the military cemeteries.

6th June 1982: Visit of Mrs. Reagan to the cemetery.

6th June 1984: Ceremony of the fortieth anniversary of the landing in the presence of Ronald Reagan and François Mitterrand.

8th January 1990: The request of the ABMC to classify the surrounding cemetery land by the sea is approved.

6th June 1994: Major ceremony of the fiftieth anniversary of the landing in the Normandy cemetery in the presence of President Bill Clinton.

24th May 1995: Last burial in the Normandy cemetery.

6th June 1996: Installation of the carillon in the cemetery of Colleville-sur-Mer.

12th September 1997: Shooting scenes of the film *Saving Private Ryan* in the Normandy cemetery.

June 2001: A project of a new Visitor Center at Colleville-sur-Mer cemetery is proposed to the Congress by two members of the House of Representatives.

27th May 2002: Memorial Day ceremony in the presence of Presidents Bush and Chirac.

26th May 2007: Opening of the Normandy American Cemetery Visitor Center.

6th June 2007: Official inauguration of the new Visitor Center during the ceremony of the sixty-third anniversary of the landing.

6th June 2009: Ceremony commemorating the sixty-fifth anniversary of the landing in the presence of Presidents Barack Obama, Nicolas Sarkozy, Prime Ministers Gordon Brown and Stephen Harper.

The endless succession of white crosses and stars mark the location of the graves of the soldiers who liberated Normandy. *Photo C. Lebastard.*

THE NORMANDY AMERICAN CEMETERY

Statues of Columbia and Marianne.

Omaha Beach.

The multiconfessional chapel.

Grave plots.

290

Flag poles.

The Memorial and the reflecting pool.

The René Coty walkway

The Time capsule

Old Visitor Center, New office of the Superintendent

Visitor Center

Vehicle park

Statue of the American youth.

The Wall of the Missing.

THE NORMANDY AMERICAN CEMETERY 291

"The Spirit of the American Youth rising from the waves" sculpted by Donald de Lue. *Photo C. Lebastard.*

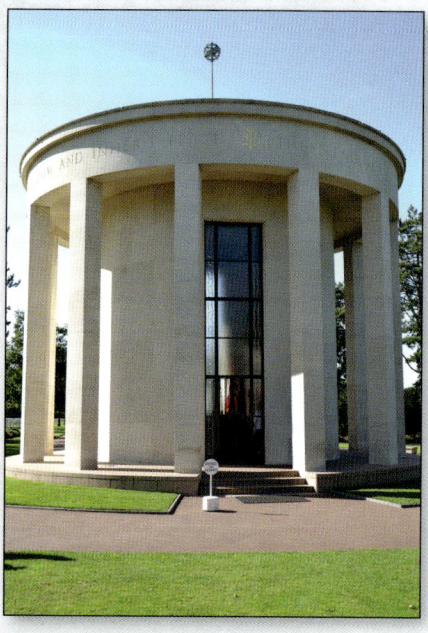

The multiconfessional chapel. *Photo C. Lebastard.*

The memorial rises behind the reflecting pool. *Photo C. Lebastard.*

On this wall were engraved the names of 1557 soldiers missing in Normandy.
Photo C. Lebastard.

The cemetery viewed from the memorial. *Photo C. Lebastard.*

The raising of the colors undertaken every morning at the opening of the American cemetery. *Photo C. Lebastard.*

The graves decorated with their flags as on every major ceremony of 6th June and each *Memorial Day* ceremony. *Photo C. Lebastard.*

The sands of Omaha Beach opposite the cemetery of Colleville-sur-Mer. *Photo C. Lebastard.*

We can see on this photograph the two flag masts of more than 80 feet which were installed between the memorial and the chapel. The two masts are not quite the same lengh to compensate for the differences in level. *Photo ABMC.*

This photograph highlights the remarkable work undertaken on the vegetation. *Photo ABMC.*

THE NORMANDY AMERICAN CEMETERY 295

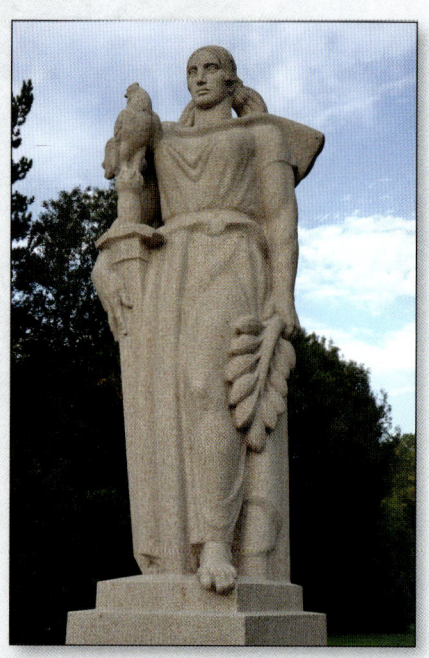

The guardian statues. Left: Columbia and Right: Marianne.
Photos C. Lebastard.

President Obama and his wife talking with Prince Charles and Prime Minister Francois Fillon in the Visitor Center on the occasion of the ceremony of 6th June 2009. *acclaimimages.com.*

BIBLIOGRAPHY

WORK INSTRUMENTS

ATKINSON (Rick), *An Army at Dawn*, An Owl Book, New York, 2003, 2 vol.

BAILEY (Ronald H.), *World War II Encyclopedia*, Time Life Books, Chicago, 1981, 38 vol.

LE CACHEUX (Geneviève), QUELLIEN (Jean), *Le Dictionnaire de la libération du Nord-Ouest de la France*, Charles Corlet, Condé-sur-Noireau, 1994, 425p.

MESSENGER (Charles), *The D-Day atlas: anatomy of the Normandy campaign*, Thames & Hudson, New York, 2004, 176p.

QUELLIEN (Jean), *La Seconde guerre mondiale*, The Memorial of Caen, Caen, 2004, 555p.

THE D-DAY LANDING AND THE BATTLE OF NORMANDY

La Bataille de Saint-Lô : 7-19 juillet 1944, United-States of America War Department, Impr. de R. Jacqueline, Saint-Lô, 1951, 200p.

Omaha Beachhead (6 june-13 june 1944), United-States of America War department, Historical Division, Washington, 1945, 167p.

AMBROSE (Stephen), *D-Day, June 6, 1944: the climactic battle of World War II*, Touchstone, New York, 1995, 655p.

BALKOSKI (Joseph), *Omaha Beach: D-Day, June 6, 1944*, Stackpole Books, Mechanicsburg (PA), 2004, 410p.

BARDE (Yves), *La Muraille de Normandie : le mur de l'Atlantique de Cherbourg au Havre*, Citédis ed., Paris, 1999, 192p.

BLOND (Georges), *Le Débarquement : 6 juin 1944*, Presses de la Cité, Paris, 1972, 312p.

BUCKLEY (John), *The Normandy campaign 1944: sixty years on*, Routledge, New York, 2006, 228p.

CARELL (Paul), *Ils arrivent ! La Bataille de Normandie vue du côté allemand*, Robert Laffont, Paris, 2006, 327p.

DEHAYS (Antonin), *Sainte-Marie-du-Mont, Code « Utah-Beach », Juin 1940-novembre 1944*, Eurocibles, Marigny, 2010, 283p.

DESQUESNES (Rémy), *1940-1944, l'histoire secrète du mur de l'Atlantique : de l'organisation Todt au débarquement en Normandie*, ed. des falaises, Fécamp, 2003, 215p.

ESTE (Carlo d'), *Decision in Normandy*, Konecky & Konecky, 1994, 555p.

HASTINGS (Max), *Overlord: D-Day and the battle for Normandy 1944*, Papermac, London, 1993, 462p.

KEEGAN (John), *Six Armées en Normandie : du jour J à la libération de Paris, 6 juin-25 août 1944*, A. Michel, Paris, 1984, 384p.

KEMP (Anthony), *6 juin 1944 : le débarquement en Normandie*, Gallimard, Paris, 1994, 194p.

KERSHAW (Robert), *D-Day, Piercing the Atlantic Wall*, Ian Allan Publishing, Hersham, 2009, 484p.

KEUGSEN (Helmut Konrad Baron von), *Omaha Beach : la tragédie du 6 juin 1944*, Heimdal, Bayeux, 2007, 215p.

LAMARQUE (Philippe), *Le Débarquement : opération Overlord*, ed. CMD, Doué-la-Fontaine, 2000, 119p.

LECOUTURIER (Yves), *Les Plages du Débarquement*, Ouest-France and Memorial of Caen, Rennes and Caen, 1999, 127p.

McMANUS (John C.), *The Americans at Normandy: the summer of 1944: the American war from the Normandy beaches to Falaise*, Forge, New York, 2004, 496p.

PATRY (Robert), *Les Opérations américaines en Normandie : 6 juin-14 août 1944*, University of Caen, Thesis completed in 1968, 308p.

QUELLIEN (Jean), *Jour J et bataille de Normandie : la Normandie au cœur de la guerre*, The Memorial of Caen, Caen, 2004, 303p.

QUELLIEN (Jean), *Les Plages du débarquement : Omaha, Pointe du Hoc, Sword, Utah, Juno, Gold, Pegasus*, The Memorial of Caen, Caen, 2002, 128p., reed. éditions OREP, 2008.

QUELLIEN (Jean), *Normandie 44*, The Memorial of Caen, Caen, 2002, 224p., reed. éditions OREP, 2010.

REARDON (Mark J.), *Victory at Mortain: stopping Hitler's panzer counteroffensive*, University Press of Kansas, Lawrence (Kan.), 2002, 368p.

RONDEL (Éric), *Les Américains en Normandie : été 1944*, Astoure, Sables-d'or-les-Pins, 2004, 172p.

RYAN (Cornelius), *Le Jour le plus long : 6 juin 1944*, R. Laffont, Paris, 1983, 274p.

WADDELL (Steve R.), *United States Army logistics: the Normandy campaign, 1944*, Greenwood press, Westport (Conn.), 1994, 190p.

THE TROOPS PRESENT DURING THE BATTLE OF NORMANDY

ANDRADE (Allan), *Leopoldville Troopship Disaster, In Memoriam*, Ft. Benning, Georgia Ceremony, 1999, 72p.

ANDRADE (Allan), *S.S. Leopoldville Disaster, December 24, 1944*, The Tern Book Company, New York, 1999, 297p.

BALKOSKI (Joseph), *The 29th infantry division in Normandy*, Stackpole Books, Harrisburg (PA), 1988, 304p.

BANDO (Mark), *101st Airborne, The Screaming Eagles at Normandy*, Zenith Press, China, 2001, 156p.

BAUMER (Robert W.), REARDON (Mark J.), *American Iliad, The 18th Infantry Regiment in World War II*, The Aberjona Press, Bedford (PA), 2004, 414p.

BENNETT (G.H.), *Destination Normandy, Three American Regiments on D-Day*, Praeger Security International, Westport (Connecticut), 2007, 222p.

BERGER (Sid), *Breaching Fortress Europe, The Story of U.S. Engineers in Normandy on D-Day*, Kendal/Hunt Publishing Company, Dubuque (Iowa), 1994, 272p.

BERNAGE (Georges), *First US army*, Heimdal, Bayeux, 2004, 458p.

COLLIN (Charles-Antoine), *Les Services de santé américains en Normandie en 1944,* Master's thesis, 2005.

DOBIE (Kathryn S.), LANG (Eleanor), *Her War, American Women in WWII*, iUniverse Inc. New York, 2003, 180p.

GAWNE (Jonathan), *Finding your father's war, A Practical Guide to Researching an Understanding Service in the World War II US Army*, Casemate, Philadelphia, 2006, 341p.

GAWNE (Jonathan), *Spearheading D-Day, American Special Units in Normandy*, Histoire & Collections, Elkar, 2001, 288p.

GAWNE (Jonathan), *Le Six juin à l'aube : les unités spéciales américaines du débarquement en Normandie*, Histoire & collections, Paris, 1998, 288p.

KERSHAW (Robert), *The Bedford Boys*, Da Capo Press, 2004, 274p.

LAMACHE (Stéphane), *La Normandie américaine*, Larousse, Paris, 2010, 191p.

SEVERLOH (Hein), WN 62: *Erinnerungen an Omaha Beach, Normandie, 6 juni 1944*, HEK Creativ Verl., Garbsen, 2002, 149p.

THERS (Alexandre), *Soldats en Normandie, les Allemands : juin-août 1944*, Histoire & collections, Paris, 2004, 35p.

THIERREE (Basile), *La Vie quotidienne des soldats américains durant la bataille de Normandie*, Master's thesis directed by Jean Quellien, Caen, 2006, 221p.

TIREL (Stéphane), *Les Structures de la 1re armée américaine dans la bataille de Normandie, leur comportement et leur évolution du 6 juin au 31 juillet 1944*, Master's thesis directed by M. Barjot, Caen, 1994, 279p.

WES (Ross), *146 Engineer Combat Battalion – Essayons*, [s.n.], [s.l.], 2006, 147p.

WHEELER (James S.), *The Big Red One, America's Legendary 1st Infantry Division from World War I to Desert Storm*, University Press of Kansas, Lawrence, 2007, 594p.

WHITLOCK (Flint), *The Fighting First, The Untold Story of the Big Red One on D-Day*, Westview press, Cambridge (MA), 2004, 384p.

BIOGRAPHIES AND TESTIMONIES

« Normandie 1944 avec les correspondants de guerre », Numerous special of *Normandie Magazine* published in 1994, *Normandie-Magazine*, Saint-Lô, 2000, 115p.

« Untold Stories of D-Day », *National Geographic*, June 2002, 138p.

AMBROSE (Stephen E.), *The Supreme Commander*, University Press of Mississippi, Jackson, 1999, 732p.

BASTABLE (Jonathan), *Paroles de combattants : le 6 juin 1944*, L.Pire, Brussels, 2008, 362p.

BAUMGARTEN (Harold), *Témoin sur Omaha Beach*, American D-Day ed., Châtenay-Malabry, 2004, 102p.

EISENHOWER (Dwight D.), *Les Opérations en Europe du corps expéditionnaire allié, 6 juin 1944 au 8 mai 1945 : rapport aux chefs d'état-major alliés*, Berger-Levrault, Paris, 1947, 363p.

GOCKEL (Franz), *La Porte de l'enfer : Omaha Beach 6 juin 1944*, Hirle, Strasbourg, 2004, 235p.

MADISON (James H.), *Slinging Doughnuts for the Boys, An American Woman in World War II*, Indiana University Press, Bloomington, 2007, 300p.

PARIS (Claude), *Paroles de braves : d'Omaha la Sanglante à Saint-Lô, capitale des ruines, 7 juin-18 juillet 1944*, C. Corlet, Condé-sur-Noireau, 2008, 328p.

PYLE (Ernie), *Brave men*, 1st Bison Books printing, Lincoln (NE), 2001, 513p.

RENEHAN (Edward J.), *The Lion's Pride, Theodore Roosevelt and his Family in Peace and War*, Oxford University Press, 1998, 289p.

ROTHBART (David), *A Soldier's Journal with the 22nd Infantry Regiment in World War II*, Ibooks, New York, 2003, 304p.

SLAUGHTER (John R.), *Omaha Beach and Beyond, The long March of Sergeant Bob Slaughter*, Zenith Press, Saint-Paul (Mn), 2007, 288p.

COMMEMORATION AND REMEMBRANCE

Les Jardins de la mémoire : les hommes et leur destin : lieux de recueillement et de mémoire des soldats de la bataille de Normandie, DIREN Lower Normandy, OREP, Cully, 1999, 48p.

« Numéro spécial du cinquantenaire : 1944-1994 », *Revue de la Manche*, numerous special, 142, 1994, 128p.

AKOKA-RAMAIN (Christine), *Normandie : l'anniversaire le plus long*, Ailleurs, Paris, 1994, p. 108-125.

BARCELLINI (Serge), WIEVORKA (Annette), *Passant, souviens-toi ! Les lieux du souvenir de la seconde guerre mondiale*, Plon, Paris, 1995, 522p.

BARRÉ (Éric), « Débarquement d'hier et d'aujourd'hui ou ce qu'en pense notre jeunesse », *Revue de la Manche*, numerous special of the 50th anniversary 1944-1994, t. 36, fasc. 142, avril 1994, p. 125-128.

BRINKLEY (Douglas), *The World War II Memorial, A Grateful Nation Remembers*, Smithsonian books, Washington, 2004, 287p.

DELOIZELLERIE (Jacquemine), *Les Lieux de mémoire de la seconde guerre mondiale dans la Manche*, Master's thesis directed by Michel Boivin, Caen, 1998, 194p.

DUTOUR (Françoise), *Mémoire et commémoration dans le Calvados de 1944 à 1994*, symposium organized by the Calvados Archive Center and the University of Caen, 1997.

ELKHAWAGA (Ahmed), *Comment les sites du Débarquement du 6 juin 1944 sont devenus des lieux de mémoire de 1945 à 1964 ?*, Master's thesis directed by Jean Quellien and André Zysberg, Caen, 2006, 129p.

ELMER (Marc), *Images-souvenirs du débarquement et de la bataille de Normandie*, L'entente nouvelle, Paris, 1963, 64p.

FOLLIOT (Guillaume), *Les Commémorations du 6 juin et de la Bataille de Normandie (1946 – 2004)*, Master's thesis directed by Jean Quellien, Caen, 2006.

FOSSARD (Brice), *Festivités et commémorations dans le Calvados, du 6 juin 1944 au 13 octobre 1946*, Master's thesis directed by Étienne Fouilloux, Caen 1988, 263p.

FOUILLOUX (Étienne), VEILLON (Dominique), « Mémoires du débarquement en Normandie », *Annales de Normandie*, mai 1986, p105-119.

FRANCK (Robert) (dir.), *La Mémoire des Français, quarante ans de commémorations de la seconde guerre mondiale*, CNRS, Paris, 1986, 400p.

HOWLETT (Roger D.), *The sculpture of Donald de Lue, Gods, Prophets, and heroes*, David R. Godine, Boston, 1990, 234p.

LEBRETON (Brigitte), *6 juin 1944-6 juin 1994, 50e anniversaire du débarquement, mémoire, hommage, reconnaissance, liberté, solidarité, paix*, Caen, 2003.

LENEVEU (Delphine), *Les Monuments commémoratifs américains du débarquement et de la bataille de Normandie dans le Calvados*, Master's thesis directed by Jean Quellien, Caen, 2007, 2 vol., 204 and 181p.

NADIN (Gilles) *et al.*, *Il y a quarante ans déjà : 6 juin 1984, le livre souvenir des cérémonies du 40e anniversaire du débarquement en Normandie*, C. Corlet, Condé-sur-Noireau, 1984, 79p.

NORA (Pierre) (*dir.*), *Les Lieux de mémoire*, Gallimard, Paris, 1997, 3 vol., 451p.

PAUVRET (Rose Blanche), *Le Tourisme et ses problèmes sur la plage d'Omaha*, Master's thesis of Geography directed by Pierre Brunet, Caen, 1967, 85p.

THE HISTORIC AREAS OF THE BATTLE OF NORMANDY

Espace historique de la bataille de Normandie : coffret pédagogique, CRDP of Lower Normandy, 1994, vol. 3, 99p.

BOUSSEL (Patrice), *Guide des plages du débarquement*, Béranger, Paris, 1964, 224p.

HOLT (Major), *Battlefield Guide to the Normandy Landing Beaches*, Leo Cooper, Barnsley, 2000, 272p.

KEMP (Anthony), *Bataille de Normandie, France : guide officiel : espace historique de la bataille de Normandie*, ed. Nouveaux-loisirs, Paris, 2004, 280p.

PLOIX (André), *Le Débarquement en Normandie : 6 juin 1944. Guide pour la visite des plages de débarquement des aires de parachutage des musées et des cimetières*, Hachette, Paris, 1964, 64p.

ROSSIGNOL (Gilles), *Le guide du Calvados et des plages du débarquement*, La manufacture, Lyon, 1994, 346p.

SHILLETO (Carl), TOKHURST (Mike), *A traveller's Guide to D-Day and the Battle for Normandy*, Interlink Books, New York, 2008, 191p.

TANTER (Joël), *Musées de la bataille de Normandie*, C. Corlet, Condé-sur-Noireau, 1998, 94p.

THE MILITARY CEMETERIES

Gardens of Remembrance, the men and their destiny, DIREN, Lower Normandy, Nouvelles Pages, 1999, 48p.

BIRABEN (Anne), *Les Cimetières militaires en France*, l'Harmattan, Paris, 2005, 214p.

BLAU (Armand), *Dans l'ombre des forêts, 26694 Dead American Soldiers at the cemeteries of Hamm, Margraten, Henri-Chapelle, Neuville-en-Condroz*, Impr. Saint-Paul, Luxembourg, 1996, 799p.

CORVÉ (Philippe), *Sur les traces de la bataille de Normandie : un guide historique et touristique du champ de bataille : les musées, les cimetières, les monuments*, Heimdal, Bayeux, 2005, 240p.

DESSENTE (Ferdinand), *Les Cimetières militaires de Neuville-en-Condroz*, A&Ω, Belgique, 1997, 155p.

GRAHAM (John W.), *The Gold Star Mother Pilgrimages of the 1930's*, McFarland & Company, Jefferson (N.C.), 2005, 229p.

GRIVE-SANTINI (Catherine), *Guide des cimetières militaires de France*, Le cherche midi, 1999.

JORDAN (William), *The Normandy American cemetery*, The pitkin guide, 2004, 22p.

MARSHALL (Georges C.), *Our War Memorials Abroad: A Faith Kept*, National Geographic Society, Washington, 1957, 38p.

OZOUF (Hugues), *Les Cimetières de guerre de la seconde guerre mondiale en Basse-Normandie, dimensions spatiales et sociales*, Geography work directed by Mrs. Fixot, Lower Normandy, 1999.

PLOIX (André), *Le Débarquement en Normandie : 6 juin 1944*, « Guide pour la visite des plages de débarquement des aires de parachutage des musées et des cimetières », Hachette, coll. Les guides bleus ilustrés, Paris, 1964, 64p.

SLEDGE (Michael), *Soldier Dead, How we recover, identify, bury and honor our military fallen*, Columbia University Press, New York, 2005, 357p.

SOURCES

MANUSCRIPT SOURCES

Archives of the Normandy American Cemetery

Databases and statistics

1C: Data on all the American soldiers buried in the permanent cemeteries managed by the ABMC.

2C: Statistics by state.

3C: Statistics of the cemetery and of the new Visitor Center.

6C: Databases of all the soldiers killed during the First World War and buried in the cemeteries maintained by the ABMC.

7C: Databases of all the soldiers killed during the Second World War and buried in the cemeteries maintained by the ABMC.

Lists

1B: The graves of the American cemetery by infantry division.

2B: The temporary cemeteries in Europe.

3B: List of the Bedford Boys.

4B to 10B: The American infantry divisions in the Colleville-sur-Mer cemetery.

11B: The four ladies buried in the cemetery.

12B: The 6th June 1944 fallen soldiers by unit.

13B: Location of the pairs of brothers.

14B: Location of the Stars of David.

15B: The Native Americans in the cemetery.

16B: The graves of the Rangers.

17B: The graves of the unknown soldiers.

18B: The American cemeteries in France.

19B: List of requests and special visits to the cemetery in 2008 and 2009.

20B. List of decorated graves in the cemetery in 2008 and 2009.

21B: Details of the temporary cemeteries given by a veteran of the AGRC on 4th October 1988.

Records

1D: Recovered soldiers.

2D: Temporary cemeteries.

3D: Plan of the cemetery in 1987.

4D: Corrections made concerning the buried soldiers in the cemeteries managed by the ABMC.

5D: The African-Americans and the women in the Colleville-sur-Mer cemetery.

6D: The Visitor Center.

7D: Miscellaneous.

8D: Mortuary Affaires.

9D: Quartermaster and GRS (The Quartermaster General and the Graves Registration Service).

10D: The carillon.

11D: *Saving Private Ryan.*

12D: Memorial Day.

13D: The *Leopoldville.*

14D: Veterans and queries.

15D: Pointe-du-Hoc.

16D: The Bedford Boys.

17D: Commanders and personalities.

18D: The monument of the 1st Infantry Division at Colleville-sur-Mer.

19D: The anniversary ceremonies.

20D: Visits.

21D: The monument at Utah-Beach.

Biographies

1S: Pfc. Mary J. Barlow.

2S: Sgt. Dolores Browne

3S: Maj. Thomas D. Howie.

4S: Billie D. Harris.

5S: Jimmie W. Monteith.

6S: Sgt. Robert J. Niland and 2Lt. Preston T. Niland.

7S: Lt. Gen. Lesley J. McNair.

8S: Tec. Sgt. Frank D. Peregory.

9S: Brig. Gen. Theodore Roosevelt Jr. and Lt. Quentin Roosevelt.

10S: Elizabeth A. Richardson.

11S: Sgt. Sam E. Sanders and T/Sgt. Gafford W. Sanders.

Photographs

1P: Old aerial photograph of the Colleville-sur-Mer cemetery.

2P: Aerial photograph of the cemetery in 1954.

3P: Old postcard of the site.

4P: Recent aerial photograph.

5P: Photograph of a coffin utilized for the burials.

6P: Photograph of one of the dummy crosses installed for the shooting of the film *Saving Private Ryan*.

Private sources

Alain Dupain

Antonin Dehays

Geert Van den Bogaert

Henri-Jean Renaud

Printed sources

Press Articles

Ouest-France from 1944 to 1981

Monday 19th May 1947: "Memorial Day".

Monday 20th October 1947: "The moving farewell blessing ceremony at the American cemetery of La Cambe".

Tuesday 13th January 1948: "An American Army carrier on fire in the Atlantic".

Wednesday 14th January 1948: "The 46 crew members of the Joseph V. Connelly are safe".

Monday 7th June 1948: "Mr. Auriol in Normandy".

Thursday 29th July 1948: "How to operate the repatriation of our soldiers fallen in Italy".

Wednesday 24th November 1948: "A cemetery guard hangs himself from a tree".

Saturday 10th and Sunday 11th September 1949: "Our beaches and the wreckage".

Tuesday 13th September 1949: "The meeting of the landing committee".

Thursday 29th December 1949: "Since yesterday at 3.00 pm, the Saint-Laurent cemetery is administered by the civil American authority".

Wednesday 7th June 1950: "The celebrations of the Allied landing in the department".

Wednesday 6th June 1951: "Seven years ago, the Allied Forces landed in Normandy".

SOURCES 311

Thursday 7th June 1951: "General Eisenhower and many Allied personalities celebrate on the Normandy beaches the anniversary of the landing".

Thursday 5th June 1952: "General Ridgway in the landing celebrations".

Saturday 7th and Sunday 8th June 1952: "General Ridgway has chaired the landing anniversary in Normandy".

Tuesday 1st June 1954: "A brilliant ceremony at the Omaha-Beach cemetery on Memorial Day".

Tuesday 7th June 1955: "The First American Division meets together at Omaha Beach".

Monday 18th July 1955: "The opening of the Pointe-du-Hoc trail gives rise to the first official ceremony".

Wednesday 16th May 1956: "A committee has been formed to assure the conservation of the Pointe-du-Hoc".

Friday 20th July 1956: "Numerous personalities at the moving inauguration of the Normandy American Cemetery".

Friday 20th July 1956: "American personalities and the 'Battle Monuments Commission' led by Admiral Thomas C. Kinkaid complete their journey to Europe aboard a special aircraft which lands them at Carpiquet".

Thursday 29th May 1958: "Memorial Day will not be marked".

Monday 2nd June 1958: "Memorial Day".

Saturday 7th and Sunday 8th June 1958: "Marshall Leclerc and Marshall Juin have chaired the fourteenth Allied landing anniversary in Normandy".

Tuesday 7th June 1960: "In the presence of numerous personalities and foreign delegations, Mr. Couve de Murville has presided in the Calvados and the Manche departments the sixteenth anniversary ceremonies of the landing".

Friday 7th June 1963: "The anniversary of the landing".

Monday 4th May 1964: "6th June 1964, 20 years after: 20 000 GI's in Normandy around Eisenhower and Montgomery".

Friday 15th May 1964: "Twenty years after… The 6th June will be on the radio waves and in the press".

Friday 5th June 1964: "Imposing Allied delegations for the 20th anniversary of the landing".

Tuesday 1st June 1965: "Memorial Day".

Wednesday 1st June 1966: "Saint-Laurent-sur-Mer: at the American cemetery a large crowd attended the Memorial Day commemoration".

Friday 7th June 1968: "The twenty-fourth anniversary of the landing, Bayeux, Omaha-Beach, Grandcamp and Isigny-sur-Mer, stages of a pious pilgrimage".

Tuesday 8th June 1971: "Grandcamp-les Bains: the 6th June ceremony at Pointe-du-Hoc".

Thursday 8th June 1972: "The twenty-eighth anniversary of the landing celebrated in the Calvados and the Manche departments".

Tuesday 28th May 1974: "The injured visitor at Pointe-du-Hoc was evacuated by helicopter to the hospital in Garches".

Friday 7th June 1974: "Thirtieth anniversary of the landing. Rangers assault Pointe-du-Hoc. Ceremonies all over Normandy".

Wednesday 7th June 1978: "From the American cemetery of Colleville to the Pointe du Hoc, the Allied landing commemoration in Normandy".

Tuesday 16th January 1979: "The landing committee: a large file to protect the historic sites".

Ouest-France, Bayeux edition, from 1982 to 2009

Tuesday 1st June 1982: "Humble testimony of Normand gratitude".

Monday 7th June 1982: "Nancy Reagan, in Normandy, at the graves of American soldiers".

Thursday 7th June 1982: "The official ceremonies of the landing".

Thursday 7th June 1984: "A vibrant hymn to freedom".

Thursday 7th June 1984: "Never again".

Saturday 7th and Sunday 8th June 1986: "The 42nd anniversary of 6th June 44: 'Let us together declare war against terrorism'".

Wednesday 10th June 1987: "At Cricqueville-en-Bessin, the future museum of the Pointe-du-hoc in a house near the site?".

Tuesday 7th June 1988: "François Mitterrand: 'Better than a memory, a lesson!'".

Thursday 7th June 1990: "Eisenhower's journey to victory".

Thursday 7th June 1990: "The son of 'Ike' on the landing beaches".

Thursday 7th June 1990: "At Grandcamp, a museum for the Rangers".

Thursday 7th June 1990: "Inauguration of the Rangers museum. Grancamp: 'We will never forget'".

Friday 4th June 1993: "Official ceremonies of 6th June 94, La Manche department will have its share".

Saturday 7th and Sunday 8th May 1994: "The preparations a month before the fiftieth, television and Ministers at Bayeux".

Tuesday 24th May 1994: "The early crowd, the landing sites are full".

Saturday 4th and Sunday 5th June 1994: "All the ceremonies of the 5th and 6th June".

Saturday 4th and Sunday 5th June 1994: "Grandcamp-Maisy honors its heroes: a monument for Frank Peregory".

Tuesday 4th June 1996: "Memorial Day ceremony at British cemetery".

Friday 7th June 1996: "A chime to remember them".

Thursday 4th September 1997: "Visit of General James Collins to the Colleville cemetery".

Saturday 13th and Sunday 14th September 1997: "Steven Spielberg films at Omaha Beach".

Saturday 13th and Sunday 14th September 1997: "Cinema: Spielberg films at Omaha".

Monday 7th September 1998: "Steven Spielberg on Omaha-Beach".

Tuesday 1st June 1999: "The veterans already at the rendez vous".

Saturday 5th and Sunday 6th June 1999: "Private Ryan's effect: 55 years on, they are landing again in force, the last great rush of the Boys?".

Saturday 5th and Sunday 6th June 1999: "The eternal children of Colleville-sur-Mer".

Tuesday 5th June 2001: "Attendance at the Pegasus memorial".

Thursday 7th June 2001: "Anniversary of D-Day: American parade at Utah-Beach".

Thursday 7th June 2001: "Pointe-du-Hoc prepares for the sixtieth".

Tuesday 28th May 2002: "Bush's Memorial Day in Normandy".

Saturday 7th and Sunday 8th June 2003: "Raffarin: 'France does not forget'".

Saturday 7th and Sunday 8th June 2003: "Ceremony in memory of the Rangers".

Tuesday 25th May 2004: "Nicole Helm saw her life ruined on 6th June".

Thursday 27th May 2004: "A military base with all the comforts for 1000 US soldiers".

Monday 31st May 2004: "6th June: Ouest-France gets ready".

Monday 31st May 2004: "39-45: Bush re-calls the American sacrifice".

Wednesday 2nd June 2004: "D-Day: between remembrance and diplomacy".

Wednesday 2nd June 2004: "Iraq in the background of D-Day".

Wednesday 2nd June 2004: "110 American choir members in the cemetery".

Saturday 5th and Sunday 6th June 2004: "D-Day: the media wave".

Monday 7th June 2004: "George bush at Colleville: America would re-do it".

Tuesday 7th June 2005: "The Minister welcomed the US veterans".

Wednesday 7th June 2006: "Lesson after waking up on Asnelles beach".

Monday 28th May 2007: "French-American friendship at Omaha-Beach".

Sunday 3rd June 2007, supplement: "A new memorial at Omaha".

Thursday 7th June 2007: "6th June: new memorial at Omaha".

Saturday 7th and Sunday 8th June 2008: "The Governor of Texas at Omaha-Beach".

Saturday 9th and Sunday 10th May 2009: "Barack Obama confirms his visit on 6th June".

Monday 11th May 2009: "Visit by Obama on 6th June: three weeks to prepare everything".

Monday 25th May 2009: "An anonymous crowd for Memorial Day".

Wednesday 24th June 2009: "The D-Day beaches, patrimony of UNESCO?".

Tuesday 6th October 2009: "Former American Artillery men in the military cemetery".

Friday 2nd April 2010: "The Superintendent leaves Omaha".

Other Press Articles

Grand Écran, No. 57, September 1998, "The Spielberg shock", p. 12-13.

La Liberté of the 27th November 2008, "Omaha-Center will open in 2010".

La Manche Libre of the 13 June 2009, "The tribute".

La Manche Libre of the 27th March 2010: "At the Pointe-du-Hoc, America starts a colossal project".

La Renaissance du Bessin of the 6th January 1978, "Carter and Giscard in the Bessin region… !".

La Renaissance du Bessin of the 2nd May 1995, "A private visit by George Bush".

La Renaissance du Bessin of the 12th September 1997, "Spielberg is filming today at Colleville-sur-Mer".

La Renaissance du Bessin of the 11th June 2004, "Flowers for all the graves".

La Presse de la Manche of the 6th June 2004, "Witness statement of Yves de la Rue".

Les cahiers espaces, "Remembrance tourism", No. 80, Paris, December 2003, 121 p.

Washington Post of the 21st October 1998, "Private Ryan' Launches New Normandy Invasion".

Printed documents collected at the Normandy American Cemetery

Escorting American War Dead, War and Navy Departments, Washington, March 1947, 25p.

Graves Registration Services: the general board, United States Forces, European Theater, [s.l.], 1945, 53p.

Graves Registration, War department Field Manual, Washington, 1945, 57p.

United States Temporary Military Cemeteries European Theater Area, American Graves Registration Command, Pictorial Historical Record, New York, [No date], 114p.

Register, American Battle Monuments Commission, [s.l.], [No date] vol. 3, 1463p.

American Memorials and Overseas Military Cemeteries, American Battle Monuments Commission.

Normandy American Cemetery and Memorial, American Battle Monuments Commission.

The American Battle Monuments Commission, World War II Commemorative Program.

NORTH (General Thomas), *Manuscript*, American Battle Monuments Commission,[s.l], [No date], [n.p.].

STEERE (Edward), BOARDMAN (Thayer M.), *Final disposition of World War II Dead 1945 – 51*, Department of the Army, Office of the Quartermaster General, Washington D.C., 1957, 710p.

Oral testimonies

Henri-Jean Renaud: he is a witness of the installation of the temporary cemeteries of Sainte-Mère-Église. His father was the Mayor of Sainte-Mère-Église during the battle of Normandy. Testimony collected on 20th April 2010.

Maryvonne Guidon: Interpretive Guide employed at the Normandy American Cemetery since 1st November 1993. Testimony collected on 24th February 2010.

Sylvie Jean: Cemetery Associate at the Normandy American Cemetery since 1983. Testimony collected on 24th February 2010.

Audiovisual documentation

4th Infantry Division, Invasion of Normandy Series – Volume VI (DVD), Combat Reels, 2006.

Tribute to a generation, dedication celebration, May 27 – 30, 2004, American Battle Monuments Commission, National WWII Memorial, Three DVD set.

ZANUCK (Darryl), *The Longest Day*, 20th Century Fox, 1962, 2h51.

SPIELBERG (Steven), *Saving Private Ryan*, Dreamworks Pictures and Paramount Pictures, 1998, 2h49.

SPIELBERG (Steven), HANKS (Tom), *Band of Brothers*, HBO, 10 episodes, 2002, 9h10.

Websites

Intranet ABMC: *Newsletters* Nos. 4 à 24: 2003 to 2010

http://images.google.com/images?q=anniversary+d-day&q=source:life (Archives of *Life Magazine*)

http://omahabeach.vierville.free.fr

http://treaties.un.org

www.6juin1944.com/veterans/tucker.php

www.abmc.gov

www.acclaimimages.com

www.archivesnormandie39-45.org

www.flickr.com

www.med-dept.com

www.qmfound.com

ACKNOWLEDGEMENTS

I would like to express here my thanks to those who have given me their help and who have also contributed to the development of this work.

I would first thank Jean Quellien for having accepted to direct this university study, for his availability and for his numerous advices. I express my gratitude to Philippe and Gregory Pique and to *OREP Editions* for having believed from the beginning in this project and for giving me their trust.

A very special thanks goes out to the ABMC which allowed me to undertake my research with confidence in one of their most beautiful locations. I would like to especially mention Daniel L. Neese, Hans H. Hooker, Charles E. Hunt, Dwight E. Anderson and Shane J. Williams who were always available to answer my many questions.

Many thanks to the very enjoyable team at the Normandy American Cemetery without whose encouragement and help this book would not have seen the light of day and who by their professionalism, always knew to guide me to the relevant documents. I would like to particularly mention Alain Dupain and Geert Van-den-Bogaert whose documents and advice were of great help. In the same way, I would like to mention Maryvonne Guidon, Laurence Guillard, Emmanuelle Hotier, Josiane Rudd-Guillemette, Sylvie Jean and Karen Lancelle for their precious help. I must also acknowledge Anthony Lewis for his intense and professional work of translation. I doubt that I will ever be able to convey my appreciation fully, but I owe to all of the team my deep gratitude.

Furthermore, I would wish to express my gratitude to the Departmental Archives of Calvados as well as Henri-Jean Renaud and Antonin Dehays for their contribution. In conclusion, I would like to thank especially my family and Jennifer Lesaque for their backing and moral support.

TABLE OF CONTENTS

General Information   p. 4
The American Organizations   p. 5
Preface of Jean Quellien   p. 7

INTRODUCTION   P. 9

FIRST PART
THE ORIGINS OF THE NORMANDY AMERICAN CEMETERY   P. 21

THE CREATION OF THE GRAVES REGISTRATION SERVICE AND ITS FIRST WORK   P. 23

ORGANIZATION OF THE QUARTERMASTER GENERAL AND THE GRAVES REGISTRATION SERVICE   P. 23

Necessary services   p. 23
The operation of the Graves Registration Service   p. 26

THE PREPARATORY WORK OF THE GRAVES REGISTRATION SERVICE   p. 31

To collect the bodies and personal effects   p. 31
Identification   p. 36

THE ESTABLISHMENT OF TEMPORARY CEMETERIES IN NORMANDY   P. 44

THE CREATION OF THE CEMETERY AT OMAHA-BEACH   P. 44

Rules to follow   p. 44
The installation of a first cemetery   p. 46
The second temporary cemetery at Omaha-Beach   p. 52

THE TEMPORARY CEMETERIES IN NORTH-WEST FRANCE   P. 55

A gradual development   p. 55
The first burials: the example of Blosville cemetery   p. 62

The gradual organization of temporary cemeteries — p. 66

- The installation of grave markers — p. 66
- The maintenance of cemeteries — p. 68
- The searches after the war and the results obtained — p. 72

Towards the establishment of permanent cemeteries — p. 75

The choices given to families — p. 75

- The first projects — p. 75
- "Tell me about my boy" — p. 77

The American Battle Monuments Commission — p. 81

- Origin of the Commission — p. 81
- The commission during the Second World War and its reorganization — p. 85

The selection of the permanent cemeteries — p. 87

- The different projects — p. 87
- The final choices — p. 91
- Are these cemeteries American territories? — p. 93

SECOND PART
The creation and organization of the Normandy American Cemetery — P. 101

The last operations — p. 103

Exhumations and repatriations — p. 103

- The preparations for repatriation — p. 103
- The progress of the exhumations — p. 107
- The return to the country — p. 111

The final burials — p. 118

- The preparations — p. 118
- The conduct of the funerals — p. 120
- Families with specific requests — p. 125

MAKING SHIPSHAPE	**p. 127**
The handover of power between the Graves Registration Service and the ABMC	p. 127
Compensation for affected farmers	p. 129

THE ARCHITECTURE OF THE CEMETERY — P. 131

ORGANIZATION OF THE BURIALS	**p. 131**
The choice of the final markers	p. 131
The installation of the grave markers	p. 136
THE BUILDINGS	**p. 137**
Construction of the chapel and facilities	p. 137
The memorial	p. 143
TO GLORIFY THE CEMETERY	**p. 146**
A place of art	p. 146
The work of Donald de Lue	p. 149
• The statue of the American youth	p. 149
• The memorial urns	p. 151
• The statues of the United-States and of France	p. 152
The setting designed by the landscaper	p. 153

THE SOLDIERS OF THE NORMANDY AMERICAN CEMETERY — P. 157

MISSING IN ACTION AND BURIED SOLDIERS	**p. 157**
General figures	p. 157
Decorated soldiers and generals	p. 163
The minorities	p. 172
Boys too young to die	p. 177
The Wall of the Missing	p. 178
The *Leopoldville*	p. 181
The Bedford Boys	p. 183
THE NEW BURIALS	**P. 186**
Quentin Roosevelt	p. 186
Gafford Sanders	p. 187
A cemetery closed to burials for families, veterans and recovered soldiers	p. 188

THIRD PART
A VITAL MISSION: TO PERPETUATE THE MEMORY OF THE BURIED SOLDIERS P. 195

THE CEREMONIES P. 197

THE FIRST COMMEMORATIVE CEREMONIES P. 197

The commemorations of the D-Day landing
before the inauguration of the cemetery — p. 197
The cemetery's inauguration ceremony — p. 200
A degree of public disinterest in the D-Day ceremonies — p. 203

THE MAJOR COMMEMORATIVE EVENTS OF THE D-DAY LANDING P. 206

The starting point of the presidential ceremonies — p. 206
The changes of the 1980's — p. 209
The ceremonies until 2008 — p. 212
The 6th June 2009: the ultimate major ceremony? — p. 217

COMMEMORATIONS THROUGHOUT THE YEAR P. 219

Memorial Day — p. 219
The "private" ceremonies — p. 222

THE ACHIEVEMENTS OF THE ABMC AFTER THE FOUNDING OF THE CEMETERY P. 224

THE PROJECTS IN COLLABORATION WITH THE CEMETERY OF COLLEVILLE-SUR-MER P. 224

The management of certain monuments — p. 224
The ABMC's wish: to protect the cemetery and Omaha-Beach — p. 228
Welcoming Steven Spielberg and shooting the film — p. 233

THE CONSTRUCTION OF THE NEW VISITOR CENTER P. 238

A congressional project — p. 238
The architecture and the symbols — p. 241

THE SPECIAL CASE OF POINTE-DU-HOC — p. 246

The protection of Pointe-du-Hoc — p. 246
Pointe-du-Hoc: an important place for Americans — p. 249
Recent works on the Pointe-du-Hoc site — p. 251

THE WORK OF THE NORMANDY AMERICAN CEMETERY — p. 253

THE MANAGEMENT AND THE MAINTENANCE OF THE SITE — p. 253

The administration — p. 253
The work teams — p. 254
The budget of the ABMC and of the cemetery — p. 257

THE DUTIES TOWARDS THE FAMILIES AND THE VETERANS — p. 258

Frequent visits — p. 258
The ABMC services — p. 261
The perception of the site by veterans and families — p. 263

THE PROVISION OF INFORMATION TO THE MANY VISITORS — p. 265

A popular tourism venue — p. 265
Public guidelines and behavior — p. 269
Sociological Inquiry — p. 270

CONCLUSION — P. 277

CHRONOLOGY — P. 281

THE AMERICAN CEMETERY (IN COLOR) — P. 289

BIBLIOGRAPHY — P. 297

SOURCES — P. 307

ACKNOWLEDGEMENTS — P. 322